Colonial Arkansas,

1686–1804

Frontispiece. Capt. Joseph Bernard Vallière d'Hauterive, commandant of Arkansas Post from 1787 to 1790. (*Courtesy of Mr. and Mrs. Howard Stebbins, Little Rock.*)

Colonial Arkansas, 1686–1804

A SOCIAL AND CULTURAL HISTORY

MORRIS S. ARNOLD

THE UNIVERSITY OF ARKANSAS PRESS · FAYETTEVILLE
1991

Manufactured in the United States of America
21 20 19 18 17 5 4

First paperback printing 1993

This book was designed by Chiquita Babb using the Minion typeface.

The paper used in this publication meets the minimum requirements of the American National Standard for Permanence of Paper for Printed Library Materials Z39.48-1984.♾

Library of Congress Cataloging-in-Publication Data

Arnold, Morris S.
Colonial Arkansas, 1686-1804 : a social and cultural history / Morris S. Arnold.
p. cm.
Includes bibliographical references and index.
ISBN 1-55728-222-6 (alk. paper)
1. Arkansas—History. 2. Arkansas—Social conditions. 3. Arkansas Post Region (Ark.)—History. 4. Arkansas Post Region (Ark.)—Social conditions. 5. French—Arkansas—History.
I. Title.
F411.A788 1991
976.7′02—dc20 91-10223
CIP

To the memory of my mother and father

The influence of the French effort, which was carried on so long, though only sporadically, and through so many disasters and failures, has long since mingled and become assimilated with the Anglo-Saxon culture of Arkansas. It has become, in its essence, much like those old disputed bones [of Pierre Lefevre]—a thing of doubtful antiquity or paternity, a legend, a myth, a remote shadowy survival, although, as late as beyond the Civil War, cases based on French and Spanish land grants—usually to French families—still occurred in the Arkansas courts. Like the French celebration of Mardi Gras, still honored by masking on the streets during the days of my boyhood—and earlier celebrated by great parades and balls—the French influence has, to all intents and purposes, disappeared. But the symbol of France, seen dimly in the great figures of La Salle and Tonti, of La Harpe, in the records of Arkansas Post, or in the mythical, unrealized Alsatian colony of John Law, serves to haunt us still, as a shadow crossing the familiar sunlight.

John Gould Fletcher, *Arkansas*

CONTENTS

ILLUSTRATIONS

PREFACE

Though I did not know it then, the seeds for this book were laid more than a decade ago when I began work on another project, namely an effort to discover what Arkansas law was like before the Americans purchased Louisiana. An earlier book, *Unequal Laws unto a Savage Race,* resulted more immediately from that original enterprise. Though that book purported to be a legal history, there was a good deal of social history in it, for it was impossible to say anything realistic about colonial Arkansas law without first understanding the economy and social structure of the colonial period. It turned out that very little real work on these last items had previously been attempted—no one, for instance, had even done a proper job of divining where Arkansas Post had been located during the eighteenth century; and that was at first a major irritation, since it meant that I had to undertake work for which I was, in many senses, ill prepared. But that irritation quickly evolved into a curiosity that, in its turn, became a kind of infatuation: Here was a place, a whole state, whose colonial history had not been written! (In the psycho-babble of the twentieth century, I came to see an irksome problem as a very real opportunity.) After the previous book appeared, therefore, though by no means immediately thereafter, I resolved to stand it on its head by writing a social, economic, and political history of colonial Arkansas in which law would figure, it is true, but merely as one cultural artifact among others. Hence this book.

Because it has evidently never occurred to anyone else to write such a book as this, its title may evoke the wrong kind of smile—calling up, even from the friendliest minds, visions of sturdy hill folk turned out in tricornered hats. "Colonial Arkansas" is not a phrase one frequently hears: Indeed, I still recall the curious ring that it left in my ears when I first heard it from Margaret Ross a decade ago. But it is nevertheless the case that the Arkansas colonial period can reasonably be made to occupy a span of almost 120 years, from August of 1686 when Henri de Tonty established a Canadian trading post on the Arkansas River, to that March day in 1804 when Lt. James B. Many of the American army received a ruinous Spanish Fort St. Estevan from Captain Caso y Luengo. It is this period with which this book mainly concerns itself, though it necessarily makes occasional relevant forays into years on either side of it. Though this book has scholarly pretensions in the sense that it is solidly grounded in far-flung archival materials, my aim has been to produce a work for the educated general reader, not a narrow-gutted monograph.

My files are embarrassingly full of correspondence with the numerous people whom I have importuned over the years, and it is a pleasure to record here my thanks to them. Among the archivists and librarians whom I owe a great deal are Russell Baker of the Arkansas History Commission; John D. Barbry, Alfred Lemmon, and Florence Jumonville of The Historical New Orleans Collection; Georgia B. Barnhill of the American Antiquarian Society; David Bosse of the William L. Clements Library at the University of Michigan; Angel Paladini Cuadrado of the Servicio Geográfico del Ejército, Madrid; Gérard Ermisse of the Archives Nationales, Paris; Gerard W. Gawalt of the Library of Congress; Robert W. Karrow, Jr., Pat Morris, and Jonathan Walters of the Newberry Library in Chicago; Bonnie Hardwick and Teri A. Rinne of the Bancroft Library, Berkeley; Rosario Parra of the Archivo General de Indias, Seville; Sally Reeves of the New Orleans Notarial Archives; and Robert R. Stevens of the Lewis Historical Library at Vincennes University. In addition, staff at the Howard-Tilton Memorial Library at Tulane University, the W. Stanley Hoole Special Collections Library at the University of Alabama, and the Hill Memorial Library at Louisiana State University provided needed assistance. Many historians have also generously shared their knowledge with me: Carl A. Brasseaux, Glenn R. Conrad, René Chartrand, Lawrie Dean, Caldwell Delaney, Marcel Giraud, Jessie Poesch, and Mildred Mott Wedel deserve special mention. Jay Edwards, Charles Peterson, and Samuel Wilson, Jr., patiently read and criticized my chapter on colonial French architecture. Dorothy Jones Core and Samuel D. Dickinson, both accomplished historians of Arkansas's colonial past, read the entire manuscript and saved me a number of errors. Mary Christina Wood gave me the benefit of her excellent editorial advice. Mrs. Elmire Villeré Drackett of New Orleans, Lt. Col. John W. Easby-Smith of Little Rock, Mr. Richmond G. Favrot of New Orleans, Mr. Thomas B. Favrot of New Orleans, Mrs. Marie Reinecke of New Orleans, Mr. and Mrs. Howard W. Stebbins of Little Rock, and Mrs. Clair Favrot Kileen of

Covington, Louisiana, graciously allowed me to reproduce portraits in their possession. I am grateful to all of these persons for taking an interest in a project that could not have been brought to fruition without their help.

Special gratitude is due Kathryn Fitzhugh and Kirk Gregory of the Eighth Circuit Court of Appeals Library, who never wavered in their resolve to comply with my constant requests for obscure books and articles. It is also a pleasure to record my thanks to the University of Arkansas Press, the Arkansas Historical Association, and the Louisiana Historical Association, for allowing me to make use here of materials that I had previously published.

Colonial Arkansas, 1686–1804

ABBREVIATIONS

AGI, PC	Archivo General de Indias, Seville, Papeles Procedentes de Cuba. Various *legajos* (bundles, abbreviated *leg.*) are cited.
AGI, SD	Archivo General de Indias, Seville, Audiencia de Santo Domingo. Various *legajos* (bundles, abbreviated *leg.*) are cited.
AHQ	*Arkansas Historical Quarterly*
ANC, C^{13A}	Archives Nationales, Paris, Archives Coloniales, *sous-série* (sub-series) C^{13A}. Various other sub-series are cited.
APLB	*Letter Book of the Arkansas Trading House 1805-1810,* National Archives, Washington, D.C.
BLC	*Before Lewis and Clark* (A. Nasatir ed., 1952).
BNP	Bibliothèque Nationale, Paris
BNM	Biblioteca Nacional, Madrid
GPHSB	*Grand Prairie Historical Society Bulletin*
LHQ	*Louisiana Historical Quarterly*
MPA	*Mississippi Provincial Archives* (D. Rowland, A. Sanders, & P. Galloway eds., 1927–1984).
SMV	*Spain in the Mississippi Valley, 1765-1794* (L. Kinnaird ed., 1946).
SRM	*The Spanish Regime in Missouri* (L. Houck ed., 1909).
VLB	*Charles de Vilemont's Letter Book* in "Memorial of the Heirs of Carlos de Vilemont . . . ," *Documents of the 24th Congress, 2d Session,* No. 89 (1837).

I

THE SITES OF ARKANSAS COLONIAL SETTLEMENT

The search for glory, knowledge, wealth, and converts drew Frenchmen into the St. Lawrence valley in the early seventeenth century. From their first settlement at Port-Royal in 1605, they expanded upriver to Quebec in 1608 and established Montreal in 1642. Though their hold on the great waterway was tenuous for most of the century, by some miracle French civilization eventually took root and grew in the wilderness: By the end of the seventeenth century, the banks of the St. Lawrence from Quebec to Montreal had come to contain a virtually continuous agricultural settlement, with farms only a few hundred yards apart and a population of about fifteen thousand. "Every few miles there was a seigneurial manor house and a mill, and eventually a steep-roofed stone church . . . To anyone travelling by river [from Quebec] up to Montreal nearly all of New France passed in review."[1]

But New France did have its hinterlands and frontier outposts. From the very beginning of the settlement effort, in fact, the people of New France had been attracted to the great wealth that could be had from trading with the Indians for skins and furs, and some local Canadian officials dreamed of a trading empire stretching from Canada to Florida or Mexico. The colonial administration in

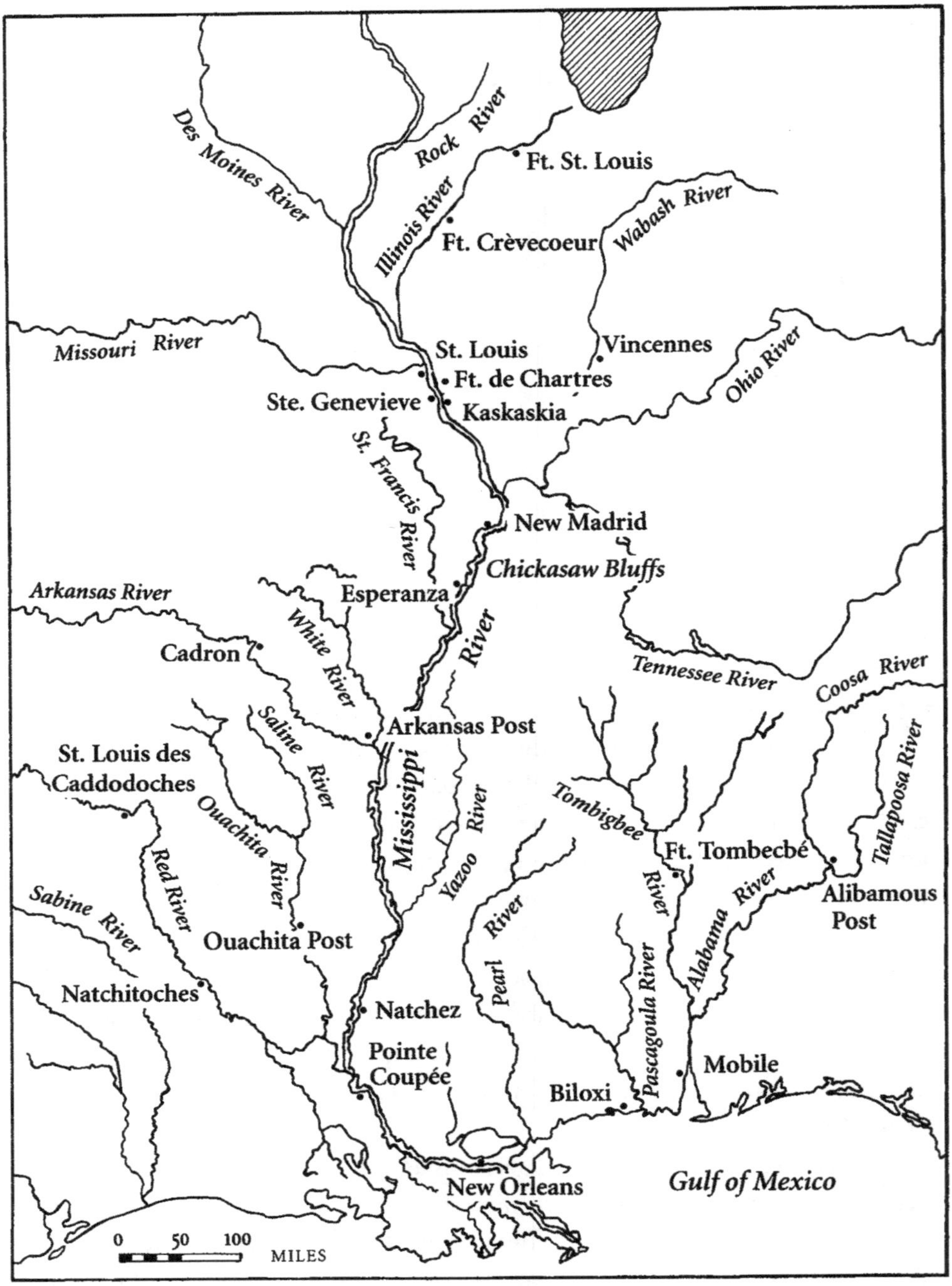

Figure 1. Map of the Arkansas region in colonial times.

France wished instead for an agricultural establishment confined at first to the great river and expanding only as population permitted. Jean-Baptiste Colbert, the French colonial minister, vigorously opposed the fur trade: "It is to be feared," he said, "that by means of this trade, the *habitants* will remain idle a good part of the year, whereas if they were not allowed to engage in it they would be obliged to apply themselves to cultivating their land."[2] Louis de Buade, comte de Frontenac, the governor of New France, nevertheless remained committed to developing this trade. In 1673 he therefore constructed Fort Frontenac on Lake Ontario, and in that very year the French made their first foray into Arkansas: Louis Jolliet and Father Jacques Marquette, the one pursuing pelts and the other in search of souls, traveled down the Mississippi, and, before turning back near the mouth of the Arkansas River,[3] they learned that the Mississippi emptied into the Gulf of Mexico. Here, then, by means of the other great river of North America, was an inland waterway route from Quebec to the Gulf of Mexico.

Though Colbert, anti-expansionist as ever, refused Jolliet the right to make a settlement in the new lands, Governor Frontenac came to view the St. Lawrence farming settlements simply as a base to serve the needs of an expanding fur trade. Frontenac's chief partner in his commercial schemes was Robert Cavelier de La Salle who in 1680 established Fort Crèvecoeur deep in the forests on the Illinois River. Two years later La Salle, Henri de Tonty, and about thirty other Frenchmen made their fabled voyage down the Mississippi to the Gulf of Mexico. In March of 1682, they spent a few days with the Arkansas Indians, who, after some initial suspicion, received them in an all-night celebration. In the square of the Indian village, La Salle planted a column bearing both the arms of Louis XIV and a painted cross; and the Quapaws, as the Indians called themselves, according to the notary in La Salle's party, accepted King Louis as "master of their lands."[4] It seems relatively clear that what the Quapaws sought most from this alliance was guns for offensive and defensive use against their enemies, chiefly the Chickasaws whom the Carolina traders had perhaps already armed in an effort to draw their trade and political allegiance. On the way back upriver from the Gulf, La Salle granted Tonty the Arkansas River region as a seigneury, and in August of 1686 Tonty settled six of his men near the Quapaw village of Osotouy about thirty-five miles from the mouth of the Arkansas.[5] This first Arkansas Post was located in what is now Arkansas County near the little

Figure 2. Henri de Tonty, *seigneur* of the Arkansas River.
(*Courtesy of the Museum of the History of Mobile.*)

community called Nady and the oxbow lake named Dumond and was the first European settlement in what, five generations or so later, would become Jefferson's Louisiana Purchase. In fact, in consequence of the New Mexican pueblo revolt of 1680, which had driven the Spanish south of the Rio Grande, Tonty's outpost was for a few years virtually the only white establishment west of the Mississippi River. Tonty made at least one unconditional land grant,[6] and probably others, from his feudal seigneury located here, and made two grants to the Jesuits on condition that they settle near his "fort."[7] This last a French traveler in 1687 described as a "french-looking house"; and another, in the same year, called it a "house built in the French fashion."[8]

Since by 1680 there were at least eight hundred fur traders called *coureurs de bois* (forest rangers) operating in the west of New France, Colbert had had to admit defeat in his effort to keep the colony limited to the St. Lawrence valley. In 1681, therefore, he had hit on the idea of licensing twenty-five such traders annually in the hopes at least of regulating their activities.[9] It was presumably pursuant to licenses (*congés*) granted to him under this trading system that Tonty had hoped to exploit the furs of the Arkansas region. In 1694, however, in an effort to concentrate the fur trade at Montreal, the colonial minister revoked the trading licenses and ordered the abandonment of all the western forts except for Fort St. Louis, which La Salle had established on the Illinois River in 1683. Tonty, of course, bitterly protested this retrenchment and was able to effect a partial rescission of these ruinous measures for a time. But the *coureurs de bois* continued in any case to operate a black market without benefit of the *congés*, and many were prepared "to turn renegade and trade out of Albany or Philadelphia rather than abandon the west."[10]

One of the casualties of these restrictive trade regulations seems to have been Jean Couture, a carpenter from Rouen whom Tonty had left in charge of his Arkansas venture at Osotouy: In 1694 he is reported in Savannah Town, spinning tales of gold beyond the Appalachians.[11] It is doubtful that Tonty's Arkansas establishment could have long survived Couture's departure. In 1699, by which time the French had certainly abandoned the region, a group of Carolina traders set out for the Arkansas under Couture's guidance; they had arrived there by February of the following year.[12] Later that spring, Pierre-Charles Le Sueur, on his way up the Mississippi, encountered one of this party who boasted that the English would soon engross the trade of the Mississippi Valley.[13]

Le Sueur had been directed to make this expedition by Pierre Le Moyne d'Iberville who had himself been sent from France in 1699 to follow up on La Salle's plan to found a colony called Louisiana on the Gulf. Louis XIV had finally become an expansionist himself, believing that it was imperative to establish trading posts and forts from the Gulf coast to the Great Lakes to contain English expansion and keep them east of the Alleghenies. Thus, "the *coureurs de bois* were suddenly transformed into useful agents of crown policy."[14] And since in 1714 there were in the Mississippi region at least two hundred *coureurs de bois* and *voyageurs* "who did nothing else during their entire lives,"[15] we cannot doubt that there were Frenchmen who ventured from time to time into the Arkansas region in the early eighteenth century to hunt and trade with the Indians, though Tonty's trading house was no longer in operation.

When Frenchmen came to Arkansas to stay, they quite naturally settled along the many navigable rivers that provided the only real transportation routes available. The Arkansas region, it is true, was criss-crossed by buffalo traces, Indian trade routes, and warpaths. Indeed, by the late eighteenth century at any rate, there were regularly traveled roads of a sort leading southward from Arkansas Post through Poste du Ouachita (Monroe, Louisiana) and Natchitoches to New Orleans,[16] and northward to New Madrid, Ste. Genevieve, St. Louis, and the Illinois country generally.[17] But these land routes were most unreliable because of floods and other impediments, and even in the best of times there were myriad streams to ford, which made the going extraordinarily treacherous.[18] Though the road from Ste. Genevieve to St. Louis was sometimes referred to rather grandly as the *camino real* (royal road), it probably accommodated, at most, only the lumbering two-wheeled, ox-drawn carts that the French called *charettes* and that would elicit so much bemused comment from American visitors. There were no wagon roads linking the settlements in Arkansas with their far-flung and distant neighbors: Only in and around Natchez and New Orleans did wagons and carriages come to be in ordinary use in colonial Louisiana. There is a story, probably true, that the first four-wheeled wagon was not seen in Arkansas Post until the summer of 1811, when one John Billingsley unloaded his from a keelboat. The wheeled wonder created such a stir "that the villagers climbed to the house tops to witness the passing."[19]

It was thus to the rivers that colonial Arkansans were forced to look for the most dependable transportation. Although low water in dry seasons and, occasionally, ice in the winter, made travel on them a somewhat unpredictable affair, much of the time the great rivers were clear. Simple two-man canoes, dugouts that Louisianians still call *pirogues, batteaux* (apparently large boats with a keel), even tall-masted Spanish war galiots, would ply the colonial Arkansas waters in search of commercial advantage and foreign intruders.[20] Going downstream was, of course, relatively easy: On the spring rises of February and March, when the Mississippi flowed at perhaps five miles an hour, only six or seven days separated the mouth of the Arkansas from New Orleans. The return trip could consume six to seven weeks:[21] Sailing up the Mississippi was sometimes possible; but contrary winds, and tall forests that blocked favorable ones, meant that most of the time the boats had to be rowed while hugging the banks where the current was slow. About all the distance that could normally be wrung from this backbreaking mode of travel was fifteen to eighteen miles a day. Cordelling, that is pulling the boat upriver by ropes, was sometimes resorted to; but along the Mississippi in the Arkansas region the necessary towpaths were hard to come by.

The Arkansas River, the most significant of the region's rivers and home of the Quapaw Indians, was quite naturally the first one that Europeans chose to occupy. As we saw, by the summer of 1686 this river had already attracted a French trading post, but serious settlement efforts were still some years away. In 1717 the entire colony was given over to the *Compagnie d'Occident*, an enterprise conceived and directed by John Law, a Scot who was the most celebrated financier in eighteenth-century France.[22] In its charter from the crown, the company obligated itself to recruit large numbers of colonists for settlement in Louisiana, and it made land grants to entrepreneurs interested in establishing plantations in various Louisiana locations, mostly along the Mississippi River since the interior regions were largely inaccessible or unsafe. The company granted one of the largest concessions, located on the Arkansas River, to John Law himself, and he soon began to make arrangements to locate a settlement at the site that Tonty's trading house had occupied.

It has been a favorite fantasy of historians of the Arkansas region for more than two hundred years that Law established German colonists on this concession, that they abandoned the region in 1722 when the news of Law's bankruptcy reached them, and that they retreated down the Mississippi eventually to settle at what later became known as the German Coast of Louisiana.[23] That this is untrue was shown as long ago as 1974 by Prof. Marcel Giraud, colonial Louisiana's most distinguished historian;[24] and yet, such is the hold that this story has had on the Arkansas mind that it has nevertheless continued to be the object of uncritical repetition.[25] It will therefore be of interest briefly to trace this tale to its source, to examine the reliability of that source, and to show that the story is demonstrably false.

Though the European population at Law's Arkansas concession could never have exceeded one hundred, the tiny settlement received considerable attention from persons associated with the company and from others. As a result, eighteenth-century material touching on it has come down to us in surprisingly

Figure 3. A view of Law's concession at New Biloxi, December 10, 1720. (*Courtesy of Newberry Library.*)

large amounts. It seems certain that, as Jean-Baptiste Bénard de La Harpe reports, the concession was established in August of 1721 by a group of indentured servants (*engagés*) of the company, skilled workmen and craftsmen whose job it was to prepare the way for the agricultural colonists (*habitants*).[26] It is true

that André-Joseph Pénigaut, who came to Louisiana in 1700,[27] states that Law's grant was first settled in 1720;[28] but as Pénigaut's assertions, especially his dates, are frequently erroneous,[29] it seems clear that he is not speaking of some earlier group but of the group that La Harpe indicated had arrived in August of 1721.[30] According to Pénigaut, though one needs to be skeptical even about this, there were one hundred men in this company, and they "had such a great amount of goods and other belongings that they loaded thirty boats with them to go up to" the Arkansas.[31] Lieutenant La Boulaye moved his troops from their position at Kappa, on the Mississippi twenty miles from the mouth of the White River, to join Law's concession on September 21.[32]

Scarcely a month later, Father Pierre de Charlevoix stopped at Kappa. He remarks that Law had recruited nine thousand Germans (a grossly inflated number) from the Palatinate to send to the Arkansas, and he allows that "it is a great shame that they did not arrive," since the country thereabouts was so fertile. He states, in fact, that there was "perhaps no place in the whole of Louisiana, except Illinois, more suited to producing all sorts of grain and pasturing animals." But all that now remained of the original grandiose scheme, he reports, were "melancholy ruins" (*tristes débris*).[33] Charlevoix's observations make it plain that none of Law's colonists had joined the *engagés* at the concession and that none was expected.

Only about a week after Father Charlevoix visited the Arkansas region, the company commissioned La Harpe to explore the Arkansas River with a view toward eventually establishing a post somewhere along its upper reaches. He arrived at Law's concession on March 1, 1722, after a voyage of more than three months from New Orleans, and found there "about forty-seven persons of both sexes," including the commandant, a storekeeper, a surgeon, and an apothecary. "Their works," La Harpe reports, "still consist of only a score of cabins poorly arranged and three arpents of cleared ground."[34] After a voyage of exploration upriver, La Harpe returned to Law's establishment on April 28 and found that one Bertrand Dufresne, whom he had installed as director at the concession, had released twenty of his *engagés* from service so that they could become *habitants*.[35] It is noteworthy that La Harpe did not record the presence of any colonists, German or otherwise, on the Arkansas; he mentions only *engagés*.

One of the persons who accompanied La Harpe on his voyage to Arkansas was Jean-François Benjamin Dumont, *dit* (nicknamed) Montigny, who was

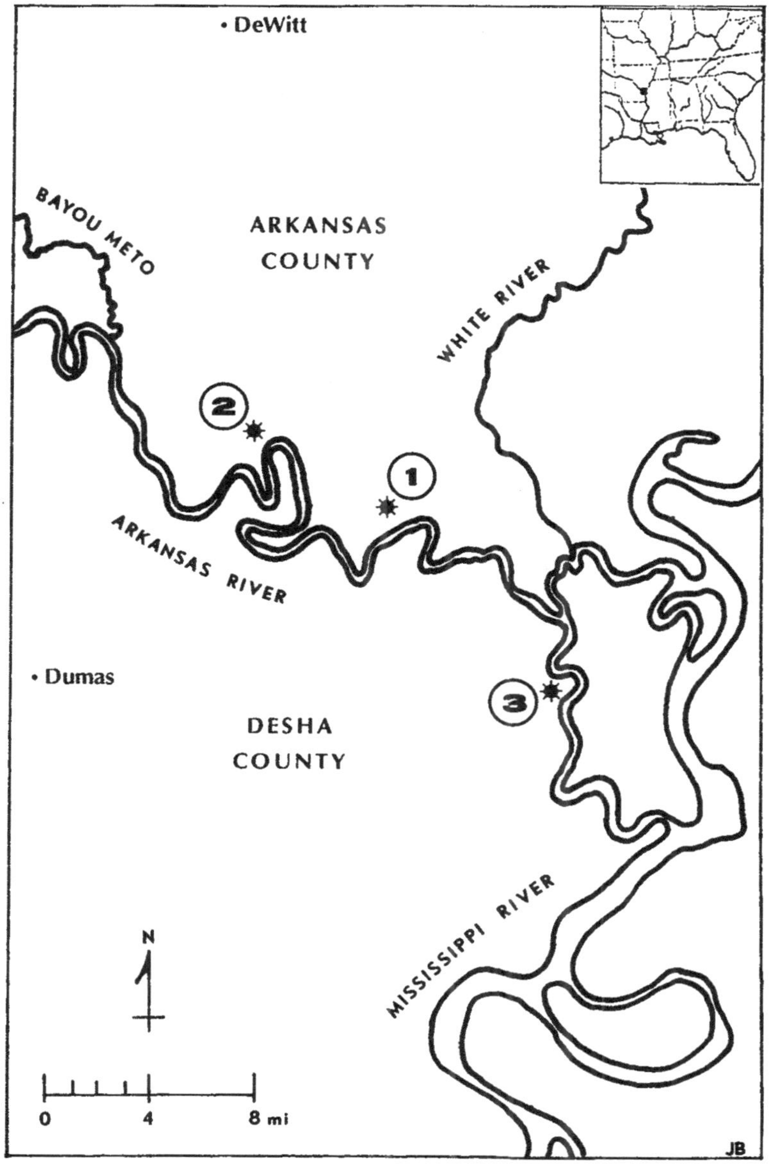

Figure 4. Locations of Arkansas Post, 1686–1991: 1. 1686–1699; 1721–1749. 2. 1749–1756; 1779–1991. 3. 1756–1779. Based on a map drawn by John Baldwin that appeared in Arnold, "The Relocation of Arkansas Post to *Écores Rouges* in 1779," 42 *AHQ* 317 (1983). (*Courtesy of Arkansas Historical Association.*)

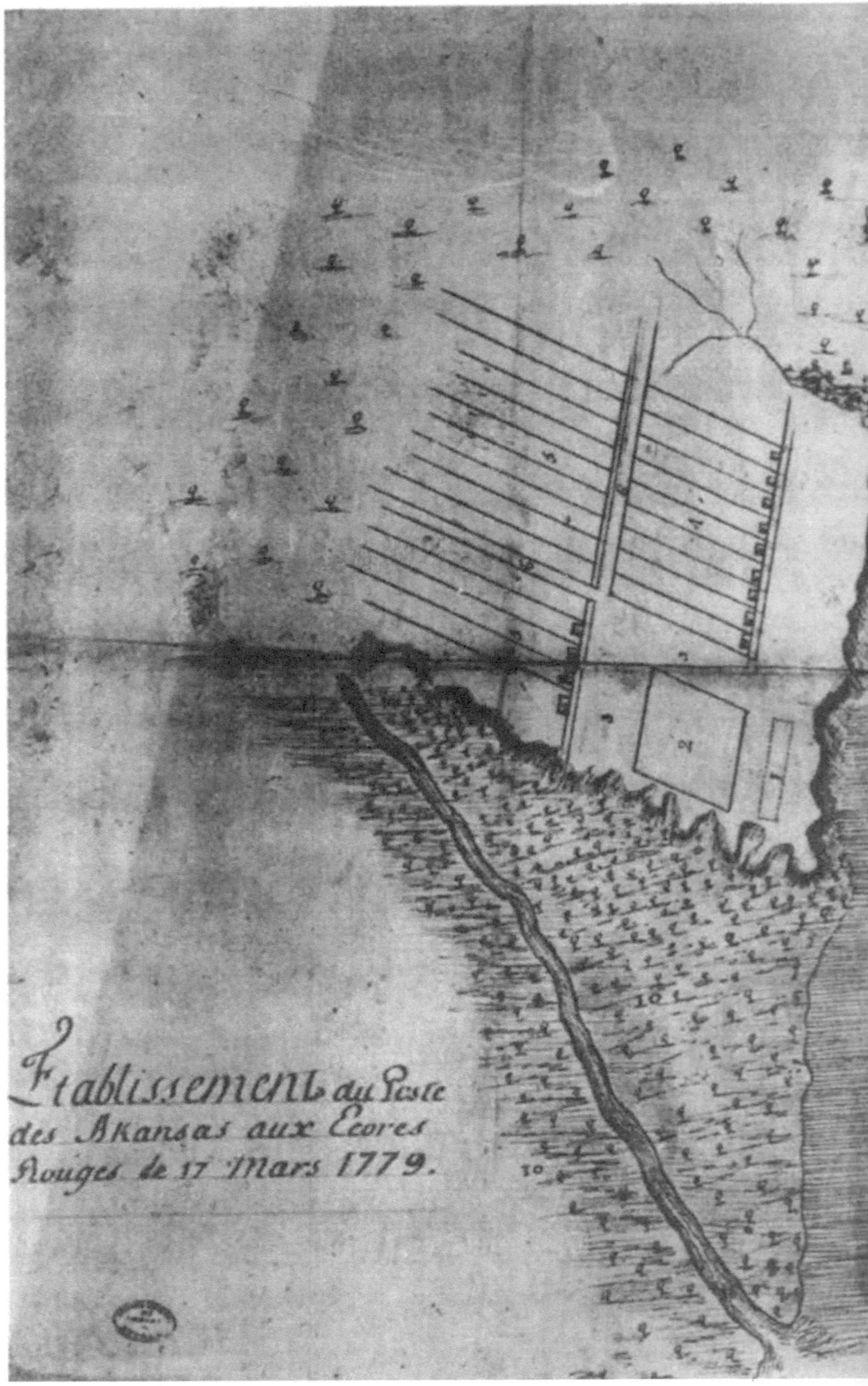

Figure 5. Arkansas Post, March 17, 1779.
(*Courtesy of Archivo General de Indias, Seville.*)

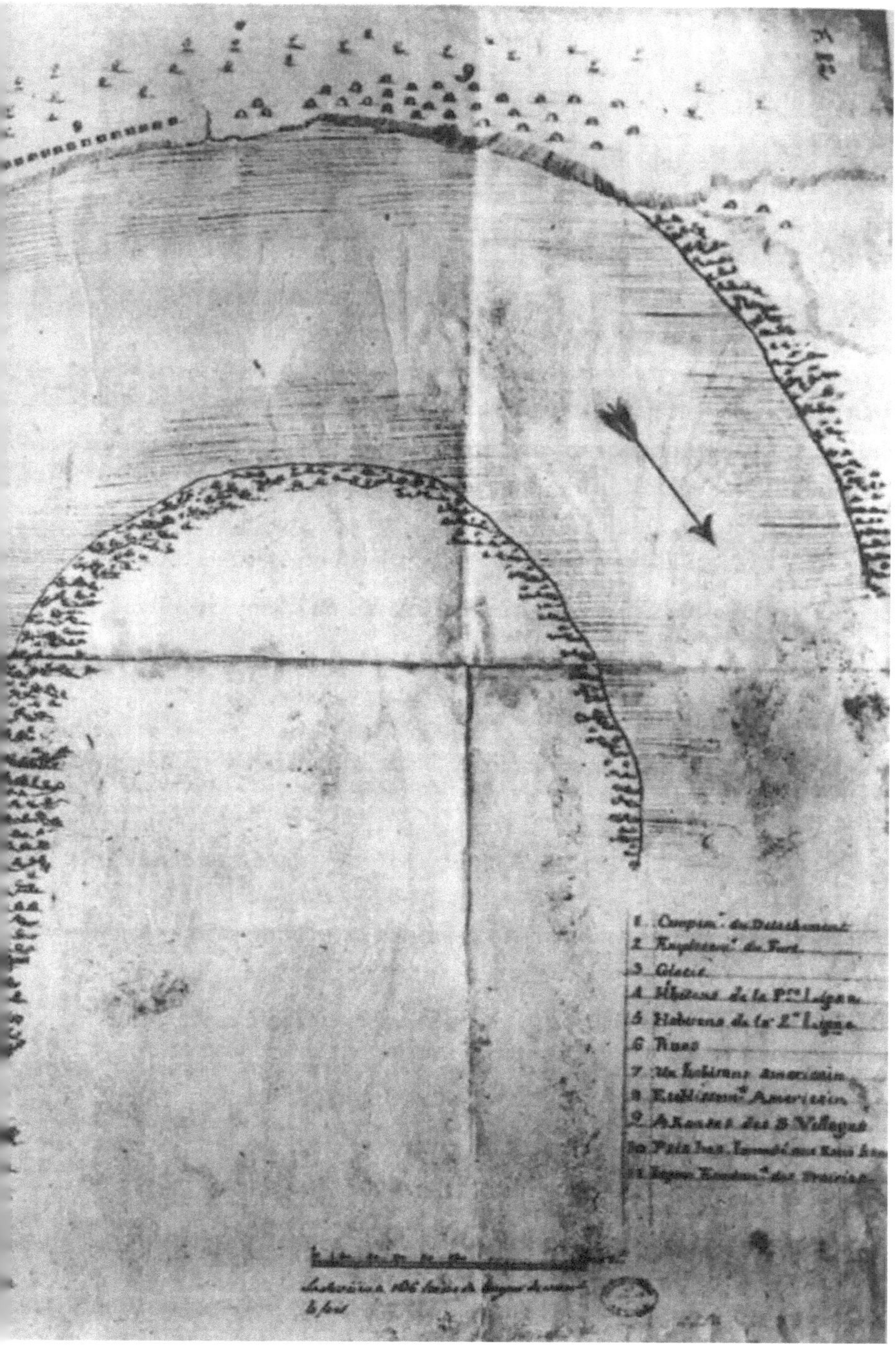
3 Glacis
6 Rues

surveyor for the expedition. Dumont has left behind a very considerable manuscript describing his experiences in Louisiana,[36] but he devotes only a little more than half a page of it to his time in the Arkansas region. He records, interestingly, that he helped the Arkansas *engagés* "beautify [the place] by the regularity of the houses that I built there."[37] He makes the further claim that the persons who settled the concession were Germans, and that when Law was disgraced the concession "fell to pieces and the Germans abandoned it and went to settle ten leagues from the capital city of New Orleans."[38] This is the first assertion by anyone that there were Germans on the Arkansas River at Law's concession. It ought to be noted at this point that Dumont did not write his manuscript until 1747, fully twenty-five years after the events that he described at the Arkansas.[39] A much-edited version of it, claiming to have been "based on the *mémoires* of M. Dumont," was published in Paris in 1753.[40] This book repeats the tale in Dumont's manuscript of Germans abandoning the Arkansas for the German Coast of Louisiana, and the story has been perpetuated by a long line of later writers, the earliest, perhaps, being Capt. Philip Pittman, who visited Arkansas Post in 1765 and published an account of it in 1770.[41]

The next observer of happenings at Law's projected Arkansas settlement was Diron d'Artaguiette, inspector general of the company, who made an official visit to the posts of the colony in 1722–1723. He arrived at the Law concession on February 25, 1723, and counted only "three miserable shacks [*baraques*], fourteen Frenchmen, and six Negroes."[42] Near the military post he reports having seen "many French *habitants,* who are all men dismissed from the concession belonging heretofore to M. Law."[43] In July of 1723, after a trip up the Mississippi, d'Artaguiette returned to the military post and took a census because, in his words, "many inhabitants had established themselves there since my last review."[44] D'Artaguiette does not say where these people had come from, or even if they had originally been part of the concession, though it is practically certain that they had.

The sources discussed are the only eyewitness accounts that bear on the events surrounding the rise and fall of Law's Arkansas colony. As we saw, only Dumont asserts the presence there of German *engagés.* The silence of the other sources on this subject would alone be enough to raise in a critical mind a suspicion that Dumont's account is unreliable. But much more important, the records of the colonial administration reflect that none of the German colonists ever reached the Arkansas. Although destined there originally, they were, in an economy move, sent directly to the region north of New Orleans that was later known as the German Coast.[45] There was, in other words, according to these documents, no intermediate sojourn for these colonists at the Arkansas concession. For those interested in the truth, therefore, the matter reduces to this: As between Dumont and contemporary colonial records, the two being in direct conflict, which ought one to believe? The choice must be made and is quite plain: Professor Giraud, after examining the evidence, states that Dumont's story is "simply ridiculous."[46]

Law's *engagés*, or some of them at least, remained behind on what are now the banks of Lake Dumond to become hunters and Indian traders, and to engage sporadically in some half-hearted and desultory efforts at agriculture. The military post, abandoned in 1725, was revived in 1731. The Chickasaws, ancient enemies of the Quapaws and for some time in the English interest, razed this settlement in 1749, as we shall have occasion to describe in greater detail in a later chapter. Soon thereafter, and probably in 1749, the French removed their village a few miles upriver to the highlands which they called *Écores Rouges* (Red Bluffs) where the Arkansas Post National Memorial now stands. Here they raised a not unimpressive military establishment, which, however, was abandoned in 1756, when the settlement and military post were moved downriver in order more easily to aid the convoys plying the Mississippi.[47] (It is likely that the Seven Years' War, in which the English and the French were beginning to engage officially the very year that this change of venue occurred, provided the impetus for it.)[48] There the settlement remained for almost a quarter of a century, when, thanks largely to the enterprise and foresight of the most able commandant Balthazar de Villiers, who wished to be shut of the floods that plagued his downriver location, the Post once again relocated, this time back upriver to *Écores Rouges*. Here the Post stayed until its disappearance as a real town in the 1940s.[49] But even as late as 1972, the Geological Survey maps reveal a ghost, an echo of a settlement with the ancient name of Arkansas Post, a cluster of three or four houses demolished in 1980 to make way for the development of the National Memorial.

Though the Arkansas Post of Louisiana was the principal colonial settlement in the state, it was not by any means the only place where Europeans gathered. Hunters and traders penetrated great distances up the Arkansas, indeed well into

Oklahoma and Kansas, in search of game and Indian trade, and they created hunting camps at strategic places along the river. Some of these camps were occupied only part of the year; many led fleeting and ephemeral existences because of hostile Indians, the seasonal character of the fur trade, and the French hunters' natural inclination toward a peripatetic life. The present-day city of Pine Bluff no doubt obscures the remains of some of these camps, though we cannot certainly call the name of any colonial Arkansan who lived there. Farther up, where the Ouachita escarpment comes up from the south to meet the water, at Little Rock, which the French called *Petit Rocher*,[50] a number of hunters seem fairly early to have achieved such permanence as was consistent with their way of life.[51] Then, too, a few more miles upstream, at what was and is called Cadron (where the Corps of Engineers, as part of the penance imposed on them for destroying the old town site, has built a rather magnificent blockhouse), hunters and traders formed a community of sorts that flickered in and out of existence during the eighteenth century.[52] Petit Jean Mountain, despite the pretty tales to the contrary, was probably named after a Frenchman (No, not a woman!) who lived or camped there and was nicknamed Little John: One with that name was killed by the Osages on the Arkansas River in 1732.[53] Other rendezvous points existed at places now difficult to locate with any confidence. Belle Point, at the juncture of the Arkansas and Poteau rivers where Fort Smith now stands, was in all likelihood one of these.[54]

Though the Arkansas River furnished the principal focus of settlement for the eighteenth-century French, it was hardly the only stream on the banks of which a few struggling Frenchmen raised their straggling huts and houses. The Red River, of course, was also an important artery of the colony, and, in 1714, the French established the post of Natchitoches there in the hopes of carrying on a lucrative trade with the Spanish of New Mexico and Texas.[55] In 1719, Bénard de La Harpe founded a small trading post and agricultural colony, sometimes called St. Louis des Caddodoches, higher up this river, just outside the present boundaries of the state of Arkansas. Its aim, and the aim of the small garrison usually stationed there, was to secure and cultivate the important allegiance with the Caddo tribes of the region and to protect against intrusions from Texas. Though the few agricultural settlers evidently abandoned this establishment in 1778,[56] apparently a small detachment of soldiers remained there until the very end of the colonial period.[57]

Figure 6. Map of the Ouachita region, 1799. (*Courtesy of Library of Congress.*)

One of the principal tributaries of the Red, which the French called the Black River along its lower course and the Ouachita River higher up, rises in the mountains of south Arkansas. Some rather dissolute French hunters operated regularly in the Ouachita region from the late 1760s, and in about 1782 Gov. Esteban Miró decided to try to impose some order on them. To that end, he sent Juan Filhiol to establish a post on the Ouachita and to try to coax the hunters into a more ordered, agrarian existence. Evidently, Filhiol first fixed his headquarters in what is now Ouachita County, at the site of modern-day Camden, which the French called *Écore à Fabri* (Fabry's Bluff), possibly after an explorer named André Fabry de La Bruyère.[58] Though two years later Filhiol moved downriver to what is now Monroe, Louisiana, and eventually built Fort Miró, a number of French, perhaps upwards of a hundred, remained in the Arkansas wilds along the Ouachita and the Saline River, its principal tributary. Even so early as 1784, one Cuvilliers *dit* Champignolle acquired a tavern license from the Ouachita Post commandant:[59] No doubt he lived on the Ouachita River in present-day Union County at what is still called Champagnolle.

The White River, which joins the Arkansas at Big Island, also became the place of residence for a few Frenchmen pursuing hunting and the fur trade. The Francoeur brothers (we have it on their testimony) lived there from 1745, presumably in White County: Francure Township was no doubt named for them.[60] By the very late colonial period, other White River settlements had been established, probably at most of the locations reliably free from floods, namely at the present sites of St. Charles, Crockett's Bluff, Clarendon, De Valls Bluff, Oil Trough, even so far up as Calico Rock and above.[61]

In 1795, when the Spanish established San Fernando de las Barrancas on the present-day site of Memphis, the New Orleans newspaper *Moniteur de la Louisiane* crowed that the new fort would afford protection to Arkansas Post and "foster new establishments between Arkansas and New Madrid,"[62] but this did not in fact happen to any significant degree. A few brave souls, a very few, did in fact settle themselves on the Mississippi bank at or near the mouth of the St. Francis River in the late eighteenth century: Sylvanus Phillips, an American, was the most famous and noteworthy of these, but no true settlement appeared there.[63]

In fact, the only other collection of colonial settlers besides Arkansas Post that might have laid colorable claim to being called a village was gathered

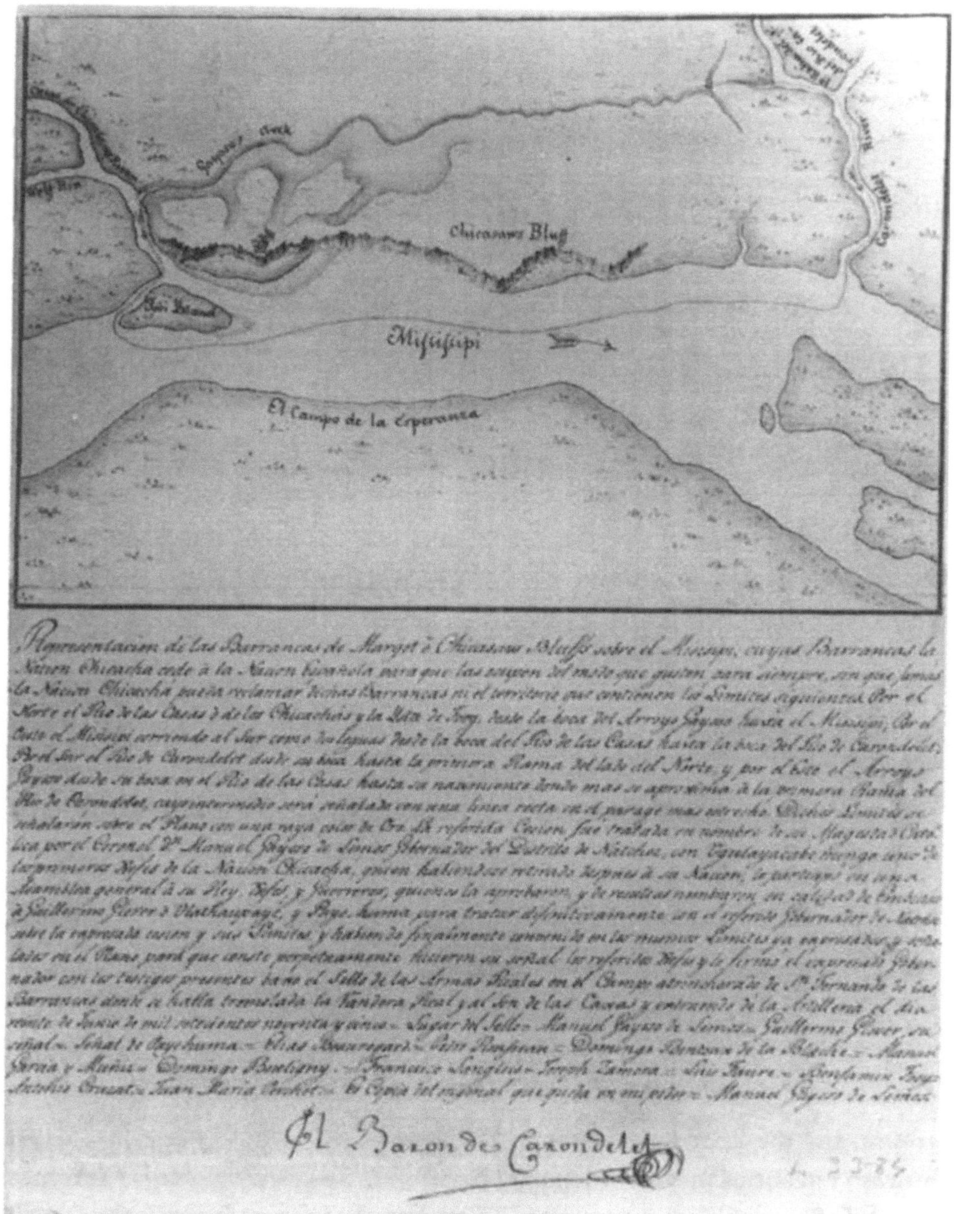

Figure 7. Map of Chickasaw Bluffs, 1795. (*Courtesy of Archivo General de Indias, Seville.*)

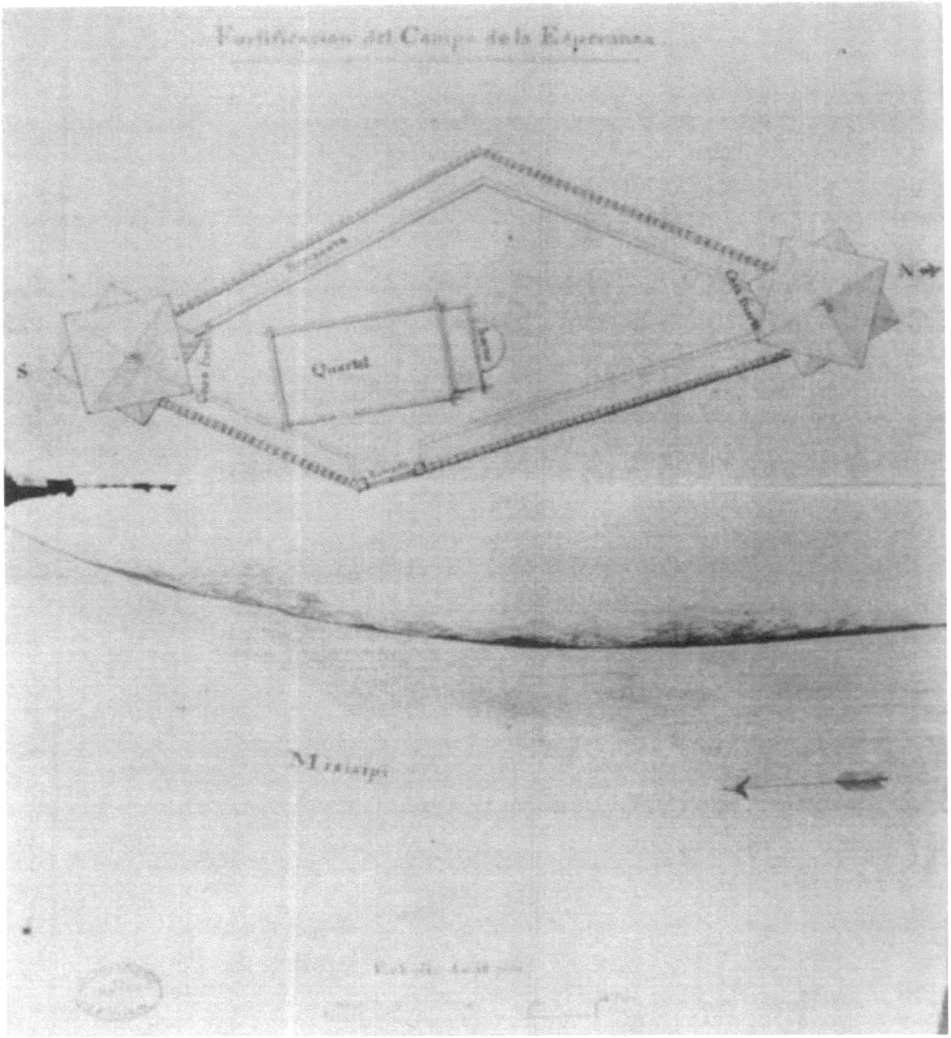

Figure 8. Campo del Esperanza, 1797. (*Courtesy of Archivo General de Indias, Seville.*)

around the tiny garrison at Campo del Esperanza (Field of Hope), which the Spanish established in 1797 when they abandoned San Fernando de las Barrancas and moved a small force across the Mississippi.[64] There were only about eight soldiers stationed there at any one time, detached from the garrison at New Madrid and commanded by a sergeant. But Esperanza was also the site of Arkansas's first naval base: A cannon launch, perhaps two, which patrolled the

Mississippi for signs of invaders and illegal immigrants, operated from there at least for a time. Each apparently had a crew of three.[65] By 1802, the commandant at Esperanza had granted over six thousand acres of land around his little fort, and up and down the Mississippi, not a little of it to one Benjamin Fooy and his relatives, and much of the rest to Spanish members of the garrison.[66] Fooy, long in the service of Spain on both sides of the Mississippi, was easily the most prominent citizen in this part of the Arkansas region in late colonial times, and he certainly became a merchant and trader of some significance. It is not true, however, that he was ever a Spanish *alcalde* (judge), as some have insisted on calling him; nor does the absurd story that Volney wrote part of his *Ruins* at Fooy's Arkansas residence find the first scintilla of support in the records.[67]

These, then, were the principal sites of European occupation in seventeenth- and eighteenth-century Arkansas. Because of the large number of transients who lived temporarily in the region, many of them illegal aliens, accurate population figures are out of the question. But an order of magnitude can be rather confidently guessed at, and it is small: Even as late as 1790, the Arkansas Post commandant reported a population at his village that barely exceeded 100;[68] it had perhaps grown to 450 by the time of the American takeover.[69] So a few hundred whites, we can reliably assume, were all that could claim to be Arkansas denizens at any time during the eighteenth century, and for most of that time that estimate will grossly exceed the true figure.

It is not that the Arkansas region lacked for grand schemes aimed at dramatically increasing its European population. After the American Revolution, the Spanish were especially keen on encouraging immigration because they quite rightly feared the encroachments of the ambitious westering American republic that they had only recently and reluctantly felt it necessary to help create. The Spanish vacillated between admitting and excluding American immigrants: They were the most obvious candidates for emigration, but they were also the most likely to be subversive.[70] In 1788, an entrepreneur named George Morgan had secured conditional permission from Diego de Gardoqui, Spain's *chargé d'affaires* in Philadelphia, to settle American colonists from the western states on a huge grant containing fifteen million acres that extended along the Mississippi from St. Como, Missouri, to the mouth of the St. Francis River. Morgan did, indeed, found the town of New Madrid in 1789, but the grant never materialized because of the opposition of Gov. Esteban Miró, who no doubt thought the whole idea too radical because of the republican form of government promised to the enterprise.[71] Another ambitious plan to populate the Arkansas region surfaced in 1799, when Carlos Martínez de Irujo, the Spanish minister in Philadelphia, sought a grant of forty thousand acres between the Arkansas and White rivers, on which he proposed to establish forty families as a barrier to American expansion. He planned to grow wheat there from which he would make flour for export to Cuba, Puerto Rico, and Caracas. A good opportunity was lost when the king rejected Irujo's project without explanation.[72]

It requires stretching considerably the ordinary meaning of words to say that the European presence in colonial Arkansas amounted to an occupation. The small number of whites who were there, however, left numerous French names strewn upon the map, and, more important, as we shall see, had a profound impact on the culture and economic life of the indigenous peoples with whom they came into contact, not to mention the animal life which, with the Indians' help, after abandoning the hope of discovering rich deposits of precious minerals, they plundered unstintingly. Their story, moreover, is full of intrinsic interest despite or perhaps partly because of the fact that they have left behind virtually no physical trace and only a very few surnames mangled beyond easy recognition.

II

THE FRENCH COLONIAL BUILDINGS OF ARKANSAS POST

Arkansas Post, the first European settlement in what would become the Louisiana Purchase, was established in the summer of 1686, less than four years after William Penn set foot in the new world to found Philadelphia. Despite this precocious beginning, which seemed to promise a kind of presumptive distinction, the Post never acquired a very distinguished reputation. This was partly due to the instability of the settlement, which, as we have seen, had to be moved three times because of floods, the danger of Indian attack, and changes in its strategic mission.[1] Nor could the size and nature of the population at the Arkansas earn it many encomia. For most of the eighteenth century, therefore, evaluations of the place were almost invariably unflattering. For instance, in 1739, Governor Bienville lamented that "our fort of the Arkansas is falling into ruins; there are only a missionary and three *habitans* there, who do nothing."[2] So, too, in 1766, Capt. Harry Gordon sniffed that "the few Banditti of Arkansas don't deserve the name of settlement."[3] In 1778, Capt. Balthazar de Villiers, who was commandant of Arkansas Post from 1776 to 1782, and therefore in a position to know, stated flatly that his post was "the most disagreeable hole in the universe."[4] And in 1796, the spy Victor Collot claimed that since the people of the

Post had "no means of defense against the Indians, who are continuously pillaging their cattle and robbing them of their industry, they are in general poor and miserable."[5] Visitors served up similar descriptions of the Post and its residents in the nineteenth century.[6]

A recent monograph expressed the view that the attachment to European legal and religious norms at Arkansas Post was tenuous at best for most of the eighteenth century, but that it improved noticeably in the last fifteen years of the colonial period.[7] Since law and religion are probably the most important manifestations of what might be called intellectual and social culture, to conclude from those findings that Arkansas Post was, until around 1790, an isolated backwater unattached to the general culture of colonial Louisiana would not seem unwarranted. It will be one aim of this chapter to explore the extent to which the Post's architecture, an important aspect of its material and artistic culture, conformed to the modes current in the rest of Louisiana during the eighteenth century, in an effort to discover whether this conclusion is in fact correct.

Sometime early in the summer of 1686, six Frenchmen built a trading house in Arkansas County on Lake Dumond, which at that time was part of the main channel of the Arkansas River. This house, near the Quapaw village of Osotouy, is the only one that we can confidently say was built at the first Arkansas Post. It was constructed at the behest of Henri de Tonty to whom La Salle had in 1682 granted a large tract of land on the Arkansas and was no doubt built by or under the direction of Jean Couture, the carpenter who was in charge of the Post. Tonty, writing in the winter of 1690–91, tells us that he left his French followers at the Arkansas in 1686 "to make a house surrounded by stakes [*entourée de pieux*]."[8] This phrase does not mean that the house was to be provided with a palisade: It is either a circumlocution for a house built of upright logs, a method of construction frequently employed in Louisiana and more commonly called *poteaux en terre* (posts in the ground); or it means that the house was to have a wall covering of stakes or vertical planks. Whatever may have been Tonty's original plan, we can advance some general observations about what the house that Couture actually built looked like, for in 1687 survivors of La Salle's ill-fated voyage of 1684 visited Tonty's post and left us some indication of its appearance.

Father Douay, one of this company, simply calls the house "French-looking,"[9] but Joutel, the leader of the group, gives a slightly more detailed description: He says that it was built of "heavy pieces of wood notched into each other, dovetailed, all the way to the top of the roof, of fine cypress and roofed with bark."[10] It is thus plain that this house was built of horizontal timbers, not vertical ones, and was therefore no doubt of the type of construction called *piéce sur piéce.* This was a method of building characteristic of seventeenth-century Canada that Canadians brought with them to Louisiana. In *piéce sur piéce* houses, the "logs were hewn into planks four to six inches wide and eight to 16 inches tall. They were tied together at the corners with full-dovetail notching to form a solid crib."[11] Prof. Jay Edwards notes that this mode of construction was frequently employed for "small rural houses" in colonial Louisiana.[12] (See Figure 9.) From Joutel's general description of Tonty's house, Samuel Wilson, Jr., has drawn the reasonable inference that the "roof was steep in the Canadian manner."[13] Joutel, Douay, and Tonty give no further details as to the appearance of the house; but Tonty at least twice does refer to his "fort" on the Arkansas, once in 1689 in a conditional grant to the Jesuits,[14] and a second time in an undated grant to Jacques Cardinal, one of the six original settlers at the Post.[15] We should not, however, be too quick to divine from these statements that Tonty's Arkansas house was provided with a palisade, though that is neither an unnatural nor an impossible inference. Certainly a palisaded house could qualify as a fort in the parlance of seventeenth-century explorers;[16] La Salle even once mentioned throwing up something he termed a fort in a very few hours.[17]

Tonty's tiny post, the population of which, so far as we can tell, never exceeded six, was abandoned by 1699 when Governor Bienville arrived on the Gulf coast to establish the colony of Louisiana.[18] We hear nothing more of European houses at the Arkansas until about eighty French workmen (*engagés*) employed by John Law arrived to establish, at the abandoned site of Tonty's post, a settlement for Law's German colonists, none of whom, because of their patron's bankruptcy and disgrace, ever settled on the river.[19]

There are several accounts of the houses and other buildings constructed by these French *engagés* after they arrived in August of 1721. On December 2 of that

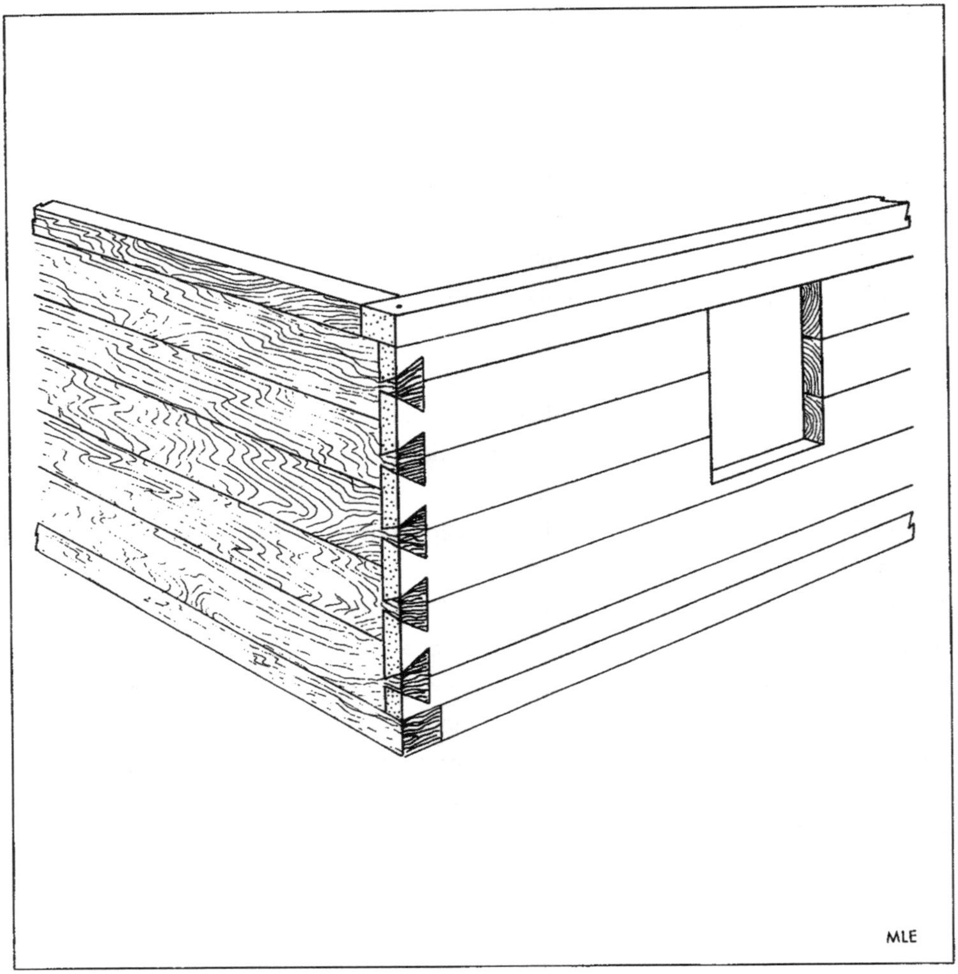

Figure 9. Pièce sur pièce construction. (*Courtesy of Prof. Jay Edwards.*)

year Father Charlevoix visited a Quapaw village on the Mississippi not more than twenty miles by land from Law's colony. It is not clear that he actually visited the colony itself, but he does locate it properly across from the Quapaw village that he calls *Kappas* on the Arkansas River, where, he says, "one sees the sad refuse [*tristes débris*] of the concession of M. Law. . . ." Father Charlevoix gives no further description, and if he actually saw the settlement, his silence with respect to what it looked like must indicate that it did not make much of an impression.[20] In March of 1722, the explorer Jean-Baptiste Bénard de La Harpe arrived with Bertrand Dufresne, Sieur du Demaine, who took over as director of the Arkansas concession. According to La Harpe, they found there only "twenty huts [*cabanes*] poorly arranged and three acres of cleared ground."[21] Almost a year later, Diron d'Artaguiette arrived at Law's concession. He said that he "did not notice anything in particular. There are only three miserable shacks [*baraques*], fourteen Frenchmen, and six Negroes." Two hours upriver by boat, at a distance of one league by land and two by water, he found the military post commanded by La Boulaye. "There is no fort there at all," d'Artaguiette observed; the commandant had "only a little hut," and there was a "sort of barn [*grange*] which serves as a lodging for the soldiers." On July 12, after a trip up the Mississippi, d'Artaguiette returned and noted that a number of new inhabitants had established themselves at the military post since his previous visit. He took a census of them, but says nothing of their dwellings.[22]

The foregoing accounts are the most trustworthy descriptions that we have of Law's colony. In 1753, a book, based, though often very loosely, on the memoirs of Dumont de Montigny and attributed to J.-B. Le Mascrier, appeared in Paris. Dumont de Montigny had indeed accompanied La Harpe up the Arkansas River to Law's concession in 1722; but this book, as demonstrated earlier, can hardly be called his contemporaneous journal, for the memoirs were written twenty-five years after Dumont's visit to Arkansas. The book reports that there was, at the Arkansas military post, "no fort at all . . . , only four or five houses built of palisades, a small *corps de garde,* and a hut that serves as a storehouse." This is not an implausible description, and it is not inconsistent with the descriptions previously noted. But this work goes on to claim that on Law's concession proper, about a league from the military post, married German workers had established themselves and begun to prosper, having already built "pavilions [*pavillons*] for the officers with huts for the workmen" and "had even constructed great storehouses [*grands magasins*]."[23] Surely this is fanciful. "Great storehouses" could hardly have escaped the attention of La Harpe and d'Artaguiette, the latter being inspector general of the entire Mississippi Company; and *pavillon* is a term of art, meaning a substantial house with a steep French roof, frequently hipped. It is not credible that La Harpe and d'Artaguiette, keeping careful records and journals, would have noticed shacks, huts, and barns and failed to see *magasins* and *pavillons.*

Except for the "houses built of palisades" that Dumont's printed book

Figure 10. Detail from a view of Law's concession at New Biloxi, December 10, 1720. (*Courtesy of Newberry Library, Chicago.*)

ascribed to the military post, which in fact did not appear in Dumont's original *mémoire*,[24] the descriptions of Law's concession and the nearby military post, though relatively numerous, give little indication of the construction methods employed by Law's workmen. The buildings were quite evidently rather crude. If the *magasins* and *pavillons* had not been figments, we could have guessed that they looked like the *magasin* with a steep hip roof that is depicted in the wonderful drawing by Jean-Baptiste Michel le Bouteux of Law's concession at its staging point at New Biloxi on December 10, 1720. (See Figure 10.) The temptation to imagine that such a house was built on the Arkansas River in 1721, however, needs to be resisted.

In 1725 the military post was abandoned, and in 1727 Father Paul du Poisson, a Jesuit missionary, arrived and took up residence "in the house of the company of the Indies, which is the house of the Commandant whenever there is one here."[25] Perhaps this house was built by Director Dufresne before he abandoned the Arkansas about 1726; in any event, Father du Poisson gives us no description of it.

Late in 1731 or early in 1732 a French military post was reestablished at Arkansas Post on what is now Lake Dumond.[26] Sometime between the reestablishment of a garrison at Arkansas and April 8, 1734, First Ensign de Coulange, who was in command there, constructed four buildings for his tiny outpost: A *poteaux en terre* barracks forty feet by sixteen feet[27] roofed with bark; a *poteaux en terre* prison ten feet by eight feet roofed with bark; a house (*maison*) *de bois sur solles* thirty-two feet by eighteen feet roofed with bark and divided into three rooms, one of which had a fireplace, with floors and ceilings of cypress; and a powder magazine built of *bois sur solles* that measured eight feet by ten feet.[28] *Bois sur solles* (wood on sills) construction utilized vertical posts, as did *poteaux en terre* construction, but, instead of being placed in the ground, the posts rested on a sill (*solle*), usually of wood, which served as a kind of foundation. This was a very common building technique in colonial Louisiana from the earliest days.[29] Governor Bienville reckoned that an "enclosure of stakes" (*enceinte de pieux*), *i.e.*, a stockade to surround the four buildings of this post, was unnecessary, since there were only twelve men in the Arkansas garrison. Instead, he suggested that "one could simply reinforce (*redoubler*) the barracks with good stakes and provide it with loopholes."[30] This was all the protection that the governor wanted to provide a remote wilderness post against threatened attacks by the hostile Chickasaw nation.

On May 9, 1749, the Chickasaws, with the help of some Abeka allies and perhaps a few disaffected Choctaws, did in fact strike the Arkansas Post. By that time, a stockade had possibly been provided the few residents of the Arkansas, because it is said that during this attack they "fled to safety in the fort, but not without the loss of six men killed and eight women and children captured."[31] But perhaps the fort referred to was simply the reinforced barracks projected in 1734. Whatever it was, it was sufficiently strong to discourage the Chickasaws from pressing their attack on it: When they lost three men, and their chief was gravely wounded, the Chickasaws retired with their prisoners.[32]

Soon after this attack, and probably in the year 1749, the French relocated their post and settlement upriver about five leagues to *Écores Rouges*, which was fifteen leagues from the Mississippi, to join the Quapaws for protection. The colonial government, no doubt greatly alarmed and embarrassed by the disastrous Chickasaw attack, caused a new fort to be built there. It was, by far, the most elaborate military establishment constructed in Arkansas up to that time; indeed, it was the most elaborate ever erected there in colonial times. No doubt some show of resolve seemed necessary to prevent further attacks and to attract and keep settlers. Some say that the fort was paid for out of the personal funds of Capt. Paul Augustin Le Pelletier de La Houssaye, commandant of the Post, in return for a five-year monopoly on Indian trade.[33] Work on this fort probably began in the fall of 1751, for an appraisal and survey of it done on March 19, 1755, lists expenses according to a contract of October 21, 1751.[34]

The stockade of this fort was 30 *toises* (180 French feet) on a side; the outside stakes stood eleven feet high after being placed in a trench three feet deep, the inner stakes five feet. It had three bastions with cannon batteries and two of the bastions had sentry boxes. Inside the enclosure were seven buildings. The most interesting, seventy-two feet by seventeen feet, seems to have contained four rooms: a hall (*salle*) and bedroom (*chambre*) for the commandant, a bedroom for the priest, and a chapel. This building was of the familiar *poteaux en terre* construction, and the survey notes that it was *bousillés entre poteaux*. This latter phrase refers to the method used to fill the spaces between the wall posts. In *poteaux en terre* construction, Professor Edwards writes, "the interstices between the wall posts were filled with a mixture of mud, lime, and Spanish moss, called *bousillage*. . . . The technique was adapted from French *colombage* (half-timber) framing, but the nogging material was borrowed from the Indians."[35] The building had two fireplaces four feet wide, one each, evidently, for the good captain and the priest. The quarters of the commandant and priest had plank floors, but the chapel evidently did not. The nine five-foot windows of the building had shutters. The roof, which was covered with clapboards or staves (*merins*), was

Figure 11. Artist's conception of Fort St. Jean Baptiste, Natchitoches. (*Courtesy of Louisiana Department of Culture, Recreation, and Tourism.*)

steep: In section it was close to an isosceles triangle, and thus would have had a pitch of almost sixty degrees. Judging from the length of the *poteaux* provided for the walls, a simple application of Pythagoras indicates that the top of the roof would have been perhaps twenty-three feet from the ground. This would have made it an imposing structure for its time and place.

The officers' quarters and soldiers' barracks, though not quite as tall, was an even larger building. It was ninety-six feet by seventeen feet and was built the same way as the commandant's house (*de la même façon que celuy du commandant*). It had plank floors and two fireplaces, one, presumably, for the officers, the other for the soldiers. Since there were two bedrooms for the officers, their fireplace was probably a double one. It had four shuttered windows and was covered with clapboards or staves. A third *poteaux en terre* building, sixty-four feet by eighteen feet, housed the storekeeper, the interpreter, the storehouse for supplies (*le magasin de vivres*), and the hospital. This one had two fireplaces, a plank floor, five five-foot windows with shutters, and an attic over the store and the

Figure 12. Reconstructed Fort St. Jean Baptiste, Natchitoches. (*Courtesy of Mr. Samuel Wilson, Jr.*)

storekeeper's bedroom, no doubt for storing goods. The bakehouse (*le bâstiment de la boulangerie*) was, as we would expect, less elaborate. It was eighteen feet by sixteen feet, of *poteaux en terre* construction, was covered with clapboards or staves, and had an oven with a six-foot inside diameter. The oven was made of mudded mortar and sat on a sill (*fait avec des torches bousillées sur un sollage*) and was covered by a lean-to (*apentis*) made of bark. Evidently the floor was dirt.

There were three other buildings at de La Houssaye's new fort: A powder magazine eight and one-half feet square made of stakes in the ground (*pieux en terre*) joined together, with a dirt floor, covered all over (*couvert pardemis*) with bark, and surrounded by a palisade fence to isolate it from the rest of the fort; a prison eight feet by seven feet, in a bastion under one of the cannon platforms, built of strong stakes (*une forte cloture de forts pieux*); and a latrine, nine feet by five feet, enclosed with stakes and roofed with bark (*La cage des latrines enclosé avec des pieux couverte d'écorces*). These three buildings had dirt floors.

All this makes for a reasonably impressive establishment. The stockade enclosed exactly one arpent (about 0.85 acre) and the amount of enclosed building space approached five thousand square feet. The building techniques seem quite *à la mode*, though the lack of amenities like galleries and glazed windows indicate that, in total effect, the Post would have to be described as provincial military Spartan. This military establishment must have borne a striking resemblance to the one constructed at Natchitoches in 1732. (See Figures 11 and 12.)

The relative grandeur of this fort makes it all the more ironic that the French abandoned it only five years after they began its construction and perhaps only a year after its completion. The government came around to the view that the Post's location, fifteen leagues from the Mississippi, made it an inconvenient *entrepôt* for convoys traveling between New Orleans and the Illinois country. Therefore, in 1756 the Post was moved yet again and yet another fort was built, this time only three or four leagues from the mouth of the Arkansas.[36] In the nineteenth century, this establishment acquired the name of Fort Desha.[37] (See Figure 13.) According to Capt. Philip Pittman, who made a reconnaissance of the

Figure 13. Sketch of the remains of the Arkansas Post built in 1756. 10 *Miscellaneous Documents of the House of Representatives for the Second Session of the Fifty-third Congress, 1893-94* 244 (1894).

Mississippi River for the English in 1765, the square stockade of this fort was about 180 feet on a side, that is, like the previous fort, it enclosed about one arpent; and it contained a three-room barracks for the soldiers, "a commanding officer's house, a Powder Magazine for the Provision and an apartment for the Commissary, all which are in a ruinous Condition."[38] Pittman wrote Maj. Gen. Thomas Gage that because of the frequent floods at this location, "all the buildings are rais'd Six feet from the Ground."[39] Apparently because of the similarity between this description and the specifications for de La Houssaye's 1751 fort, Stanley Faye thought that Pittman had pawned off a description of the 1751 fort for the fort as it existed in 1765.[40] But there are some interesting differences, including the omission in Pittman's description of a chapel and priest's *chambre;* and we know in fact that the fort built in 1756–58 did not have a proper chapel, for Father Louis Carette, the resident Jesuit missionary at Arkansas Post, resigned in disgust partly because of that fact.[41] Furthermore, all eighteenth-century French forts in Louisiana would have been very much alike, given the similar needs of soldiers and the military's penchant for uniformity. The dimensions of the stockade would have naturally suggested themselves, not only because they were the dimensions of the old fort, but also because the stockade was exactly one arpent on a side.[42]

In any case, in 1758 maintenance and repairs of "the buildings and other dependencies of the Post of Arkansas" were required.[43] A hut twenty-six feet by eighteen feet was built outside the fort *en poteaux en terre.* It was enclosed with stakes and roofed with shingles (*bardeaux*) with a *bousillage* fireplace, and was for the use of the Indians when they came to the Post on business, as they frequently did. Several other huts, originally constructed as temporary quarters for the soldiers and residents of the Post (*domicilez du poste*) while the fort was being built,[44] were refurbished because they had rotted and been damaged by wind (*un coup de vent*). They were to be used to house persons in the convoys that called at the Post on their way to and from the Illinois country. A lean-to was affixed to one of the gables of the bakehouse to house the garrison's baker. It was made of *poteaux en terre* and roofed with shingles. It was also said to have been covered by a double row of stakes (*entouré de pieux à double entourage sur les unes des autres*). The oven's mouth, made of *bousillage,* and its sill were also repaired. Many of the *poteaux* in the walls of the old storehouse were replaced to prevent rotting. Some equipment was included in the bill for repairs, including levels, buckets, and so forth, the most interesting perhaps being a nineteen-foot ladder for "climbing up the roofs of the buildings, either for repairing them or the chimneys, or in case of fire." Ditches for drainage and sanitation were also provided.

This is about all that can be advanced with any confidence about the buildings of the Arkansas Post of 1756.[45] It is certainly true that the houses there were, as Pittman said, raised above the ground, as both Étienne Layssard, the storekeeper, and Balthazar de Villiers, one of the Post's commandants in the 1770s, comment on that fact.[46] The only other reference to architecture in the commandants' letters from this period is the mention in 1774 of a gallery on the commandant's house that had fallen in.[47] This, the first mention in the Arkansas sources of a common eighteenth-century Louisiana architectural feature, comes rather late, since galleries were introduced into the colonial architectural canon in the 1720s by creoles from the West Indies.[48] Maps of Pascagoula in 1726 and Mobile in 1743 "show raised cottages completely surrounded by broad galleries."[49] Since the Arkansas Post built in 1756 was flooded so frequently and since the population consisted mostly of hunters,[50] the apparent lack of architectural sophistication at the Post during this period is not surprising.

A considerable lift to the prospects of our struggling outpost was provided by its removal in 1779 back to the high ground at *Écores Rouges.*[51] De Villiers's 1779 map of this post shows thirty dwellings spread over a distance of about three hundred yards along a horseshoe bend of the river.[52] (See Figure 5.) Only seventeen of these dwellings—de Villiers calls them houses (*maisons*)—were built by French *habitants;* the other thirteen belonged to Americans fleeing the American Revolution, and de Villiers calls them huts (*cabans*). Since the whole settlement was constructed in a little more than three weeks, it could not have included anything very grand. On his map, de Villiers projected a fort in the shape of a rhombus, about 240 feet on a side; but no fort was in fact built at this new Post until 1781, when the *habitants,* greatly fearing an attack by the Chickasaws on account of Spain's alliance with the Americans during the revolution, built one of their own, which de Villiers dubbed Fort Carlos III. The Chickasaws did in fact attack this fort in 1783 and it withstood the onslaught, but in 1788 it had fallen into the river, making necessary yet another makeshift effort by the *habitants.*[53] In 1796, Victor Collot, the French spy, observed this evidently amateurish effort and sneered: "Two ill-constructed huts, situated on the left, surrounded with great palisades, without ditch or parapet, and containing four six-pounders, bear the name of fort."[54]

When the Americans took over the Spanish fort of San Esteban on the Arkansas in 1804, however, the inventory revealed that a new military establishment had been built. There was a stockade containing four buildings: A commandant's house thirty-six feet by sixteen feet, "with two galleries, two closets at the ends of that on the back," divided into two rooms with a "double clay chimney"; a barracks fifty feet by twenty feet, likewise with a "double clay chimney"; a storehouse "supported on props" forty-five feet by twenty feet; and a kitchen (*i.e.,* bakehouse) twenty feet by twelve feet. All of these buildings were roofed with shingles. The commandant's house was said to be in very bad condition and the storehouse in poor condition.[55] The design of the commandant's house,

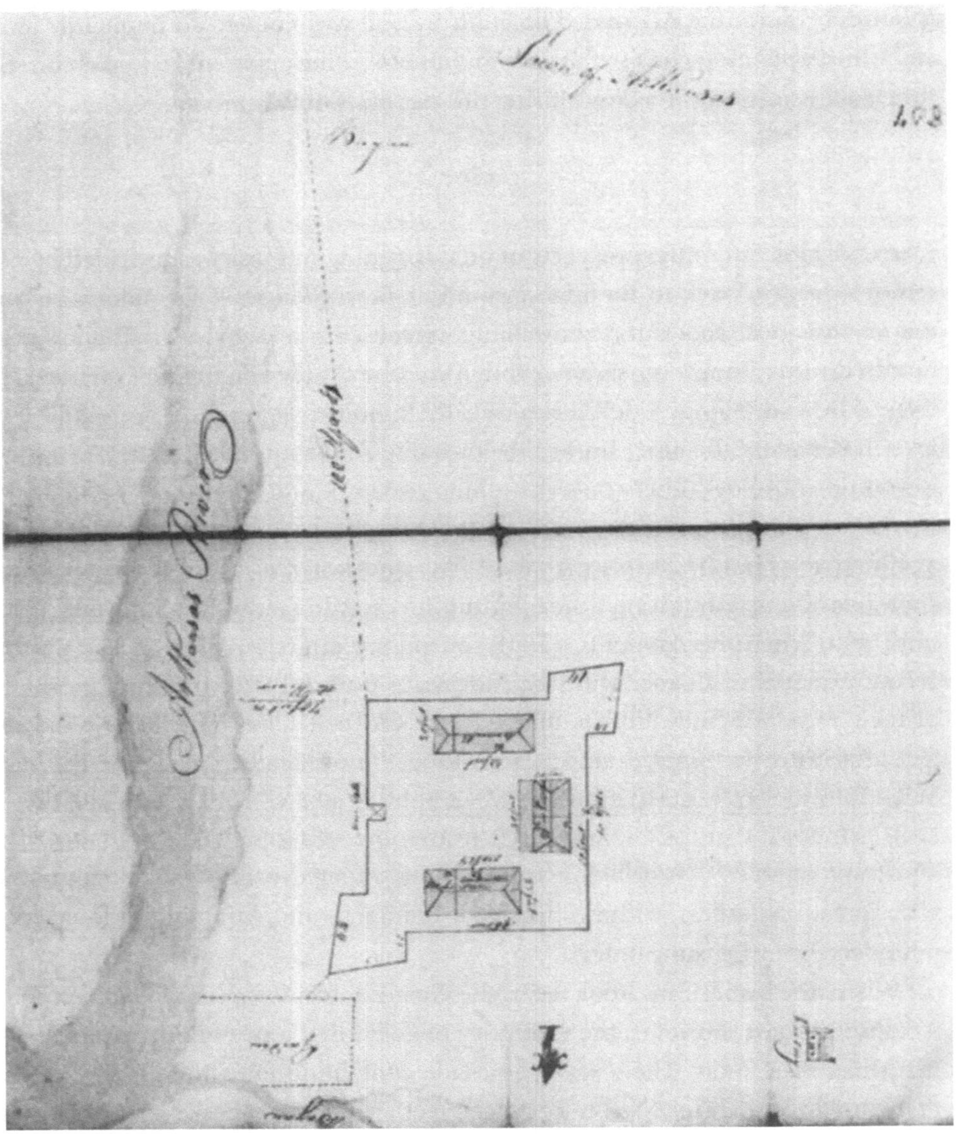

Figure 14. Map of the Fort of the Post of Arkansas in 1807. RG 107, War, Records of the Office of the Secretary of War, National Archives, Washington, D.C.

evidently built in the late 1790s, nevertheless indicates that a kind of architectural maturity had overtaken the remote military post of *Los Arcos.* The enclosure of part of a back gallery, remarked on in the inventory, is a feature of eighteenth-century Louisiana architecture noticed by Professor Edwards as early as 1750, and a floor plan from about 1770 virtually matches the commandant's house.[56] We learn, moreover, from a plan of this fort made in 1807, that all the buildings contained in it had hip roofs.[57] (See Figure 14.) This is the only real proof of what we would have had anyway to guess, for hip roofs were a regular feature of Louisiana houses from the very beginning of serious architectural effort there. They were derived from Quebec and ultimately from Normandy.[58]

It is, moreover, relatively clear that during the late 1780s and the 1790s, as the population tripled to about 400, free and slave,[59] and the commercial importance of the Post grew, the architecture of the *habitants* had matured in quite a striking way also. In 1793, when the population was only 220, free and slave, Pedro Rousseau, captain of the Spanish war galiot *La Flecha,* put in at the Post of Arkansas: He reports that the village proper, which was upriver from the fort, contained "about thirty houses with galleries around, covered [*i.e.,* roofed] with shingles, which form two streets." (Perhaps these are the two *rues* marked on de Villiers's 1779 map, and, perhaps too, they are the Front and Main streets of the early nineteenth-century American settlement.) Down the river, Rousseau says, there were "a dozen quite pretty houses [on lots] of four by four arpents, where there are very beautiful fields of wheat on the highland."[60]

While this is the only eighteenth-century description of the French houses at Arkansas Post that has come down to us, there is more than a little available from the nineteenth century that confirms Rousseau's observations. In 1806, for instance, a deed of land at the Post recited that the land contained "a house of *colombage* thirty feet in length by twenty with galleries all around completely covered with shingles. . . ."[61] There can be little doubt that this house was built in the eighteenth century. William F. Pope, private secretary to a territorial governor, reports that when he came to the Post in 1832, "many of the houses erected during Gov. De Villemont's administration [1794 to 1802] were still standing and were built after the French style of architecture with high pointed roofs and gables and heavy exterior timbers, and high chimneys." They were, he says, at the time he first saw them, in an advanced state of dilapidation. "In many instances," he observes, "tall chimneys had fallen down, and trees of considerable size were growing out through the roofs and chimney places."[62] Washington Irving confirms Pope's 1832 description of the forlorn old Post of Arkansas. He landed there on November 15 of that year and found it a "decayed, ruinous

Figure 15. Interior and exterior views of the Becquette-Ribault house, Ste. Genevieve. (*Courtesy of Ms. Margaret A. Wilhauk.*)

88 4 13

Figure 16. Interior and exterior views of the Bolduc house, Ste. Genevieve.
(*Courtesy of J.M.C. Photo Service.*)

place"; he was especially taken with "an old Spanish wooden building, with piazza." He also noted "French buildings, with casement—piazzas."[63] In "The Creole Village," a story that Irving wrote based largely on observations made at the Post, he describes the dwelling of one of his characters as follows: "It was an old ruinous Spanish house, of large dimensions, with verandas overshadowed by ancient elms. The house had probably been the residence, in old times, of the Spanish Commandant."[64] Irving goes on to say that "[m]ost of the houses [at the Post] were in French taste, with casements and rickety verandas. . . ."[65] W. H. Halliburton, the noted Arkansas antiquary who came to Arkansas Post in 1845 to live, quotes Pope's description as accurate and concludes: "To this description the writer adds that the greater number of these buildings had their floors from four to six feet from the ground, with galleries on all sides."[66] These descriptions, taken together, demonstrate that in the late eighteenth and early nineteenth century the Post consisted of raised *colombage* houses with encircling galleries, some with exposed exterior timbers, others covered completely with shingles, the most advanced state of colonial Louisiana provincial architecture. (See Figures 15 and 16.)

Pope recounts a duel, precipitated by a quarrel that occurred at a hotel, that took place in Arkansas Post in 1820. According to an account of this duel, which Pope had caused to be written out for him, the hotel "was of French architecture, with a wide, open hall, and porches, alike open, extending in a circle all around the building." One of the participants in the quarrel, the account went on to say, gave chase to the other, and they commenced "running around the circular porch and through the hall."[67] Perhaps this hotel was a hybrid of the American dog-trot and French colonial vernacular styles and was built after the American occupation.[68] It is certain, in any case, that colonial Louisiana building styles did not go out of vogue when the Americans assumed sovereignty over Arkansas. In 1809, for instance, the Arkansas Post merchant James Scull contracted with Daniel Mooney to build a house fifty feet by thirty-two feet "and to erect a gallery over each side of the house ten feet wide. . . ."[69] Thomas Nuttall drew a rather crude likeness of what may be a house with a hip roof and gallery at Cadron in 1819. (See Figure 17.) Pope reports, moreover, that in 1832, when he stopped at Montgomery's Point at the mouth of the White River, there was a hotel there which "was elevated some distance above the ground on high brick pillars, and had wide verandas on all sides."[70] This building was surely built after

Figure 17. Detail from a drawing in T. Nuttall, *Travels into the Arkansa Territory during the Year 1819* (1821).

the American takeover, probably after 1821 when Montgomery sold out at the Post and moved to the White River.[71] It appears, in fact, that houses with galleries all around and interior chimneys were still being built in Arkansas County close to the Post as late as 1880. (See Figure 18.)

Though no French-colonial Arkansas house still stands, more than a few of Arkansas's eighteenth-century and early nineteenth-century buildings survived, although in various states of repair, well into the nineteenth century. Indeed, Halliburton records that "[a] number of these houses were standing at Arkansas Post and on the river a few miles below" until the Battle of Arkansas Post, in January of 1863, "when all the houses at the Post as well as those on the river below were destroyed."[72] A drawing of this battle shows houses built of vertical logs with galleries front and back. (See Figure 19.)

Figure 18. The Menard house, Nady, Arkansas. *(Courtesy of Mr. Ray W. Menard, Tulsa.)*

There are other, vaguer and more general nineteenth-century references to the old colonial buildings of Arkansas Post,[73] but many of the foregoing accounts are specific enough to indicate that Arkansas Post became, in the last ten years or so of the colonial period, a place that was in tune with the building vogues of its more sophisticated neighbors in Ste. Genevieve[74] and St. Louis[75] to the north and New Orleans to the south.[76] This is a rather remarkable feat, but it agrees nicely with what we know occurred with respect to the observance of both religious and legal niceties at Arkansas Post in the last decade of the eighteenth century; for in 1796 a parish was for the first time established there and a chapel finally built, and in the 1790s legal proceedings took on an attention to detail that they had not theretofore exhibited.[77]

We cannot at this distance tell, of course, how well built or finely crafted the buildings at Arkansas Post were in the late eighteenth century: Such details are

Figure 19. Detail from a *Leslie's Weekly* illustration entitled "The Investment of Fort Hindman, Arkansas Post, Ark. . . . January 11th, 1863."

lost virtually beyond recall. Only two surviving travelers' accounts bear even remotely on these matters. Late in 1738, during the Second Chickasaw War, Father Vitry visited Arkansas Post and commented on Father Avond's accommodation there. He calls it "a makeshift hut" and notes that "the walls are made of split log, the roof of cypress bark, and the chimney of mud, mixed with dry grass which is the straw of this country." Father Vitry also states that though he "had lived elsewhere in such houses . . . nowhere did I have so much fresh air. The house is full of cracks from top to bottom."[78] This, of course, confirms the observations already advanced about the rudimentary state of architecture at the Post during the first part of the eighteenth century, but tells us nothing directly of later conditions there. As for the later period, in 1834 the Englishman G. W. Featherstonhaugh passed through the Post and reports that it contained a "few straggling houses, principally occupied by some descendants of the ancient

French settlers, who live in the same comfortless way that the same class does at Carondolet."[79] Carondolet, a village south of St. Louis established in 1767, had early on acquired the nickname *Vide Poche* (Empty Pocket) because of its poverty. What Featherstonhaugh meant to convey by his comparison of the Post with Carondolet can probably be gathered from his description of the latter village, which he had seen a few months previous to his visit to the Post. "It is a poor, poverty-stricken place, containing some inconvenient wooden houses," he said of Carondolet, "whose inhabitants are precisely what they were one hundred years ago, not having made the least progress in the useful arts. They . . . appear not to have one earthly comfort in their houses."[80] But Featherstonhaugh's visit to the Post occurred when it was in steep decline, so his remarks tell us little, if anything, about the state of affairs in the late eighteenth century, during what may well have been the Post's golden era. It needs to be kept in mind, in any case, that many Arkansas residents traveled to New Orleans and St. Louis and would have seen the architectural styles and refinements current there. Indeed, François Ménard, the leading Post merchant in the 1780s, had a house in New Orleans in the *Rue de la Madame Boisclare;*[81] and the census of 1791 already listed a carpenter and a *menuisier* (cabinetmaker) among the 151 souls, white and black, in residence at the *Poste d'Arkansas.*[82] Mr. James Scull's house, built in or about 1809, was certainly far from crude, for it had chair rails and baseboards in every room.[83]

Most of the houses at the Post at any rate seem to have been rather modest affairs of two rooms, built on the so-called medieval model: A *salle* or general purpose living/dining room, and a *chambre* or bedroom. Gov. James Miller in 1820 asserted that "the houses generally have two rooms,"[84] and the first office of the *Arkansas Gazette,* according to one report, was located in such a house.[85] But a few of the dwellings were more capacious: Samuel Treat, American Indian factor, wrote in 1810 of a house with two large rooms and two additional bedrooms "on and above the piazza,"[86] and the commandant's house at the end of the colonial period, as we saw, had the usual *salle* and *chambre* plus two *closets* made by enclosing portions of the back gallery.[87]

In size, the houses of which a record has survived ranged from 228 square feet for Father Pierre Janin's humble rectory *cum* chapel[88] to Pierre Lefevre's *maison principale* of about 800 square feet with galleries all around it. Lefevre's house was surrounded, probably, by a palisade fence, and included in its curtilage an orchard, no doubt with apple and peach trees, and several outbuildings, among which were a sawmill, a grist mill, and kitchen.[89] This house would have been a little larger than the Becquette-Ribault house in Ste. Genevieve (about 700 square feet) and somewhat smaller than the Bolduc house (1,100 square feet) in the same town. (See Figures 15 and 16.) The average house at Arkansas Post in the late colonial period measured about 550 square feet, which is not significantly smaller than the average of 600 square feet reported for colonial Ste. Genevieve,[90] larger than the 450 square feet of the very earliest houses in St. Louis,[91] and about the same size as those in French Kaskaskia.[92] These are, to be sure, small houses; but they are somewhat more capacious than they might at first appear, since the French foot was approximately 12.8 inches. (One therefore needs to multiply areas derived from French measurements by about 1.15 to convert them to English equivalents.) Furthermore, covered galleries added most effectively to the living space, for, in addition to protecting the walls of the house from rainwater and thus from rot, they provided a place to gather and even to sleep when weather permitted, as it frequently did in the Post's relatively balmy latitudes. Galleries would probably have increased Pierre Lefevre's useable space, for instance, by more than 1,000 square feet, which was more area than was available inside the house. It needs to be recalled, too, that his kitchen was a separate building altogether.

Nothing very reliable can be said about the inside of these houses, since no description is available; but we are probably right in assuming, from what we know of the rest of the colony, that the walls in the best of them would have been plastered or, at the very least, whitewashed like the outside.[93] We may doubt, however, though it is by no means impossible, that any of the Post's houses contained the highly polished walnut floors, "waxed and as smooth and bright as a mahogany dining table" that Amos Stoddard reported at St. Louis.[94]

Such furniture as these houses contained was no doubt simple and functional, and probably made for the most part by the owners of it or by local craftsmen, though it is likely that a few pieces would have made the trip upriver from New Orleans, especially with the families of the commandants and other military officers. The loss of the Post archives, which contained a large number of estate and debtors' inventories, makes it difficult to say with anything approaching precision how the Post's houses were furnished. Surviving records and journals do sometimes refer fleetingly to tables, chairs, and beds, but give no

Figure 20. Armoire made in St. Louis, *ca.* 1780.
(*Courtesy of Missouri Historical Society, St. Louis.*)

hint as to their style or construction. A 1771 inventory, that chance has rescued from destruction, records a walnut armoire, a cupboard (*alhazena*), and a walnut table owned by Marie Montcharvaux at Arkansas Post.[95] A fairly large number of eighteenth-century creole armoires have survived, enough to give some confidence about what Madame Montcharvaux's looked like.[96] (See Figure 20.) Perhaps her cupboard was what the French called a *buffet,* usually a hutch with drawers above and cabinets or shelves beneath.[97] François Ménard's 1791 will reveals that he kept his business papers in a *bureau,* a desk, which, in its simplest form, could have been merely a table with a drawer;[98] but it could have been a good deal more elaborate. By the late colonial period, some Post denizens could evidently boast of a great deal of furniture: In 1810 Pierre Lefevre had a large walnut armoire with copper hardware, a "yellow wood" (bodark) armoire with iron hardware, a wild cherry desk with copper hardware, a walnut chest of drawers, a big walnut table, a cypress table, a wild cherry table, three chairs, two cypress benches, and a bed with two small mosquito nets.[99] We see and hear nothing of wall decorations, though as early as 1727 Father du Poisson had an engraving of Saint Regis hanging in his room to help awe and convert the Quapaws.[100]

We cannot for a moment, of course, entertain the thought that the Post was a center of style, or, probably, that it achieved as a general matter even the cultural levels of colonial Ste. Genevieve. As usual, Thomas Nuttall, the priggish English botanist, intrudes to prevent such a thought, even if our common sense would not have. Nuttall can usually be counted on to hammer our little creole village with a terrible invective, and he does not fail us when it comes time for him to speak of the architecture there. "The houses," he complained, "commonly surrounded with open galleries, destitute of glass windows, and perforated with numerous doors, are well enough suited for a summer shelter, but totally destitute of comfort in the winter."[101] Nevertheless, it is possible after examining the surviving sources to appreciate what John James Audubon meant when he spoke of the time in the late eighteenth century when the Post of Arkansas "could have been called an agreable Small Town."[102] And the Post and its houses were at least impressive enough to W. H. Halliburton for him to remark that, even as late as 1845, "all the citizens of Arkansas County outside of the village of Arkansas Post, without exception, lived in unpretentious log-cabins."[103]

III

THE SORTS AND CONDITIONS OF MEN AND WOMEN

The class structure at the eighteenth-century *Poste aux Arkansas* was intriguing and full of interest for the social historian. The Post was ruled by an itinerant gentry, namely the commandants who frequently styled themselves "Judge Civil and Military" of the Post, and who usually remained in residence for only three or four years. They were, almost to a man, provided with high-sounding names: Louis-Xavier-Martin Delinó de Chalmette, Paul Augustin Le Pelletier de La Houssaye, Joseph Bernard Vallière d'Hauterive, and Charles Melchior de Vilemont furnish good and typical examples. Though the particle "de" in the name is not an unequivocal signal of gentle birth, and though some people affected it without right, it nevertheless creates a working presumption that a person using it belonged to a family that was of the landed gentry. Just to make sure that everyone correctly perceived his quality, the Arkansas commandant from 1739 to 1748 in official documents styled himself Jean-François Tisserant *Ecuyer* de Montcharvaux.[1] The monicker "Ecuyer," *i.e.,* Esquire, furnishes a clear indicium of social status. At least four military officers stationed at the Arkansas, moreover, were or went on to become knights: de La Houssaye, Alexandre Chevalier de Clouet, Captain de Gamon Chevalier de La Rochette, and Étienne de Vaugine Chevalier de Nuysement.

Figure 21. Louise Favrot de Clouet. (*Courtesy of Mr. Thomas B. Favrot, New Orleans, and Mrs. Clair Favrot Kileen, Covington, Louisiana.*)

Most of these military officers were, judging from the letters they wrote, quite well educated people. The French and Spanish that many of them employed, at any rate, would receive reasonably high marks from eighteenth-century grammar masters; though occasionally their correspondence contains some phonetic vernacular that, in order to comprehend it, needs to be read out loud, and listened to as it reenters the mind. These gentry have left behind, too, some evidence of a rather refined taste. For instance, Louise Favrot brought to her 1761 marriage with Alexandre de Clouet 2,000 *livres* worth of furniture and silverware, and he endowed her at the same time with furniture valued at 14,500 *livres*.[2] In 1769, de Clouet left his Arkansas command to go to New Orleans long enough to supervise his mother-in-law's succession, and he bought seven silver table settings and two silver gravy spoons at her estate auction.[3] At the same sale, his wife Louise bought prodigious quantities of her mother's clothes, including "a dress and skirt of iridescent taffeta, a dress and skirt of satin with flowers on a grey background," and two corsets of dimity. She also bought more than two dozen napkins.[4] We cannot say with certainty that the Post commandant's table was set with any of the fine accoutrements with which the good chevalier and his wife outfitted themselves on this day; but it is difficult to believe that some at least of the couple's silver, furniture, and fine clothes did not find its way up the river during de Clouet's two-year residence there. We know, too, that Madame de Clouet understood the demands of *noblesse oblige*, for she acted as a nurse when an epidemic struck the Post in the fall of 1769, and she left behind some ornaments for the Post chapel when she and her husband departed for New Orleans later that year.[5] Étienne de Vaugine also had tastes, and possessions to match, that one would not expect to encounter on the frontier. He married in 1752 at Arkansas Post, and when his wife died twenty years later he caused an inventory to be made in order to partition their community property. It included a walnut tester bed on stag feet with bed curtains of yellow satin, two sideboards, a sofa with stag feet, a lot of silver plate, and large amounts of tableware and table linen. Just as revealing as what Vaugine owned was what he owed: One of his creditors was "Monsieur Pinard, tailor of Paris," to whom he was indebted to the tune of 120 *piastres*.[6]

The French and Spanish colonial governments attracted people of this quality to govern and protect the forest posts of Louisiana by conceding them the right to trade with the *habitants* and the Indians in their neighborhood. Sometimes, though this was ordinarily contrary to colonial policy, officers even sought and received a monopoly of trade with certain tribes. For instance, in 1758 Étienne Layssard wrote to the governor in New Orleans with much bitterness about the Post commandant's claim to exclusive trade with the Quapaws, an arrangement that he thought clearly illegal.[7] A trade monopoly, of course, was the most lucrative of trading privileges since, without competition, the holder could charge a monopoly price for his goods. Competitive capitalism was much riskier: Capt. Balthazar de Villiers, in common with many other commandants, was engaged in it, and it evidently ruined him, for he died bankrupt and in 1782 his wife, at the behest of his creditors, even spent some time under arrest just before his death. Among other disastrous investments, de Villiers had extended credit to American refugees from the revolution, who sought and obtained asylum at the Post: He outfitted them for the hunt but evidently most of them never returned. De Villiers's financial woes, which plagued him throughout the latter part of his career, no doubt contributed to his extreme dissatisfaction with his post. It was, he said, *le réduit le plus désagréable de l'univers*—the most disagreeable hole in the universe.[8] But then, de Villiers was speaking of the Post located, as we saw in chapter one, in the flood plain in Desha County. For him, therefore, his duty station was a literal slough of despond.

Other officers, however, had a much higher opinion of the Post, especially after its final relocation. Pierre-Joseph Favrot, for instance, a well-educated member of one of the most distinguished of colonial Louisiana families, who had spent a few years as a young officer at Arkansas Post, in later life aggressively sought the commandantcy there, though unsuccessfully.[9] Favrot's anxiety to return to Arkansas probably indicates that the Post was quite profitable for a number of the military personnel who were stationed and in business there. Among these evidently were Capt. Fernando de Leyba and Francis Vigo, a soldier of the garrison, who were partners in a fur-trade concern that operated far up the Arkansas as early as 1774.[10] Vigo was even able to enlist the aid of the governor in New Orleans in arranging leave to go upriver to wind up some business of his and Leyba's after Leyba's transfer to St. Louis.[11] Another officer who seems to have made quite a financial success of his stint at the Arkansas was Ignacio Delinó de Chalmette, the commandant of the Post from 1790 to 1794, who accumulated a fortune there and at Nogales (Vicksburg), though the New Orleans grandee Joseph de Pontalba affected for a time, and for unstated reasons, to find this in some measure scandalous.[12]

There were, in addition, a few members of gentle families at the Post during the eighteenth century who were not attached to the military. André Fagot de La

Figure 22. Francis Vigo. (*Courtesy of Vincennes University.*)

Garcenière was one of them. Educated in France, and fluent in French, English, and Spanish, he seems to have operated as a kind of *de facto* notary at the Post during the Spanish regime and certainly as an official one after the American takeover.[13] Colonial Louisiana was, moreover, sufficiently democratic to allow for the gentrification of some of the merchant class at the Arkansas: Proof of this lies in the very occasional titles of respect accorded them in the eighteenth-century censuses and militia lists. The militia officers, all merchants, were denominated "Don," whether or not they were born to the manor: They were officers and, therefore, gentlemen.[14] The widow of merchant François Ménard ventured to call herself "Doña Maria" in a 1793 petition dealing with her husband's succession,[15] no doubt because she was certainly the richest person at the Post at the time, and, with nine slaves, had been the largest slaveholder two years previously.[16] So, too, one encounters Don José Bougi in the 1798 census.[17] Joseph Bougy was an important farmer and merchant at the Post, and, as owner of eleven slaves, the largest slaveholder there in 1793.[18] When the British naturalist Thomas Nuttall arrived at the Post in 1819, he brought a letter of introduction to Bougy, itself a sign that Joseph was a prominent person. Nuttall remarked that he "soon found in [Bougy] a gentleman, though disguised at this time in the garb of a Canadian boatman." Bougy was the only Frenchman at the Post for whom Nuttall could find a kind word: He said of him that the Post "owes much to his enterprise and industry."[19]

The most prosperous of the merchant class, whether or not they affected the titles of the gentry, were no doubt considered their social equals. There were, however, never more than four or five of these at any one time at the Post. To acquire some idea of their economic condition, it is instructive to look fairly closely at one of them, Pierre Lefevre, who removed to Arkansas from Vincennes in 1788 or 1789. His loss is our gain: We can gauge his standard of living rather accurately because, unfortunately, he went bankrupt in 1810 and the inventory of his debtor's estate has survived. In addition to five tracts of land near the Post totaling over one thousand acres, he owned, as we have seen, a house in the colonial Louisiana West Indies style with galleries all around and measuring thirty-five by twenty-two French feet. He also had a barn, kitchen, other outbuildings, an orchard, a sawmill, and a grist mill. Inside his *maison principale* he had some quite interesting furnishings.[20] Pierre was definitely, before his downfall, among the *hauts bourgeois* of colonial Arkansas.

Agriculture grew only slowly at the Post, despite the fertility of the soil there on which many visitors were moved to remark. By 1722, Law's workmen had managed to clear only about three acres and had reaped only an insignificant harvest; but for the arrival of a relief boat from downriver that year, the little settlement would have found itself in real difficulty.[21] About two decades later, activity at the Post had come to a virtual standstill: "Our fort of the Arkansas," Governor Bienville wrote, "is falling into ruins; there are only a missionary and three *habitans* there who do nothing."[22] If these *habitans* were growing anything, it must have been merely for their own subsistence. A few years later, however, an inventory reports "1600 pounds of tobacco from the 1743 crop";[23] it is a reasonable guess that this was grown for sale locally and downriver.

Early in the Spanish period, Commandant de Clouet attempted to encourage his settlers to make more serious agriculture efforts, but it must have been extremely difficult for him to do so: At the downstream location to which the Post had been removed in about 1756, floods provided continual discouragement to European and aborigine alike. In fact, they produced no crop at all from 1763 to 1767 because of the fear of floods. Nevertheless, in 1768 de Clouet wrote the governor that he was setting a good example for his *habitants* by planting a garden to "show the people that the earth yields everything to those who are not lazy." He also encouraged his population to build ovens; there was not a single one when he arrived, he maintained, but now there were already four. De Clouet even made the *habitants* promise to erect a common fence around their fields, to create, in other words, what is somewhat misleadingly called a common field.[24] This type of agricultural arrangement, practiced in rural France from medieval times and in the Illinois country, though not in Canada or in lower Louisiana, did not, despite its name, involve communal ownership of the land. Instead, strips of land individually owned were surrounded by a fence to keep out the animals, and the community was obligated to repair and maintain it: It was thus the fence, not the field, that was common. There is no indication in his later letters that de Clouet's common fence ever materialized, despite his good intentions. There is in fact no evidence of the existence of this kind of agricultural arrangement at any of the locations of Arkansas Post at any time. De Clouet knew that his situation near the mouth of the Arkansas was a hopeless one for agriculture, and he recommended the removal of the Post upriver, no doubt to *Écores Rouges,* where his *habitants* could safely plant and harvest tobacco, corn, and cotton.[25]

During the French period, the garrison of the Post, not being able to rely on local supplies, had to have its flour imported from the Illinois country, which regularly sent its surplus downriver to New Orleans during years of good harvests. Early plans to settle the Arkansas River region in 1716 noted that it would have to "draw its corn and wheat from Illinois."[26] Indeed, it is right to think of the Illinois settlements as the "granary of Louisiana,"[27] as they not infrequently produced three times as much food as they could use. As early as 1731, Kaskaskia merchants shipped over one hundred thousand pounds of flour downriver,[28] and in 1733 and 1736 six thousand pounds of this Illinois export flour found its way to the tiny garrison at the Arkansas.[29] Documents recording similar shipments in 1772, 1773, and 1774 survive,[30] and even after the Post was moved to *Écores Rouges* in 1779 self-sufficiency remained an elusive goal, because of bad harvests, droughts, and the small number of farmers. For instance, in the spring of 1783, Capt. Jacobo Dubreuil wrote to the governor that there had been no harvests at all since the removal, and the whites and Indians alike were reduced to eating roots from the mountains.[31] After the American Revolution, the Post was frequently forced to look for supplies not only to the Illinois but also to Natchez;[32] sometimes the commandant resorted to the simple expedient of making purchases from American vessels loaded with Ohio flour that were traveling the Mississippi on their way to New Orleans.[33]

There was never a substantial agricultural class at the Arkansas, as the continual complaints by the commandants there make absolutely plain. Late in 1787, however, three French farming families from Illinois, including that of Joseph Bougy, doubtless refugees from the Northwest Ordinance, did settle in Arkansas, and Captain Vallière reported that they had cleared their land and planted, reaped, and ground their first wheat crop.[34] This is the earliest mention of a flour mill at the Arkansas: It would have been horse-powered. In 1791, the census asserts that there were twenty-six farmers (*cultivateurs*) at the Post, but in fact only fifteen of these persons report a crop, and their total agricultural output is a mere 315 bushels of wheat and 4,700 bushels of corn. Five German Protestant farmers only recently arrived, perhaps from Vincennes, produced almost two-thirds of the wheat crop.[35] One of these immigrants, Michael Wolf, so impressed the French spy Gen. Victor Collot with his industry that he earned a fairly extensive notice and eulogy when Collot came to write his book. "A single farm," Collot wrote, "belonging to Mr. Wolf, a German, evinced what might be expected from a country this fertile. He was employed in gathering his corn harvest, which yielded him two hundred fold. The quality of the wheat was certainly equal to that of the best departments of France; which leaves no doubt, that under a government favorable to agriculture, this cultivation would be attended with the greatest success."[36] Perhaps it was some of Mr. Wolf's wheat that found its way from the Arkansas to Ouachita Post for trial there late in the century.[37]

In 1793, much the same picture of the agriculture practiced at the Arkansas emerges. There are now forty households, twenty-seven of which report a crop, and the production of wheat has increased quite dramatically to almost 2,000 bushels; but six German Protestant households grow 60 percent of it, and five French families almost all the rest. These same five families grew 50 percent of the corn produced that year.[38] In 1794, the wheat crop has decreased to about 1,300 bushels; three German Protestant families have produced one-third of it, and four French families 40 percent.[39] Two years later, the wheat crop again decreased, this time to around 1,050 bushels, and only ten households of approximately sixty report growing it. The three German families remaining at the Post produced only 25 percent of this year's crop and four French families 60 percent.[40] In 1798, the wheat output fell just below 1,000 bushels, partly, for unknown reasons, because the Germans grew nothing at all. Six hundred of these bushels, more than 60 percent of the total, were produced by four French households, three of them headed by widows, in a town containing almost one hundred households and nearly four hundred persons.[41]

One can appreciate from the foregoing that serious agricultural effort was not indulged in by many of the denizens of the Arkansas; and many of those who did exert themselves in that way were also merchants. It is safe to conclude that there were never more than eight or ten real farmers at any one time at the Post in the colonial period. It is therefore doubtful that the Post was able to sustain itself at any time during the colonial period. Although the state of the agricultural art, and the number of people engaged in it, certainly increased during the last decade of the eighteenth century, John Treat, writing from the Post in 1805, notes even at that late date that "agriculture here is yet in its infancy," even though the ground was quite fertile: The land, he said, "had been constantly sown with the same kind of grain, only half cultivated and never to have received any manure." In the same year, he reports gloomily that "Indian Corn produces well but from the multitude of both Crows, and Black Birds which destroy'd it the Year past, the raising it has been altogether relinquished." Most families raised cotton for home consumption, he said, and there was some attempt to

GROSS AGRICULTURAL OUTPUT OF ARKANSAS POST, 1791–1799, IN *MINOTS* AND *CARROTTES*

YEAR	WHEAT	CORN	TOBACCO	VALUE*
1791	301	4,628	———	$5,230
1793	1,825	4,015	395	$7,961
1794	1,240	1,250	850	$4,367
1796	1,020	960	470	$3,353
1798	947	1,200	200	$3,244
Avg.	1,066	2,410	373	$4,830

*Based on 10 *livres* (two dollars) per *minot* for wheat, 5 *livres* (one dollar) per *minot* for corn, and 6 *reales* (75 cents) per *carrotte* of tobacco. These prices were fairly typical for Arkansas during the 1790s, though they could of course vary widely because of the uncertainties of the harvests. A *minot* was a little more than a bushel.

produce it in commercial quantities; but there was no gin at the Arkansas until late in 1805.[42]

An indication of the state of agriculture at the Arkansas in the 1790s is the value of the gross agricultural output revealed by the five censuses extant from that period. As the accompanying table shows, the average total crop was worth perhaps forty-eight hundred dollars a year. The relative insignificance of this figure can be demonstrated in two ways. First of all, in 1795 the tiny village of Carondolet just south of St. Louis, with a population of only 182, a little more than half that of the Post at that time, produced 30 percent more wheat than the Post did a year later and more than twice the corn.[43] (And this despite the fact that Carondolet's nickname was *Vide Poche* [Empty Pocket] because of its poverty!) Second, we have it on reliable authority that revenues from the fur and skin trade at Arkansas Post with the Osage tribe alone averaged $18,750.00 annually in the waning years of the colonial epoch,[44] almost four times the average annual gross agricultural output for the same period. That source also reveals that the Osages were bagging game in staggering quantities in late colonial times: The average annual shipment derived from them contained over forty thousand French pounds of deerskins, along with the pelts of twelve thousand raccoons, five hundred bears, twenty-five hundred to three thousand beavers, and three hundred otters.[45]

Figure 23. Quapaws hunting, killing, and smoking buffalo.
(*Courtesy of The Historical New Orleans Collection.*)

The surviving colonial documents make it plain beyond cavil that the vast majority of the population of the Arkansas was engaged in hunting or the fur and skin trade in one capacity or another. We hear of *bourgeois* (trading-post managers) and their *engagés* (hired hands) as early as 1749;[46] most of them stayed beyond the reach of the commandant and census-taker whenever possible. Some operated independently of any formal arrangement with others. In 1726, the census-taker, speaking of the Arkansas population of perhaps thirty persons, had asserted that "all the *habitants* were poor and lived only by hunting wild animals";[47] and a 1746 report said of the twelve Arkansas *habitant* families that "their principal occupation is hunting, curing meat, and commerce in tallow and bear oil."[48] In 1765, Capt. Philip Pittman had reported that the people of the Arkansas subsisted "mostly by hunting, and every season send to New Orleans great quantities of bear's oil, tallow, salted buffalo meat, and a few skins."[49] About a decade later, Commandant de Villiers described the Post as "a place of residence for merchants and a meeting point for the hunters who come here to equip themselves . . . paying their debts and then equipping themselves anew or taking their catch to town."[50] He also remarked pointedly that "the hunters [are] for the most part people of bad behavior who could soon be replaced by more useful colonists" if only he could provide a more suitable town site.[51] But even as late as 1796, long after the Post had been moved back to the Grand Prairie, Capt. Charles de Vilemont asserted, with some exaggeration, that all his male *habitants* were hunters.[52] Trade in the products of the hunt and supplies for hunters was effected at the Arkansas mostly by barter, the only significant source of specie at the Post being the Spanish military payroll in the form of silver coins. But this pay was frequently late, and in 1771 Capt. Fernando de Leyba informed the governor that "the money now used on the post bears my signature." Evidently, Leyba's written promises to pay the soldiers' salaries and for flour were being circulated as currency.[53]

Of worldly goods the hunters of the Post were almost entirely bereft. For instance, when Luis Lefevre, a poor relation of the well-to-do Post merchant noticed before, executed his will, he recited as his only possessions his gun (*fusil*) and his clothes.[54] Indeed, the commandants more than once in their letters remarked on Arkansas residents who owned nothing but their *fusils*. A revealing 1770 inventory of a fugitive Arkansas hunter, who had become a gunsmith for the Caddo Indians in about 1763, notes that he owned two boats, three Indian slaves (one of whom, no doubt, was his concubine), large quantities of bears' oil, tallow, skins, "flat sides" (dried buffalo flanks), deer hides, and two hundred salted buffalo tongues.[55]

An interesting manifestation of the primacy of hunting and the fur trade in the economic life of the Post is the collection of regulations produced there aimed at governing the relationship between hunters and their merchant suppliers. These the commandant and the governor promulgated from time to time in consultation with the hunters and merchants; their chief concern lay in outlining priorities among the creditors of the hunters, namely their *engagés* and various suppliers.[56] It is instructive to compare them with the elaborate agricultural regulations dealing with common fields that were produced in Ste. Genevieve and Kaskaskia where farming was the most prominent pursuit of the inhabitants.[57] As we have seen, there is no evidence whatever for the existence of common fields at the Arkansas.

After the hunters, the next rung on the Post's social scale was occupied by the free mulattoes and the free blacks. The 1791 and 1793 censuses record two mixed-blood ladies whose names are Marianna and Jean; their occupation is listed as seamstress.[58] (In eighteenth-century New Orleans, as elsewhere, "seamstress" was a euphemism for prostitute.) These are the only free mulattoes to appear in the Post records. The censuses also report a handful, never more than three, of free blacks, but next to nothing can be said about them except that one named Pedro Menard produced a corn crop of twenty bushels in 1796.[59]

Below these last in the social scheme of things were, of course, the slaves. Almost all of these were black, though Indian slaves were far from unknown. When the Spanish assumed sovereignty over Louisiana, they outlawed the future enslavement of Indians, but the owners of Indian slaves had their property rights in the Indian slaves they owned at that time preserved. In 1789, a "savage" belonging to Capt. Joseph Vallière was baptized:[60] Since the Indian's age is not given, we cannot tell if, as seems most unlikely, he was enslaved at the time of the cession to Spain, or if, as frequently happened elsewhere in Louisiana, he had been enslaved later despite the Spanish law forbidding it. In any case, slaves at the Post were never numerous: In 1798, in a total population of 393 they numbered only 56, all black.[61] The low percentage of slaves in the colonial Arkansas population is further evidence of the lack of serious agricultural effort there, since in the colony as a whole the eighteenth-century population was typically half slave.

The slaves of the Arkansas unfortunately led virtually unrecorded lives, except for an occasional lamentation in a letter complaining of their having run away. On one such occasion, a very interesting situation arose when the Quapaws were asked to give up five slaves that had escaped from their St. Louis owners. The Indians at first claimed that the slaves were presents, but then asserted that they had been freed under their law "because a man of the slaves' color is born to freedom as soon as he enters the house of a chief."[62]

Many of the black and mulatto slaves of Arkansas Post were no doubt engaged in agricultural work. Most of the French farmers of late eighteenth-century Arkansas had a few slaves to help in their fields; but no one, so far as the record goes, ever owned more than the eleven of whom Joseph Bougy could boast in 1794.[63] The German Lutherans, interestingly, though excellent farmers, owned no slaves at all, a fact that makes it almost certain that they were conscientiously opposed to slavery. But the slaves at the Post were not by any means all field hands. In 1789, for instance, Capt. Joseph Vallière's house servants served dinner to an American visitor, and it is likely that they were black slaves.[64] So, too, in 1793 Capt. Pedro Rousseau put in at the Post to have the rudder of his galiot repaired, and Vallière supplied him with an old black artisan who soon had him on his way with newly manufactured parts.[65] Since Captain Rousseau paid the artisan directly with a draft on the treasury in New Orleans, it is possible that the old man was a free person of color. Evidently, blacks also worked as laborers for the merchants, dressing and packing hides and loading carts and boats. In 1793, for instance, the widow Ménard had nine slaves, but she produced no crop, and the census lists her as a merchant, not a farmer.[66]

It is likely that the population at Arkansas Post was small enough during most of the eighteenth century to make for a relatively egalitarian society. Class differences, however, did manifest themselves in a number of ways, especially, as we would expect, in the choice of marriage partners. The gentry of the Post were interconnected in a complex and extremely interesting fashion. To take but three examples: Françoise Marie Petit de Coulange, daughter of Post commandant Pierre Petit de Coulange, was the mother of Charles Melchior de Vilemont, commandant of the Post from 1794 to 1802; Étienne Vaugine, an officer at the Post, married Madame de Gouyon, sister-in-law of Post commandant de La Houssaye; and Marie Félicité Vallière, daughter of the Post commandant from 1787 to 1790, became the wife of François Vaugine, who was the son of Étienne and an officer in the Post militia. If the gentry tended very much to intermarry, the French hunters and some of the merchants frequently formed unions with Indian women, partly because they could find few white women who wanted to share their lives, partly because of the commercial advantage that such connections afforded. The Indians in general welcomed these affiliations: Neither the French hunters nor the peoples whom the French upper classes insisted on calling savages seem to have had the slightest hesitation about mixing their blood. The church had not at first countenanced these liberal attitudes toward miscegenation, not principally on racialist grounds, but, ironically, from a fear that the French hunters would corrupt and debauch the Indians, drawing them away from the teachings and discipline of Christianity. We shall see that the eighteenth-century Arkansas church was not well established, and in the end it decided that it was better to sanction these kinds of marriages than to tolerate the concubinage that would be rampant without them.

As a result of probably five generations of such marriages at the Arkansas, by

Figure 24. Françoise Marie Petit de Coulange de Vilemont.
(*Courtesy of Mrs. Elmire Villeré Drackett, New Orleans.*)

the end of the eighteenth century many of the European families there were of mixed blood or at least had mixed-blood collateral relatives.[67] Some late colonial writers even attribute the survival of the Arkansas European settlements to the fact that the French, far from disdaining their Indian neighbors, took up with them in the freest and most intimate way.[68] However that may be, the late colonial records reveal a surprising variety in the tribes into which the hunters and traders married themselves. The Quapaws, of course, furnished a principal source for wives, but many other tribes made similar contributions: One sees Osage, Paduca, Kansas, Abenaki, Loup, and Cherokee women joined in marriage with Arkansas Frenchmen in a six-year period alone.[69]

The sad truth is, however, that many of these Indian women had probably been *de facto* slaves, and some of them had no doubt actually been purchased from Indian captors. Nor were white women exempt from this kind of cruelty. For instance, Indians had stolen Jacinta María de Torres at Santa Rosa de Lima de Abiquiu, a Spanish settlement forty-five miles north of Santa Fe; she was lucky enough to find a reasonable husband in Raymond Vessière, who purchased her at the Post in 1775. One María Benancia was not nearly so fortunate. She had been captured in a Comanche raid near Santa Fe, and a trader named Andrés Labonhanda bought her and promised to free her by marrying her; but he proved to be a drunkard who repeatedly beat her. "He said I was his slave," she wrote to the governor, "telling me that I was not his wife." She had cost him good money, Andrés told her, and "could do whatever he pleased." The unfortunate María begged the governor to allow her to marry another man, for her master was threatening to "take her to the forest and sell her for double the price she cost him." While the governor's response is not recorded, María apparently later took up with her fellow Spaniard Martin Serrano, a soldier at the Post. Presumably, he was the man whom she had assured the governor could keep her "in the state of life which God and the Church command."[70]

Another way in which social stratification is noticeable at the Arkansas has to do with food and drink. While the hospitality offered strangers in the early days of the Post was no doubt somewhat primitive, we are able to say certainly that by 1789 a visitor to the Post commandant could expect to be regaled in rather high style. On a fine spring day in 1789, a "Kaintuck" named John Halley, in the company of his patron, called at the Post and Capt. Joseph Vallière received them with a great deal of kindness. At 7:30 A.M., the commandant's servants brought his guests what we have learned to call a continental breakfast, that is, bread, butter, and coffee. At half past twelve on the same day "dinner" came on. "We had a variety of Dishes out of Venison and a fine ham," Mr. Halley writes with evident satisfaction, and "some Roast, fried stakes, some stued with wine, stued with earbs *etc.*" The boatman continued: "Our drink was wine and water. After we had eat very harty of the meats, the wa[i]ters cleaned of[f] the different dishes and set on some fine oald cheese and butter with bottles of wine and glasses."[71]

Of course, most of the residents of Louisiana's *Poste aux Arkansas* would not have had house slaves to attend their tables, as the captain did, and would not have served up the fancy fare that he, his family, and guests seem regularly to have enjoyed. The lower orders, for instance, relished cornbread, while the French upper classes found it particularly odious. *Gru* or *sagamite* seems to have been another favorite of the lower sort: This was a boiled corn mush seasoned with bears' oil or tallow. *Gru,* Father du Poisson reveals, was frequently used as a bread substitute: "A spoonful of *gru* and a mouthful of meat go together."[72] Most people would not have had ham and beef, of course, as Vallière did, but meat of other kinds was usually plentiful, since the woods and prairies were alive with deer, bears, and buffalo; and the skies were thick, in season, with pheasants, ducks, and bustards. Then, too, wild grapes, mulberries, and plums were free for the taking if one were not among the fortunate few of the Arkansas who by the end of the eighteenth century had an orchard. Eggs were not altogether lacking even absent a barnyard: Father du Poisson reports in 1727 on turtle-egg omelettes that he found most satisfactory.[73] The ingenuity and creativity of the residents of the Post who could not afford imported wines were engaged in producing drinks in a surprising variety. "Sang," evidently the fruit punch that the Spanish call sangria, was apparently well known at the Post.[74] Eggnog was also a favorite: Mr. Halley relates that one day in 1789 "the boys went out in a canough among the willow bushes and brought in about a peck of ingeon hens [cranes] and black birds eggs, 275 in number, out of which we had some fine egg nog."[75] An Arkansas delicacy enjoyed by all the classes and much in demand in New Orleans and even Madrid was salted buffalo tongues.[76] The Indians of lower Louisiana counted alligator tail a great delicacy,[77] though these beasts rarely ventured as far north as Arkansas Post. Perhaps this was just as well: A Mons. de Pagès reported that when he visited Natchitoches in 1767 "the foul odor of the urine and excrement of the alligators infects the air [and] our biscuit was poisoned by it to the point that while eating it we thought we were chewing rotten and infected bread."[78]

The social structure at the Arkansas must surely have lent an extraordinary texture to the daily life there. A polyglot population of mixed religious and social background, many even of mixed racial composition, must have made the old Spanish Post a most intriguing place. A person spending only a day in the last decade of the eighteenth century at the fort and village would almost certainly have heard at least five languages spoken—French, Spanish, German, English, and Quapaw—and probably another Indian tongue or two. It is an incongruous time and place in which to encounter so cosmopolitan, if somewhat unsophisticated, a population.

As was the case throughout colonial Louisiana, the denizens of Arkansas Post were extremely fond of drinking, billiards, cards, and dancing; and the love of these diversions was a shared characteristic of all the social classes there.[79] In 1770, the commandant remarked that there were two licensed *cantinas* at his post and numerous clandestine taverns within his bailiwick. For a time around 1780, while de Villiers commanded, there had been a billiard room at the village; the merchants had been very much opposed to it because the hunters lost all their money there and thus could not pay their debts. When, therefore, early in 1784, one Pierre Trusserau asked permission to establish a billiard parlor, Commandant Dubreuil refused: The governor backed him up, but cautioned that "all forms of amusement should not be suppressed at isolated posts like yours." Late in 1785, however, an importunate Trusserau at last succeeded in gaining the governor's permission for his billiards enterprise.[80] He may have had competition for a time, since Marie and Jean Jardelas operated a billiard parlor in the center of town, probably as early as the late colonial period.[81]

Other forms of gambling also flourished, and, to hear Captain Leyba tell it, there were even professional card sharks about. In 1773 he complained to the governor of a man named Clermon "whose only cargo in his pirogue is a pack of cards by means of which, and by his extraordinary skill, he strips the hunters of their possessions, leaving them without the means either to continue their journey or meet their immediate needs."[82] Very late in the colonial period, François Marie Perrin du Lac passed through the little settlement and remarked that when the hunters returned every spring from the annual hunt they passed their time "playing games, dancing, drinking, or doing nothing, similar in this as in other things to the savage peoples with whom they pass the greater part of their lives, whose habits and customs they acquire."[83] Matters remained basically the same in 1807: One A. Stewart, who had been a soldier at the Post for three years, wrote that the village was mostly French and that the inhabitants were "remarkably fond of amusements, particularly of dancing, cards, and billiards." He also noted that "the inhabitants frequently have balls, the novelty of which has induced me to attend them often." He was unchivalrous enough to say that "the ladies, tho not perfect Venuses, bear the usual degrees of comparison of handsome and ulgly, with me, and perhaps they would with you, if you had not seen a deaseant female in two or three years. They are fond of flattery!!!"[84]

The creation of Arkansas Territory in 1819 brought numerous visitors to Arkansas Post, and they all felt a need to comment on the amusements pursued by the *habitants* there, for apparently it was these that most obviously set the Arkansas French apart from their observers. James Miller, the first territorial governor, wrote his wife shortly after his arrival at the Post in 1820 that the French "are at this place very fond of Balls and Loo parties. Saturday and Sunday nights are the fashionable nights for their parties to meet, and they never disperse until after daylight." The governor very much disapproved of such goings-on on the Sabbath, and thus refused to attend; so the obliging *habitants* held some balls on nights that did not offend his Protestant sensibilities. "They have one young lady," Miller reported in describing his experiences at these balls, "a Mamselle Don Carol; the rest of the ladies are married, from twenty to seventy-five years of age." He then gave an overall appreciation of the scene: "The houses generally have two rooms, one room for dancing, the other to play Loo in and beds to lay the young sucking children on. [A] married woman is almost disqualified to attend a ball without a child; they nurse as unconcerned as at home in their nursery. They have one fiddler who can play but one tune [and] they can dance but one figure, which is a kind of reel or cotillion. [T]hey commence at dawn and hold on until day light, when each of the fair sex saddles her own pony, mounts and trudges home. The men generally hold on longer at the card table. At these card tables I have seen Grandfather, Grand-mother, son and daughter, and granddaughters all engaged in gambling as eager to make money as if playing with any one else. It is not uncommon to lose 150 or two hundred dollars in a night, or they may win. This appears to be their worst vice and it is a great one—I have discouraged it since I have been here. . . ."[85]

A few months earlier, the Presbyterian missionary Timothy Flint had given an equally censorious account of the Arkansas French and their worldly diversions. He preached at the courthouse every Sunday to a congregation that he reckoned as "principally French." "They are," he said, "in such circumstances polite, and seem attentive." But they had a distracting habit that annoyed him greatly: "The French people generally came to the place of worship," he complained, "arrayed in their ball-dresses, and went directly from worship to the ball. A billiard-room was near, and parts of my audience sometimes came in for a moment, and after listening to a few sentences, returned to their billiards. Nor is here the only place, where the preacher has to endure the heart-wearing agony of having an audience interchanging their attention repeatedly between the sermon and the billiard room, in the delivery of one discourse."[86] Protestants were not the only ones to complain about the Sabbath activities of the French at the Post. One Sunday morning in 1832, Father Ennemond Dupuy became quite upset because many Post *habitants* were "busy at the gin mill, others trying or selling their horses, others playing billiards."[87]

Thomas Nuttall, resident at the Post at almost the same time as Flint, also found the French there addicted to pastimes that he considered both noteworthy and unworthy. "The love of amusements here," he wrote, "as in most of the French colonies, is carried to extravagance, particularly gambling, and dancing parties or balls. But the sum of general industry is, as yet, totally insufficient for the support of anything like a town."[88] These kinds of amusements were so universal throughout the old province of Louisiana that Washington Irving, in a story inspired by his visit to Arkansas Post in 1832, was moved to relate that while walking through the town he "heard the sound of a fiddle from the mansion of Cooper Martin, the signal, no doubt, for a joyous gathering."[89] But this was an entirely fanciful invention, for, as Irving himself tells us, by the time he visited the Post, the French portion of it was mostly in ruins and the French, all but one or two families, had moved upriver to Jefferson County.[90]

IV

THE STATE OF CULTURE, SCIENCE, AND RELIGION

The literacy rate at the Arkansas demonstrates that the general state of education there was lamentably low, though no lower than in parts of rural eighteenth-century France. In 1796–97, during his first six months as parish priest at the Arkansas, Pierre Janin asked forty-eight godparents to sign their names to baptismal certificates: Only ten of them, or about 20 percent, could do so.[1] There is evidence, moreover, that the level of literacy did not improve as the colonial period wore on.

There were, nevertheless, always a number of Post residents interested in culture and learning. Pierre-Joseph Favrot, sometimes called the creole Pepys (something of an exaggeration, to be sure), was, as we have seen, an officer at the Post for a few years beginning in 1768; and we have concrete evidence of his interest in instructing the young because of the educational handbook that he produced for his sons some thirty years after he left the Arkansas. This small manual indicates what the upper-class Louisiana creole thought a gentleman should know: Arithmetic, grammar, modern and classical languages, and the arts (drawing, music, and dance) all find a place here, as do the physical sciences, geography, and history. Favrot pointedly noted that Latin was "absolutely necessary to anyone from a good family."[2] He and a few others like him clearly

Figure 25. Pierre-Joseph Favrot. (*Courtesy of Mr. Richmond G. Favrot, New Orleans.*)

would have wished for educational opportunities for the children of Arkansas Post. Ignacio Delinó de Chalmette, commandant at the Post from 1790 to 1794, for instance, was no doubt among these, for in later life he repeatedly enjoined

Bernard de Marigny to "get educated—a man without education is only half a man."[3]

Instructing the young at Arkansas, however, posed a real difficulty for those interested in such refinements. Sometimes the local priest, when there was one, provided some rudimentary instruction. Writing on Christmas Eve of 1752 to the governor in New Orleans, Commandant de La Houssaye asked permission to have his young brother-in-law assigned to Arkansas Post, and assured the governor that he would "try to give him a good education with the help of the Reverend Father Carette who has offered it to me."[4] The Sieur de Livillier, de La Houssaye's brother-in-law, was in fact dispatched to the Post, with, however, the caveat that some schooling in New Orleans, presumably at a later date, would be preferable.[5] In 1792, Father Pierre Gibault was at work giving religious instruction to the young people of Arkansas Post, an enterprise that probably required providing some elementary reading lessons.[6] But there seems never to have been a real school at the Post, though it is entirely possible that toward the end of the eighteenth century a vagabond schoolmaster or two, for which the province did not entirely lack, may have wandered through and stayed for a time in exchange for room and board. Home schooling, too, was common in the colony.[7]

Serious education being for the most part unavailable at Arkansas Post, those seeking such advantages for their children simply had to apply elsewhere. François Ménard, a frontier merchant, self-made and the richest man at the Post in the late eighteenth century, therefore sent his illegitimate daughter Constance to the famed school of the Ursuline Convent in New Orleans, where there were upwards of 180 students enrolled at the end of the colonial period. Ménard even left her a trust fund for her support and maintenance there.[8] Marie Félicité Vallière de Vaugine, daughter of Post commandant Joseph Vallière, also attended school at the Ursuline Convent. This institution, at least at first, was more of a finishing school than a serious academic enterprise, but it has been claimed that "most of the ladies of the colony were educated there and few [of them] went to Europe to be educated after its establishment, and their domestic virtues have won the warmest encomiums." For that reason, we are told, "a long list of the most distinguished men of the colony sought their brides among the pupils of the Ursulines."[9] Whether other Post *habitants*, at least in any numbers, were able to send their children off to school is doubtful, because of the expense involved.

Figure 26. Father Pierre Gibault. (*Courtesy of Missouri Historical Society, St. Louis.*)

The simple truth is, of course, that most of the people at Arkansas Post during the colonial period had more immediate concerns than the fine points of Latin grammar and the nuances of natural science: They were busy enough keeping body and soul together in the demanding economic and physical environment of the Arkansas River. From a list of burials at the Post between 1793 and 1799 a number of interesting facts are exposed to view, even though the sample is quite small. Based on these data, one-fourth of those born at the Post died before their first birthday, and one-third before age ten. A mere one-half achieved the age of twenty-one, and the average life expectancy at birth was only twenty-six years. Those who managed to survive to age ten could, however, look forward with some confidence to arriving at the ripe old age of thirty-nine.[10]

Books receive no mention in the hundreds of letters left behind by the Post commandants. It is nevertheless likely, judging from what we have learned of the rest of the province,[11] that the gentry of the Post had at least a few books to amuse themselves with and to provide entertainment and instruction to their children. We know, in fact, that in 1780, less than two years after giving up his command at the Arkansas, Capt. Fernando de Leyba owned a library of almost seventy volumes at St. Louis. Although Leyba probably purchased a part of this collection at auction in St. Louis,[12] it is altogether possible that he had had some of these books in his possession when he was resident at the Arkansas. Pierre-Joseph Favrot, moreover, as one would expect of a man interested in education, had a rather extensive library at his death, which included a twenty-eight-volume set of the works of Buffon, the French naturalist and writer, as well as dictionaries and works on history, the theater, Spanish law, and world travel.[13] It is not impossible that he had brought a few of these books or others with him when the governor assigned him to his brother-in-law's detachment at the remote Spanish post of *Los Arcos* in 1768.

It appears that the state of literary culture was not especially high anywhere in the colony. For instance, there was only one printing press at any one time in the entire eighteenth-century province of Louisiana, and the first one was not at work until the end of the French period: The earliest surviving Louisiana imprint is a broadside of 1764 announcing the cession of Louisiana to Spain.[14] The output of this press, located of course in New Orleans, was apparently not large: Only eighty-nine items produced by it seem to have survived. Fully 60 percent of these are broadsides, and almost one-third of all the surviving issues come from the twenty-day French interregnum in December of 1803, when Pierre de Laussat, the French legate, made a grand Gallic show of accepting the retrocession of the colony. The lone literary efforts were three poems by Julian Poydras de Lalandes dedicated to Gov. Bernardo de Gálvez and published from 1777 to 1779.[15] A newspaper, a well-produced and interesting weekly called the

Figure 27. Marie Félicité Vallière de Vaugine. (*Courtesy of Lt. Col. John W. Easby-Smith, Little Rock.*)

Moniteur de la Louisiane, did appear in 1794 in New Orleans:[16] But visitors claimed that it never had as many as eighty subscribers at once, and those mostly Europeans and other foreigners.[17]

No doubt the odd copy of the *Moniteur* made its way up the great river to the

Post of Arkansas. Its readership there, however, could not have been large. Indeed, Washington Irving remarks of the French of Arkansas that they had no use whatever for newspapers: They criticized American newcomers because "they trouble themselves with cares beyond their horizon and import sorrow thru the newspapers from every point of the compass."[18] In fact, Samuel Treat, American Indian factor at the Post in 1805, did just that, for in his letters he frequently makes requests for newspapers to be sent to him. Treat may have been rather bookish, for shortly after he arrived at the Post he noted with relief that it was not at all a disagreeable place to live, as long as there was some decent reading matter about to sustain oneself. "There is little doubt," he wrote, "(though sequester'd from the gay world) a person with a well chosen Library may render his situation far from being uncomfortable."[19]

In this state of affairs, it cannot surprise us that colonial Arkansas produced no writers or poets—at least no trace of them has come down to us. But, rather surprisingly, some eighteenth-century poetical notice of the place has survived. During the period 1728 to 1742, Jean-François Benjamin Dumont, *dit* Montigny, was at work on an epic poem called *The Establishment of the Province of Louisiana.*[20] It is not a great work. One eighteenth-century French bibliophile complained that "the verses are execrable, though they contain singular things"; and Dumont's modern-day editor allowed that "poor Dumont was not, alas, even a third-rate poet."[21] But any literary reference to Arkansas, though only thirty-eight lines long and no matter how badly executed, merits attention.

Our poet Dumont accompanied La Harpe up the Arkansas River in 1722, and calumniates the entire venture by asserting that its main object was to search out a fabled *rocher de topaze*—a cliff of topaz. He remarked sarcastically that at the time of their voyage this lapidary marvel must unfortunately have been "obscured by florid grass or by mist; for . . . despite all our travail, all that came [of our effort] was that we saw a lot of pretty country, good and quite excellent for all manner of crops." The explorers did, he said, find marble and slate, even some rock crystal; and he concludes with the observation that "it is a great shame that such beautiful lands are only the lot of so many barbarous and savage nations, and that there are not enough refined folk able to settle in this charming country."[22]

This is probably the place to record another early literary effort with an Arkansas connection. Half a century after Dumont visited the Arkansas country, Jean-Bernard Bossu published a somewhat better poem than Dumont's, though in no discernible meter, which he asks us to believe he wrote to record a speech made by a Quapaw whom he encountered in the Illinois. Bossu asserts that "[t]he *Akanças* really have a poetic bent," and goes so far as to claim that "their simple elegies are worthy of the sensitive and exquisite Ovid." It seems that Bossu's Quapaw, an envoy to Fort de Chartres and the grandson of one of La Salle's 1682 expeditionaries, was king of a ball given in his honor at the fort in 1756. His queen and partner was a fourteen-year-old French beauty, of course named Manon, by whom he was of course deeply smitten, and whom he innocently tried to persuade to remove a scarf that covered her bosom. The girl, Bossu credibly reports, blushed and demurred. The Indian "said not a word," Bossu claimed, "in reply to the expostulations that each country has its customs, and that it would be the vilest impropriety for a French woman to expose her bosom, although it was very natural for an *Akanças* lady to do so." After collecting his thoughts for a time, the Indian unburdened himself of a short speech that Bossu was moved to render into seventeen rhymed couplets. It began: "Why, young Manon, do you keep imprisoned with such severity this white, new-born breast, which no mortal has seen, whose just bloomed bud no hand has plucked? Let them breathe, tender creatures, alas! innocent victims, why do you stifle them?" After much rather predictable babbling about alabaster globes, capering tender does, and the like, the poem ends with this injunction: "If, to prevent the unhappiness of your lovers, you wish to punish their view while sparing their hearts, then veil your beautiful eyes, cover then this mouth whose lustre sets us afire and whose sound touches us; and, certain of the blows that your charms inflict, never again expose yourself to the view of mortals!"[23] As amatory poetry goes, this effort is perhaps not deathless: But as an early example of cross-cultural anthropology by a Frenchman familiar with the Arkansas country it is fascinating and delightful. We nevertheless might be right to guess that Bossu's poetry tells us a great deal more about eighteenth-century Frenchmen and Frenchwomen than their Indian contemporaries.

The appreciation of the sciences at the Arkansas was apparently rather primitive, judging from the level of the medical arts practiced there, though we get only the most occasional and fortuitous glimpses of them. Like the legal profession,

Figure 28. The Quapaws welcome Bossu.
(*Courtesy of The Historical New Orleans Collection.*)

on the continent of Europe the medical profession was bifurcated. Physicians formed the truly learned half; university-educated, their job was the diagnosis of disease and illness and the prescription of cures. Surgeons, on the other hand, were craftsmen who, like other craftsmen, learned their skills mainly through apprenticeship, though in 1743 an ordinance was passed that required surgeons to possess a master of arts degree. Gov. Alexandro O'Reilly's decree of February 12, 1770, thus correctly divided medical duties: "Medicine proper," he explained, "is the science of recognizing diseases and the relation that they have with remedies, and of prescribing the latter together with diet"; surgery, on the other hand, involved "the general use of the hands and of exterior remedies."[24]

We hear no talk whatever of physicians (*médecins*) in Arkansas, but this is hardly surprising since there were never more than a handful of them in the whole of Louisiana. During the French period, however, surgeons receive frequent mention: La Salle even had one with him when he visited the Arkansas region in 1682,[25] and a surgeon and apothecary were among the eighty or so whites who reached Law's concession in August of 1721.[26] A surgeon seems also to have been a regular feature of the French army detachment at the fort, for such persons are often encountered in the records.[27] Surgeons were not, evidently, particularly learned, as one would have guessed. In 1748, an Arkansas Post surgeon named Lefevre deserted to join a trade expedition to Santa Fe, where his Spanish captors reported that he was also a barber and a tailor.[28] (Note the overlap of skills: All three callings required cutting and sewing.) The fort built in 1751–55 did, however, have a hospital in one of its buildings,[29] so there was evidently some attempt being made to address the matter of medical treatment with seriousness.

For a time, François Ménard served the Spanish garrison at the Post as surgeon,[30] but he resigned in 1770, and we find no further mention of medical personnel at the fort for the rest of the century. Interestingly, in 1791 an American surgeon named Benjamin K. Adams accompanied a wounded man from Arkansas Post to Natchez; when officials at Natchez interrogated him about why he had left the Post, he said that "he was not happy there and there was no work for a person with his skill in the said place."[31] Adams seems to have found Natchez much more to his liking, and his faculties seem to have been more in demand there, for in 1794 he is styling himself "Doctor of Physic" in the Natchez records and contracting to cure the lame.[32]

Thomas Nuttall, the British botanist who visited the Post in 1819, confirmed Dr. Adams's assessment of the state of things at the Arkansas. "French quackery," he reported, "has hitherto been preferred to the advice of a regular physician."[33] No doubt home remedies played a large part in the treatment of illness, and Jean-Bernard Bossu reports in 1770 that the Arkansas French consulted Indian medicine men on occasion.[34] He also tells a tale, possibly true, of an Alabaman medicine man who had tried to inoculate Arkansas Indians against smallpox, had botched the job, and had found himself tied to the stake for his trouble.[35] Perhaps, too, the French of the Arkansas, like the Indians, sometimes repaired to the place now known as Hot Springs to take the healing waters.[36]

Probably the most interesting of the Indian remedies that Bossu recounts was a fumigation technique that, he assures us, was "a sure cure for rheumatism, gout, gravel, and other infirmities." He asserts that he saw a European cured of gout by this method at the Arkansas. "The medicine man," he says, "boiled in a cauldron all sorts of simples, leaves of red and white laurel, balsam, citronelle, sassafras roots with branches of pine and white candleberry. . . ." Then, "the savage doctor placed the cauldron under a canopy made with hoops over which he stretched a tanned deer skin to concentrate the vapor of roots and fragrant herbs . . . and had the patient put his sore foot immediately above the cauldron." The result: "[T]he European completely recovered."[37]

While we may be forgiven some twentieth-century skepticism about the efficacy of the medicine man's decoction, it is also well to remember that the remedies known to eighteenth-century European medicine were frequently no more scientific than his. In fact, the Quapaws sensibly eschewed bloodletting, much employed in Europe, because "blood must be preserved as it is the source of life."[38] European medicines and treatments aimed mainly at expurgating the body of "bad humors," so emetics, diuretics, diaphoretics, and the like provided the cures of preference. As it happens, chance has allowed to come down to us a list of the medicines that Post surgeon François Ménard had on hand on January 4, 1770. The good doctor had twenty-seven remedies in his medicine chest, among which were various ointments, salts, and balms, diaphoretic antimony, absinthe, verdigris, aloe, gum drops, and elderberry cough syrup. The most exotic of his medicines were Spanish fly, snake powder, and crawfish eyes; probably the most effective remedy on hand was half a pound of *quinquina,* the Peruvian bark from which quinine was made. But some of the remedies, in

Figure 29. Bossu cures an Indian. (*Courtesy of The Historical New Orleans Collection.*)

improper doses, could do positive harm: Ménard's mercury medicines (*panacés mercurielles*) were no doubt among these.[39] In fact, in 1756 one Teissière, the storekeeper at the Arkansas, was relieved from duty because, it was said, he "had had the misfortune to lose his mind as a result of a sickness"; and his superior guessed that this was "the effect of mercury which they made him use, no doubt without taking all the necessary precautions for this remedy." The authorities judged that Teissière's "madness [*folie*] up to the present had not been bad" but, nevertheless, since they did "not have the necessary commodities to treat these kinds of sicknesses," they thought it best to send Teissière "to Rochefort where he could perhaps find a cure."[40] Whatever their efficacy and side effects, the amounts of the medicines that Ménard possessed were extremely small, usually only an ounce or two of each, and the Post seems to have suffered from a lack of adequate medical supplies during the Spanish period. In 1797, for example, Captain de Vilemont sent a sick soldier to New Orleans with the explanation that "there were no remedies in this post for his ills."[41]

Virtually the only product of Louisiana's colonial press that can aspire to being called a book appeared in 1796, but it can maintain no straight-faced claim to originality for it was for the most part a compendium of a medical work published in Madrid in 1786. This most interesting book (or pamphlet: It contains only forty-nine pages) came provided with a rather grandiose title: *Medicines, and a Digest of the Method of Mr. Masdevall, Medical Doctor of Charles IV, King of Spain, to Cure all Epidemic, Putrid, and Malign Illnesses, Fevers of Different Kinds, etc. and to Prevent Them.*[42] Who its editor was does not appear, though some connection with Father Antonio Portillo of New Orleans may be presumed, since on page seventeen of this work he is said to have used Dr. Masdevall's method to good effect. It is likely that the publication of this book was related to the first appearance of yellow fever at New Orleans in the year that it was brought out.[43] However that may be, the shortage of doctors in Louisiana had provided some of the impetus for its publication, for its subtitle states that it is intended "for the use of families deprived of physicians." The text asserts as well that it was published "particularly for the inhabitants of colonies exposed to the malign influences of the climates that they inhabit, and deprived of the help of prudent and careful physicians";[44] and it assures the reader that the application of the cures that it contains is "within the reach of everyone, even those of mediocre intelligence."[45] More expansive guarantees appear later on: "Rarely," the author exudes, "will the physician who knows how to follow the instructions that I give lose the glory of curing his patients. The understanding of this method requires little talent; it only requires someone of moderate brightness; it is not necessary to have studied medicine. As long as he knows how to read and understand what is written, he can effect cures more effectively than any physician."[46] Recipes, in Latin with a French translation, for all the necessary prescriptions are provided. Such a work would have found a ready readership, one suspects, among a few *habitants* in the remote Arkansas country.

All the large claims for Dr. Masdevall's cures that the book makes cannot be enumerated here. It will have to suffice to reveal that the author promises the virtually instant defeat of a long list of fevers, but "principally . . . those that come from corrupt air or from miasmas that always infect cemeteries, prisons, hospitals, ships, and watery and marshy places."[47] This association of sickness with swamps and stale air was a commonplace of eighteenth-century medicine. It is tragically ironic that swamps did in fact increase the incidence of fevers, but for a reason that colonial doctors could not guess, namely the disease-bearing mosquitoes which infested them. It is doubly ironic that complaints about fevers and mosquitoes should have so frequently appeared in each other's company in colonial Louisiana documents.

Arkansas Post, in all of its various incarnations, was situated in or near the alluvial plain of the Mississippi, and the generally low and swampy environment of course bred hordes of mosquitoes, about which visitors to the Post often complained bitterly. Father du Poisson, writing from Arkansas in 1727, lamented that mosquitoes had "caused more swearing since the French came to Mississippi, than had been done before that time in all the rest of the world."[48] Some sixty years later, an American boatman named John Halley, probably a "Kaintuck," called at the Post, and, after having been "treated with a great deal of complaisance and plenty of [drink]" by a local Frenchman, "went to bead after 2"; but he reported that he "slep very little, the misquetars being very troublesom."[49]

A generation later, in 1819, the missionary Timothy Flint gives a vivid and moving account of the abject misery that these ubiquitous pests created. He said that most of the time that he spent at the Post "was, from a hundred circumstances, a time of gloom and dejection." Everyone in his family, except himself, was sick. "The lives of two," he said, "were in jeopardy for a number of days. All the neighbors were sick, and many were dying about me." It seems probable that

Flint had been unlucky enough to arrive at the Post during a yellow fever epidemic. He went on to recount: "The air was excessively sultry, and the musquitoes troublesome to a degree, which I have not experienced before or since. I was obliged to rise from my bed at least ten times a night, for forty nights. I slept under a very close musquitoe curtain. I would soon become oppressed for want of breath under the curtain, and when I drew it up and attempted to inhale a little of the damp and sultry atmosphere, the musquitoes would instantly gather on my face in such numbers that I was soon obliged to retreat behind my curtain again. Thus passed those dreadful nights, amidst the groans of my family, calls for medicine and drink, suffocation behind my curtain, or the agony of musquitoe stings, as soon as I was exposed to the air." Not only did the mosquitoes render the nights intolerable, but during the day if one sought refuge under a shade tree the pesky insects, "which during the heat of the day, took shelter in the shade, would rise in countless swarms from the grass to attack. . . ." Flint and his family could not even take their food "until a fire, kindled with the most offensive materials, and under the table, dispersed its suffocating fumes to drive [the mosquitoes] away." (Father du Poisson had reported the use of smudges against mosquitoes almost a hundred years earlier.)[50] The *habitants* used to joke about the subject of mosquitoes, Flint said, and "urged this incessant torment as an excuse for deep drinking. A sufficient quantity of wine or spirits to produce a happy reverie, or a dozing insensibility, had a cant but very significant name,—'a musquitoe dose.'"[51] It is thus easy to understand why the 1810 inventory of Pierre Lefevre's debtor's estate reveals that he owned a bed outfitted with two mosquito nets.[52]

Flint came to the conclusion that "[t]he valley of the Arkansas, with very little exception, is sickly. Remittents and intermittents are so common, that when a person has no more than simple fever and ague, he is hardly allowed to claim the immunities of sickness, and it is remarked that he only has the ague. The Autumn that I was there, it appeared to me that more than half the inhabitants, not excepting the creoles, had the ague."[53] So, too, in 1809, an American soldier noted that the diseases at the Post were "mostly intermittent fevers and other trifling complaints."[54]

Historians have long recognized that the church often provided help to the state as an agency of social control and dispute settlement. In Louisiana, as elsewhere, the church certainly aspired to be a partner with the secular government in creating and maintaining a moral order. "Today religion joins with the law," one observer of Louisiana noted: "The one suppresses bad thoughts, the other restrains guilty hands."[55] But the resources of the Louisiana church were simply no match for its ambitions, and nowhere was that truer than in the remote Post of Arkansas.

One of the means to which the French resorted in order to attract the loyalty and trade of the Indians of Louisiana was the creation of missions to convert and minister to them. Across the Mississippi, contemporary Anglo-Americans were well aware of the part that the Jesuits played in the French effort to gain the affection of the Indians. One New Englander, greatly alarmed by Law's plans to colonize Louisiana, warned in 1720 that French colonization would result in the disaffection from the English of the Indians inhabiting "the inland countries."[56] Law's colonists, he feared, would "cut off all Intercourse and Traffic between us and the Indians";[57] and in the event of a war with France the Indians on the west side of the river could prove potent allies for the French.[58] He knew of the missionaries' work: "In every tribe there are some missionary priests, and tho' few or none of the savages have ever been made thorough converts to the truths of the *Christian* religion, yet in all other matters they look upon these good Fathers as Teutular *Gods,* and give themselves up entirely to be directed by their Counsels."[59] The author concluded his estimation of the danger that the missionaries posed by noting sarcastically: "In short, Sir, he ought to be a *cunning* man that treats with the *Indians,* and therefore the *French* leave that business to the Jesuits."[60]

Even before the grand plans of Law's *Compagnie d'Occident* were laid there was a missionary among the Quapaws. The first missionary to take up residence in Arkansas was Father Nicholas Foucault who established himself there in 1700.[61] He was also the first martyr of Louisiana: He left Arkansas late in July of 1702 in the company of two soldiers and two Koroa Indians, and the Indians murdered him along the way under the pretext "of punishing the aged priest for leaving. . . ."[62] Serious missionary efforts were evidently not made again until John Law's colonizing plans were laid. At that time, the Jesuits undertook to provide a priest for Arkansas; but the Capuchins grumbled that "the Jesuits promise more than they can keep,"[63] and events proved them right. The priest destined for Law's Arkansas colony died on the journey from New Orleans,[64] and only after Law's director Bertrand Dufresne abandoned the concession in 1726 were the Jesuits able to furnish a replacement. In 1727, Father Paul du Poisson came to Arkansas; in the interim the place had enjoyed only an occasional visit from the peripatetic priests of the region.[65] Two years later the Jesuits sent Brother Philip Cruez to help du Poisson, but he died in November of 1729 of sunstroke.[66] That very month du Poisson himself perished in the massacre at Natchez: The Natchez Indians burst into the chapel there while he was praying and cut off his head with a hatchet.[67] Again the Arkansas was without a priest and had to be content with the episodic visits of wandering missionaries.

The only priest of the French period who stayed long enough to have much of an effect was the Jesuit Father Louis Carette who took up his post in 1750.[68] In August of 1758 he left in despair, taking the church records with him. Over the years, the good father had become increasingly disgruntled with the state of affairs at the Post of Arkansas. For one thing, there was no chapel at the location to which Captain de Reggio had moved the Post in 1756, and no effort was being made to provide one. But the event which precipitated Carette's departure involved the irreligious inclination of his French communicants. The commandant's dining room was the only place now to say a mass, "not a very suitable place, not only because it was a dining room, but on account of the bad conduct and freedom of language of those who frequented it."[69] The room was open to everything, even the fowls of the Post; and after one mass a hen, flying over the altar, knocked over the chalice, and sacrilegious remarks followed. One person exclaimed: "There! The God's Shop is upset." "To these sentiments," Father Watrin wrote of the Arkansas flock, "corresponded a life as little Christian."[70] Father Carette auctioned off his belongings, paid his debts to the store, and left in despair for New Orleans.[71] Watrin noted dejectedly that Carette had "labored to correct the morals of the French, but reaped hardly any fruit from his toil."[72]

The French never sent a replacement for Carette, and with the suppression of the Jesuit order in Louisiana in 1763 came the end of any possibility of resident priests for Arkansas for a considerable time: The number of priests in Spanish Louisiana was small and was not augmented until settlement became extensive enough to support parishes. Shortly after O'Reilly took command, he wrote a memorandum outlining the religious needs of the colony and indicating where he planned to send priests, but he omitted mention of Arkansas altogether.[73] It was simply too remote and too tiny.

In 1770, to hear the Arkansas commandant tell it, there was still no real chapel, much less a priest, at the Post. That year Capt. François Demasellière requested permission of the governor to convert the "building where public praying is done" into a shelter. It was, he said, only a one-room building, "unadorned by any religious goods . . . where the chaplain used to sleep."[74] (This building had, no doubt, been Father Carette's house.) Some of the inhabitants had a slightly different version: To them, the building was indeed a chapel. As to the lack of adornments there, they wrote to de Clouet, Demasellière's predecessor, to inquire what ornaments had been there when Demasellière assumed command. There had been candlesticks and an altar cloth they knew; but now their chapel was bare. What, they wanted to know moreover, had become of the presents for the chapel that Madame de Clouet had left behind?[75]

After the creation of Ste. Genevieve Parish in 1770 the pastor there occasionally ministered to the people at Arkansas; and in 1790 responsibility for the Arkansas country was transferred to the newly created parish of New Madrid.[76] It was not possible at first for the new parish to devote much time to the pastoral care of its nearest southern neighbor, about 250 miles distant from it by water. Beginning in September of 1792, however, Father Pierre Gibault, the famous patriot priest of the west, spent almost a year at the Post as a missionary from New Madrid Parish.[77] A year after Gibault's departure, Father Sébastian Flavien de Besançon, a French Capuchin and refugee from the French Revolution, arrived to take up the mission at the Post. He remained in residence only about eight months and the Post commandant complained that the priest had neither a chapel nor the power to confess.[78]

The year 1796 was an important one in the ecclesiastical history of Arkansas, for it marked the creation of the first canonical parish ever erected there. Its pastor was Pierre Janin who fled the revolution in France and arrived in Philadelphia in the fall of 1794, armed with documents from the Bishops of Angers and Zanora attesting to his ordination and good character. Bishop John Carroll of Baltimore assigned him in January of the next year to the parish of Kaskaskia in Anglo-American Illinois. After only about a year in that post, Janin asked to be demitted to the Diocese of Louisiana and the Floridas, crossed over to Spanish Illinois, and went down to New Orleans. Bishop Luis Peñalver y Cárdenas, upon learning that Janin did not like big cities, decided to send him to minister to the faithful at *Las Arcas.* The people of the district of Arkansas and its surroundings had, according to the bishop, "no other pastor who can administer the sacraments of baptism, marriage, penitence, eucharist, and extreme unction," so it was apparent that their need was great. Bishop Peñalver instructed Janin, after getting the permission of the Post commandant, to "build a small house in which to celebrate the holy sacrifice of the mass, administer the sacraments, and keep the books" and other records of the parish. Furthermore, the bishop lent the new pastor ornaments and other necessary equipment for his Arkansas church: From the chapel of the church at Cole's Creek (near Natchez) he provided a purple stole and a black stole, some altar cloths, some corporals, a *singulo,* and an amice; and from the bishop's own chapel came a curved (or arched) altar, two brass candlesticks, a china baptismal font, some glass cruets, a glass saltcellar (for solemn baptism?), and three purificators.[79]

It was, therefore, a reasonably well equipped priest who arrived at the Arkansas in August of 1796, probably unannounced but with a letter of introduction from the bishop to Capt. Carlos de Vilemont, the commandant of Arkansas Post. As we saw, the bishop had expressed the hope that Janin would construct a house, but such a project probably put too great a strain on the resources on which the good father could hope to call, even though the bishop had exhorted the Arkansas faithful to "attend to and provide aid to their minister" when he requested it. It is likely, therefore, that Janin took up residence in a vacant house provided by the commandant or Post *habitants* soon after his arrival.

What is certain is that when Father Janin arrived at the Post one of his first concerns had to be to provide a church for his parishioners. In fact, according to de Vilemont, a month after his arrival Janin had already written a memorial on behalf of the *habitants* asking Bishop Peñalver to request the government to build a church at the Post. The *habitants* wanted a place "where they could attend to divine offices with the decency that they require, a place that can hold a greater number of people than the small living room [*sala*] in the priest's house where they are now celebrated." The cost of such a building, they reckoned, might reach sixteen hundred dollars.[80] Governor Carondolet responded, vaguely, that "we shall see to building a church and a rectory [*maison curiale*]" at the Post, but nothing whatever seems to have been done for another two or three years.[81]

The house that served the little community as church and presbytery was indeed unsuitable. In March of 1799, Father Janin informed the intendant that his rectory (*casa curial*) was "so run down and deteriorated as to be no longer habitable with any convenience. . . ." Janin's tiny accommodation, according to him, amounted to "no more than an apartment eighteen feet long by ten feet wide, to which is attached a small room eight feet long by six feet wide": The "apartment" served as the chapel and the other room as the priest's sleeping quarters. Since its sills were rotten, he believed that rebuilding the house was absolutely indispensable, and he also requested the construction of "a kitchen that at the proper time will serve as a lodging for the priest's servant." In addition, Father Janin asked for galleries around his house, a staircase (steps), and a new fireplace. He did not think that the remodeling and new construction would cost more than four hundred dollars.

The intendant, probably relieved that the good priest had lowered his sights and had focused on a more manageable project than building a new church, promptly sent Janin's petition to the chief engineer of the province for an estimate of how much the proposed work would cost. Within the week, on April 8, 1799, the chief engineer responded with an elaborate estimate, including the number of posts, rafters, and so forth necessary to remodel the premises, provide a running gallery (*galeria corrida*) around it, and build a "little kitchen ten feet by ten feet" containing a double oven. All this could be done, he estimated, for a little more than 431 dollars. Two days later, the Royal Hacienda of the province approved the project and the intendant gave the order to execute the works.[82]

These improvements were evidently indeed made, but the little parish was nevertheless about to suffer a decided setback, for in September of 1799 the bishop concluded that the St. Louis parish urgently required Father Janin to replace Father James Didier, the pastor there, who had recently died. Janin's services at the Illinois parish were "more necessary . . . than at the Arkansas," the bishop and intendant reckoned, because of the larger population at St. Louis;[83] besides, they noted that Father Janin's knowledge of French, Spanish, and English would stand him in good stead with the polyglot population there.[84] Father Janin left a few days after saying Christmas mass in 1799, and the Post never again had a resident priest. Not until about 1835, the year before statehood, would there be another Roman Catholic parish anywhere in Arkansas. Of course, with the American takeover in 1803, Louisiana would no longer have a state-subsidized church; and only four of the thirty-five clergymen in the old Spanish colony chose to remain.[85]

The absence of much connected religious activity in Arkansas, and the impermanence of resident priests at the Post, meant that one effective alternative to social control by the state was altogether lacking. The truth is that for most of the eighteenth century the church was quite weak and ineffective throughout Louisiana, even in the supposedly civilized precincts of New Orleans. When the diocese of Louisiana and the Floridas was created in 1794, Luis Peñalver y Cárdenas was named its first bishop,[86] and on December 22, 1795, he made extensive inquiries into the moral and spiritual health of his diocese. He found it none too good. Father Joaquín Portillo of New Orleans reported to him that more than half the people in his city lived in open sin.[87] Don Jasper de Aranda thought Portillo's estimate conservative, for he told the bishop that most of the people lived in public concubinage and that all the blacks did; he often found it necessary, he said, to preach to the inhabitants that they were worse than pagans.[88] There were parents, he claimed, who, as soon as their sons arrived at the age of puberty, gave them a black woman or mulatto girl. Slaves did not get married, he reported, and their offspring were very numerous.[89]

Bishop Peñalver's instructions to the parish priests of Louisiana are very interesting for the light that they shed on the functions that he expected his pastors to fulfill. They were to encourage all parishioners who were ill for three days to make a will and were to urge all married people to live together. All those living in concubinage were to be compelled to separate. He instructed the priests, moreover, to avoid discords and controversies and to mediate "whenever such a position does not offend God"; and they were to advise their parishioners to do the same in all "injuries and disputes."[90] The bishop also told his pastors that the commandant was the most important person in their parishes. That was partly because the cooperation of the commandant was frequently necessary to effect a moral order tolerable to the church. For instance, if those living in concubinage failed to separate, the priest should, according to the bishop, report them to the civil authorities for punishment in accordance with the secular law.[91] Likewise, if slaveholders worked their slaves on days of obligation, the local pastor must tell the commandants to enforce the sabbath laws.[92]

Examples of the cooperation of church and state in the late eighteenth century are relatively numerous. When Paul de St. Piare, pastor at Ste. Genevieve, complained to the bishop of drunken Indians who committed great crimes in his parish, the bishop replied that the commandant should enforce the laws against selling liquor to Indians. "Preaching is insufficient," he said, "if civil authorities do not help."[93] When in 1797 advice was sought from the vicar-general of St. Louis on what to do about a blasphemer, he advised threatening the offender with the civil authorities. As an alternative, he suggested sending him to New Orleans to the ecclesiastical court for punishment. Even this alternative, however, could involve secular authorities since only they had the power to arrest those who would not appear voluntarily in church tribunals.[94] The state's monopoly on force was also important when it came to having to deal with married persons who refused to live together and who attempted to effect an escape from the parish. In such a case, Bishop Peñalver instructed his priests to solicit the help of the royal justice—the commandant in places like Arkansas Post.[95]

Because the church did not exert a sustained force over a significant period of time in the Arkansas country, it is not surprising that very little has been left behind to indicate what influence it was in fact able to bring to bear. All that has survived are marriage, baptism, and burial records, most of them from 1796 and after.[96] We cannot, therefore, tell what effect, if any, Father Janin was able to give to the bishop's instructions. But there is some interesting detail to be gleaned from such documents as have survived, and they reveal both a conscientious determination to bring the settlement into line with canon law and a practical willingness to compromise with the conditions of the frontier.

Since they usually had no resident priest, future spouses in Arkansas apparently stipulated in their marriage contracts that they would regularize their union *in facie ecclesiae* at the earliest opportunity, and then simply began living together as husband and wife. It is clear that the *habitants* regarded the signing of this contract as a kind of civil marriage. This view could only have been reinforced by the fact that the commandant "passed" the contracts in his capacity as surrogate notary and official witness. In 1793 Father Pierre Gibault married five couples who had previously contracted marriage "before witnesses" (one of whom, presumably, was the commandant) due to the lack of a priest in the area.[97] Several of these couples also recognized certain children as their own, thus allowing them to take advantage of the post-marriage legitimation rule of the civil and canon law.[98] In 1797, Father Janin married two couples who had previously "married in the presence of the commandant of this post."

Interestingly, the record of that marriage notes that in 1797 Bishop Peñalver had waived the necessity for publishing the banns for marriages previously contracted in this fashion.[99] Of course, these unions were otherwise of no legal effect; it could not be clearer that in this period such couples were not married in the eyes of either the church or the state.[100]

Juan Filhiol, the commandant at Ouachita Post, had got himself into serious difficulty witnessing these kinds of contracts, probably because an important family had complained about the "marriage" in this fashion of their daughter to an Indian whom they decidedly disliked.[101] In 1801 the bishop had haled Filhiol before an ecclesiastical court to explain why he had allowed these forward marriage contracts and participated in their execution. Filhiol replied simply that that had been the custom and that he had stopped doing it when a parish priest was appointed for his post in 1799. In the end, the bishop's tribunal sensibly held that all Filhiol had done was witness a civil contract between parties, and it therefore acquitted him. Filhiol had not actually officiated at a ceremony; he had only acted as a surrogate notary. Evidently the commandants in these kinds of instances were wise enough not to pronounce any words purporting to create a marital bond.

Other entries in the Arkansas church records indicate that many of the inhabitants had been cohabiting without even the benefit of a contract to regularize the arrangement when a priest should next appear. At least that is a plausible inference from the records of marriages in which parents recognize children and make no mention of a prior contract.[102] This presumption seems especially strong in cases where the illegitimate children are numerous and of a fairly advanced age.[103] Such a state of affairs is, in the nature of things, not at all surprising. Clearly, the inhabitants of Louisiana, and of Arkansas in particular, were not especially devout. It is a tribute to the persuasiveness of the priests of Arkansas that they were able to impose as much spiritual order on the place as they were.

In one respect, however, it appears that the teachings of the church had no impact at all: The Quapaws evidently remained attached to their old religious ways despite the best efforts of the missionaries to convert them to Christianity. Jean-Bernard Bossu attempted to gull the credulous into believing a fantastic tale about how he had converted some Indians in Arkansas to Christianity by exposing the fakery of a medicine man who had awed the Indians with a talking

Figure 30. Bossu destroys an Indian idol.
(*Courtesy of The Historical New Orleans Collection.*)

idol. It is a revealing story, accompanied by a most amusing picture, but without doubt a wholly fanciful one.[104] Nor, interestingly, were the black slaves thoroughly Christianized, judging from the fact that no records of the marriages of blacks have survived. It is just possible that no such records were kept or that they have been lost; but records of the baptism and burial of blacks do survive in fairly large numbers, and this makes both of these possibilities less likely. It would not, in any case, be a cause for wonder if slaves did not marry in regular fashion. The church, of course, regarded regular marriages as every bit as necessary to the health of black souls as of white ones, but there is evidence that the attitude of slaveowners made such marriages difficult and often impossible to effect. In 1795, for example, Father Felix de Quintanar, the Capuchin pastor of Galveztown, complained to the bishop that the slaveowners themselves officiated at the marriages of their slaves and just laughed when he offered to marry them for free. The owners claimed that what they did was "the usage not only in this town but in all the colony."[105] The bishop wrote back instructing the priest to get the commandant to help him persuade slaveholders not to officiate at slave marriages.[106]

Change in this custom must have come slowly if at all. No doubt slaveowners wanted no competition when it came to authority over their slaves and resented any attempt to dilute it. In 1801, the pastor of Attakapas noted that census-taking in his district was difficult because slaveholders did not want to reveal their holdings.[107] Clearly any intrusion by external authority into the master-slave relationship was going to meet with great resistance. This was evidently true in Arkansas as well, although the number of slaves there in the eighteenth century could not have much exceeded sixty.[108]

V

WAR AND THE MILITARY

The old Post of Arkansas, though it was certainly from the beginning an Indian trading post, takes its name not from its commercial activities but from the fact that it was a military establishment. It is usual to say, as we have indeed said, that Arkansas Post was founded in 1686, but the European settlement on the Arkansas did not in fact acquire that name until after a garrison was established there in 1722 to protect the Frenchmen at Law's concession. Before that time, the Arkansas outpost does not seem to have had a name: Tonty simply referred to his trading house, French quarter, or fort at the Arkansas, and Law's concession had no name other than his to distinguish it. It thus appears that the military mission of the Arkansas settlement provided it, in many people's minds, with its primary *raison d'être.* Even so late as 1802, an American resident of New Orleans describes Arkansas Post "as almost altogether military,"[1] something of a distortion to be sure. The number of soldiers at the Arkansas was small except in times of extraordinary danger when the Post sometimes received reinforcements. The first garrison, established in 1722, consisted of Lieutenant La Boulaye and seventeen men.[2] The government recalled this tiny force from the river in 1725 after Law's bankruptcy.

During the early French period it is likely that the soldiers stationed at the Arkansas and their Quapaw allies had the most to fear from the Chickasaws, who lived in villages in northeast Mississippi but regularly ranged into Alabama, Kentucky, Tennessee, and even Illinois. It seems that the enmity between the Quapaws and the Chickasaws was of long standing: In 1673, Marquette and Jolliet reported a Quapaw village on the east bank of the Mississippi, and its apparent disappearance before La Salle's 1682 visit may well have been due to Chickasaw expansion.[3] However that may be, the Chickasaws' alliance with the English was firm and unshakable and that alone would have made the French, and thus the Quapaws, the Chickasaws' sworn enemy.

The Arkansas Post soon was drawn into the struggle between the French and the English for dominance of North America. This contest for empire of course manifested itself in a number of places, but the lower Mississippi River region was an important theater for it. The British of Carolina were particularly interested in the Arkansas region because of the strategic importance of the Arkansas River and because of the abundance of skins and pelts to be had there: The skin trade was extraordinarily important to the Carolina economy throughout most of the eighteenth century.

In 1729, the flourishing French settlement at Natchez, the second most considerable in the whole province, was completely destroyed by the Natchez Indians, who massacred most of the *habitants,* a total of almost three hundred men, women, and children. The attack and its aftermath, even by the standards of eighteenth-century Indian warfare, were particularly gruesome: Pregnant women had their stomachs slashed open and their fetuses ripped out; the men's heads were severed and arranged in rows, even stacked like cannonballs. Governor Périer suspected (some say manufactured) a general Indian conspiracy at the root of this disaster and in retaliation soon devised a grisly barbarism or two of his own: He entirely annihilated the Chaouachas, a tiny and wholly inoffensive tribe near New Orleans, and burned a Natchez woman to death at the capital's *place d'armes,* now Jackson Square. These acts horrified the colonial administration in France, but it did approve of the governor's plan to pursue and altogether exterminate the Natchez. Périer was unable to consummate this genocide but did finally inflict such heavy damage on the tribe that its remnant was forced to take refuge among the Chickasaws.[4] These efforts and others of the Chickasaws to undermine the French in Louisiana in general, and in particular

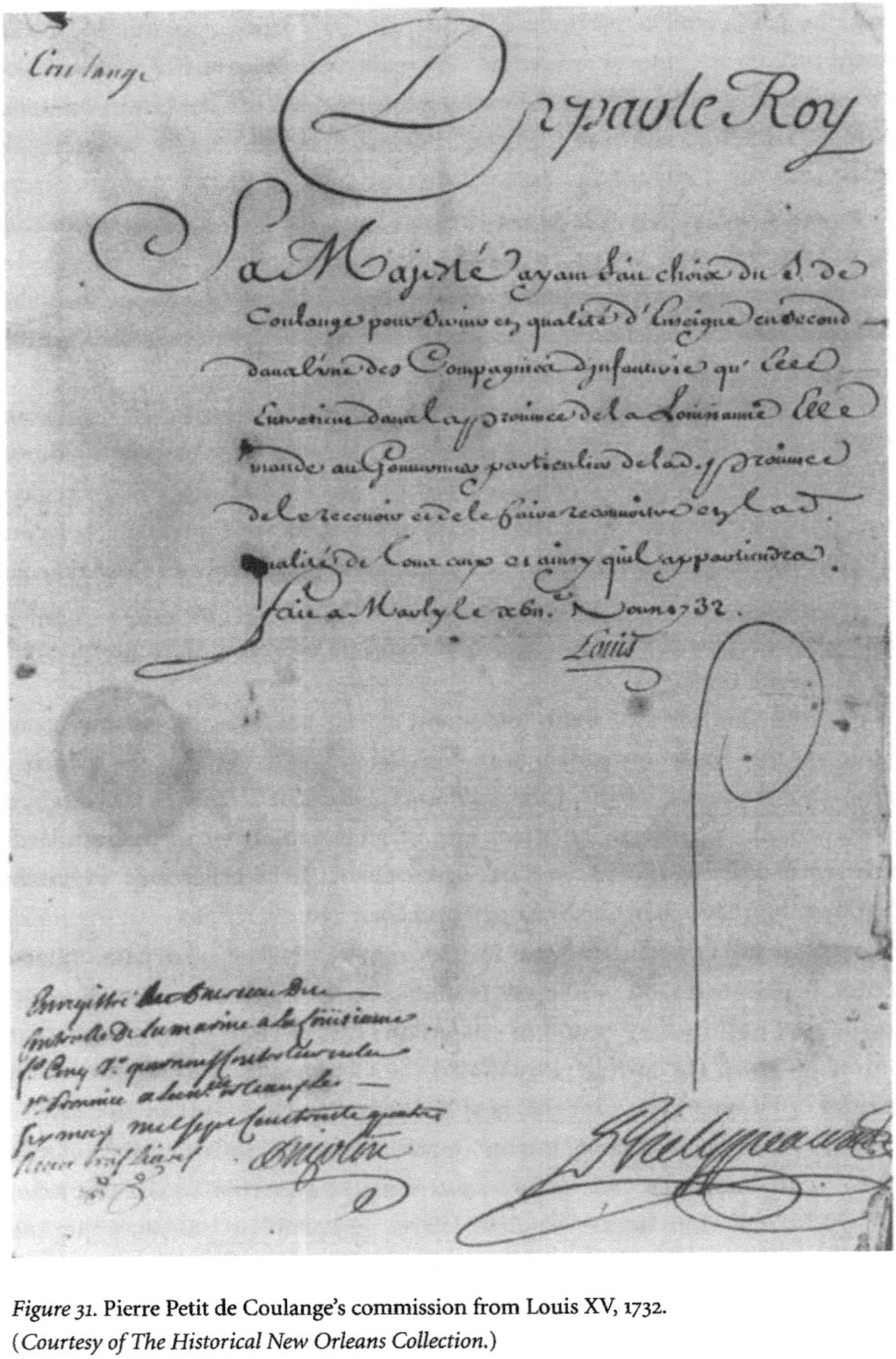

De par le Roy

Sa Majesté ayant fait choix du S. de Coulange pour servir en qualité d'Enseigne en second dans l'une des Compagnies d'infanterie qu'elle entretient dans la province de la Louisiane elle mande au Gouverneur particulier de lad. province de le recevoir et de le faire reconnoitre en lad. qualité de tous ceux et ainsy qu'il appartiendra. Fait a Marly le [illegible] 1732.

Louis

Figure 31. Pierre Petit de Coulange's commission from Louis XV, 1732.
(*Courtesy of The Historical New Orleans Collection.*)

to enlist the Quapaws in a pro-British alliance, account for Périer's resolve to strengthen his tiny Arkansas community which in 1727 consisted of only about thirty Frenchmen. In 1731 the governor sent the Sieur de Coulange up to the Arkansas with a considerable contingent of seventy men to form a settlement there; but the Natchez attacked and forced him to retreat downriver after two men were killed and two others wounded.[5] Later that year, therefore, Périer ordered de Coulange to establish a garrison at the Arkansas, an enterprise in which he finally succeeded.[6] He erected some buildings at the Post, but since he had only twelve men assigned to him, the governor reckoned that a palisade was not necessary.[7] By 1733 the governor could write proudly that de Coulange had "made himself so beloved that [the Quapaws] have been at war [against the Chickasaws] for two years, although I have had nothing to give them except promises."[8] In fact, one of the Quapaw parties had killed two Chickasaws and burnt another to death in their village.[9] The Chickasaws responded by stepping up their attacks on the convoys on the Mississippi.[10]

Governor Bienville, Périer's successor, decided to engage in war against the Chickasaws in deadly earnest. To that end, he conceived a grandiose plan of attack on their villages that involved a force of Quapaws as well as troops, militia, and Indian allies from the Illinois and New Orleans. De Coulange's cousin, Joseph Louis Boucher de Grandpré, who became commandant at Arkansas in 1734,[11] was to lead the Quapaws into battle, but due to faulty communications he arrived too late with his main force. Twenty-eight Quapaws, members of an advance party, did however join the battle at the Chickasaw Bluffs under the command of Pierre d'Artaguiette of the Illinois. The short of it is that d'Artaguiette too hastily committed his army and advanced into a Chickasaw ambush. Despite resistance from the Iroquois and Quapaws, who alone among the Indian allies stood their ground and fought, the Chickasaws cut the French army to ribbons and burned alive those unlucky enough to have survived. De Coulange was evidently among those who suffered this hideous death. Bienville's own army of the south, unable to make the original rendezvous, later met defeat as well.[12]

With his prestige shattered, Bienville set about devising an extraordinarily elaborate scheme to avenge this disastrous dishonor to French arms. One of the important figures in his plan was the Sieur de Vergès, an engineer whom Bienville charged with the task of discovering a land route from the Mississippi to the Chickasaw villages over which to transport cannon, mortars, and other equipment for a siege. De Vergès arrived at Arkansas Post on October 21, 1738, with sixteen soldiers, one officer, and four cadets and enlisted the Quapaws in his effort. With their help, de Vergès did considerable reconnoitering and located a route to the Chickasaws on the Mississippi's east bank a few miles above the mouth of the St. Francis River. From the banks of the Mississippi to the high ground that marked its banks during the spring floods was about sixteen miles, de Vergès said, and at that point he reported encountering a trace ordinarily used by the Chickasaws to travel to their villages: There were signs of horses about, fresh signs, so de Vergès and his men withdrew, but not before noting that the ground was firm enough for gun carriages to use it. Only four more days travel, the Quapaws told him, would bring them to the very Chickasaws themselves, though this proved inaccurate.[13]

A route having been located, Bienville's plan took shape. In the summer of 1739, four new companies arrived from France to form the nucleus of a southern army, to which Bienville would add his regular troops and militia from the lower Mississippi. From the north, from Illinois, the new commandant La Buissonière would lead 40 soldiers and upwards of 150 Illinois and Kaskaskia Indians, and from farther north yet, from Canada, 400 men were promised. The Illinois and Natchitoches posts were to supply two hundred horses, cattle for food, and eighty pairs of oxen for drawing the carts to be used in transporting war supplies. The staging area, the place at which all these forces and supplies were to be gathered, was to be a fort constructed in Arkansas just below the mouth of the St. Francis River.

Governor Bienville had sent de Vergès and a Captain Coustilhas with workers and soldiers to build this fort, called Fort St. Francis, in September of 1738; they were also to build there the carts and wagons necessary to transport the cannon and other war supplies. Augmented by two other groups later sent to help, the complement at Fort St. Francis had swollen to about three hundred men by the middle of May in the following year.[14] The fort, a square with a bastion in each corner,[15] was intended to contain "lodgings for officers, barracks, two warehouses, a bakehouse with three ovens, a powder magazine, a hospital, and kitchens,"[16] but the records do not reveal whether all these buildings were in fact constructed. In any case, in August it was decided to abandon de Vergès's route to the Chickasaws in favor of one from the Chickasaw Bluffs, and by the middle

Figure 32. A Louisiana military drummer, *ca.* 1740. (*Courtesy of Canadian Parks Service.*)

of the month Fort Assumption had been built there.[17] Men, animals, and tons of war matériel had to be transported, not, of course, without some loss, especially to the animals which had to be driven overland to what is now West Memphis and transported across the Mississippi by boat.[18]

In October, a larger Canadian force of Frenchmen and Indians, amounting to almost five hundred men, appeared at the Bluffs,[19] and when Bienville joined his army there in the middle of November it must have been twelve hundred strong, the largest force that the French would ever assemble in Louisiana. But even so huge an army as this could not give Bienville a victory. Incredibly, the road to the Chickasaws could not at first be found; and Commandant Montcharvaux came from the Arkansas with the news that most of the cattle and horses from Natchitoches, needed to draw the heavy artillery, had been stranded for a time at the Caddo village, exhausted and ravaged by hunger; a few of the horses had arrived at the Arkansas River in very bad condition and all the rest had perished.[20] Just as bad, the cannon and ammunition rusted into uselessness in the damp Louisiana winter, a winter against which everyone, from Indian ally to colonial official, had warned Bienville repeatedly. The Chickasaws were amazed by Bienville's indecisiveness and inactivity, while most of the Indians allied with the French, including the Quapaws, wandered off in disgust early in 1740. Just as Bienville had resolved to abandon the effort entirely, the Chickasaws sued for a bogus peace that he gladly accepted. Bienville immediately embarked for New Orleans, and on the way downstream he ordered Fort St. Francis destroyed. He tried to bluff the French government into accepting the enormous expense and the loss of life occasioned by this adventure as the cost of an alleged victory: The French show of arms had cowed the Chickasaws, he reassured his superiors, and they would soon descend into a submissive docility.[21] But the Chickasaws resumed their raids on French shipping on the Mississippi and the Post of Arkansas in the summer of 1740 was warned to be on its guard.[22]

The Quapaws had stood resolutely with the French through two disastrous campaigns against the Chickasaws. Despite these failures, they continued stoutly to resist the constant blandishments of the British to come and settle among them.[23] It is, nevertheless, easy to believe Governor Vaudreuil's complaint that when he arrived in the colony he found the Quapaws in a state of lethargy with respect to further operations against the Chickasaws. Vaudreuil had somehow stirred them to action, however, and in 1744 they brought him two Chickasaw scalps, five in 1746, and two more in the spring of 1747. The governor explained to his superiors that the Quapaws were of great importance to the French because they lived closer to the Chickasaws than any of their other allies. He therefore ordered Commandant Montcharvaux to pay them generously for the scalps that they produced.[24]

These vigorous actions and others against the Chickasaws would soon bring a furious retaliation. At dawn, on May 10, 1749, a band of about 150 Chickasaws, Abekas, and perhaps a few dissident Choctaws in the English interest, struck the Arkansas Post. Unluckily for the French, the Quapaws had only recently removed their villages to the high ground at *Écores Rouges* because of the great flood of 1748; and so the twelve men of the garrison, their officer 1st Ens. Louis-Xavier-Martin Delinó de Chalmette, and the few Europeans in residence were forced to face the onslaught on their own. These few Frenchmen were taken entirely unawares, perhaps because the Chickasaws' scout, or so Father Vivier says, was a drummer recently deserted from the Post itself: Certainly, knowing the routine of the place and its topography, he would have known too the best means to effect a surprise. The Chickasaws captured six men and eight women and children outside the fort, but they abandoned the siege of the fort itself when a lucky cannon shot wounded their great chief Payah Matahah. That same shot, however, proved unlucky for the six male prisoners: James Adair, a British trader who lived among the Chickasaws, tells us that the Chickasaws, despairing of their chief's life, "according to their universal method in such a case . . . killed most of their unfortunate captives . . ." The women and children were spared and divided between the Chickasaws and Abekas. The French ransomed three of these slaves from the Chickasaws, and some or all of the others were eventually released to the English in Charleston.[25]

Some twenty-five years after the fact, James Adair exulted in print about this raid. His Chickasaws, he boasted, had "attacked and burned a large village . . . though under the command of a stockade fort."[26] This claim contains some puffery, since just three years before the attack the government had reckoned that there were only about twelve male *habitants* and ten slaves at the Arkansas.[27] Still, the incident had greatly alarmed the whole province, especially since some reports had it that three Englishmen had led the attack and that some Choctaws had participated in it. There was a very real fear that the disaffected among the Choctaws, whose numbers were large, would join with

Figure 33. A Louisiana private and sergeant, *ca.* 1725–1735. (*Courtesy of Canadian Parks Service.*)

the Chickasaws in an effort to destroy the entire colony. The governor therefore moved quickly to ensure the safety of the Arkansas French: He immediately ordered the Post moved upriver to join the Quapaws at *Écores Rouges*, as the Quapaws themselves requested, and also ordered a new fort to be built there.[28] Incredibly, however, he did not reinforce the garrison. Indeed, by 1751, because of desertions, the garrison consisted only of Delinó, a corporal, and six soldiers; and when Delinó descended unbidden to New Orleans in that year the soldiers sacked the government store and deserted to Texas. Vaudreuil soon replaced Delinó with Lt. Paul Augustin le Pelletier de La Houssaye, assigned him a full company of fifty men, and ordered him to build a new and elaborate establishment, which he did. In 1756, however, no doubt because of the beginning of the Seven Years' War, the Arkansas fort was moved downriver to Desha County, and the regular garrison of fifty men was temporarily reinforced that same year by another company of fifty or sixty men under the command of the Chevalier d'Erneville.[29] This was surely the largest number of troops ever assigned to Arkansas Post. The troop strength seems to have returned to fifty men a year later and evidently remained at that level until the Spanish took over.

As had been the case during the years of French rule, while the Spanish held sway in Arkansas the European population there was too small and the garrison too impotent to intimidate seriously anyone with a hostile intent: The number of soldiers varied between fifteen and twenty during the first years of Spanish occupation.[30] A large military contingent was not necessary because after the British occupied that portion of Louisiana lying east of the Mississippi (except, of course, for New Orleans), and renamed the southern part of it West Florida, they discouraged Chickasaw raids across the river, preferring instead a policy of peaceful co-existence with their new Spanish neighbors. After the peace, the French even persuaded the Quapaws to allow the British to pass unmolested up the Mississippi to take over the Illinois country east of the Mississippi from the French commandant there.[31]

Though the end of the Seven Years' War brought an end, until the American Revolution, to open hostilities, the British in West Florida nevertheless continued their attempts to seduce the Quapaws away from their new Spanish masters. The total European population of West Florida could not have exceeded fifteen hundred at the time the English first occupied it, and some of the French *habitants* of course migrated to New Orleans or elsewhere in Spanish Louisiana rather than live under the British flag. But the British soon began an aggressive immigration effort. Though Natchez was virtually unsettled in 1765, it soon sprang into prominence: Between 1766 and 1769, the British made thirty-nine land grants, some of them huge, in the Natchez area. Movement to Natchez, which began as a trickle in 1767, became a boom in five years,[32] and one of those who settled there during this period of expansion was John Bradley, who in 1770 operated Natchez's only trading post.[33] Commandant Demasellière of the Arkansas reported that in that year Bradley had told the Quapaws of the executions of the five French revolutionaries in New Orleans, news that had greatly shaken the Quapaws' already tenuous attachment to the Spanish. Demasellière had countered Bradley's reports with a stupid lie that the Quapaws could not possibly have believed: The French had requested these executions, he said, because the five had lost their minds.[34]

The loyalty and affection of the Quapaw Indians was of course absolutely essential to the continued existence of the Arkansas settlement, and during the French period the alliance had been firm and unshakable. In fact, generally speaking, the French could not find sufficient encomia to heap upon the Quapaws. In 1758, for instance, Governor Kerlérec described them as "without doubt the bravest of all those nations which are dependants of this continent," and he praised them because they had "never varied in their attachment to us." Of all the Indian nations, the Quapaws were, he said, "the only one which has never soaked their hands in French blood," and, he continued, "although proud and haughty with their enemies, the Arkansas are good, affable and in full accord with the French."[35] A few years later, Father James Didier rhapsodized that "the Arkansas are barbarous in name only according to what I heard from the mouth of Mons. de Kerlérec . . . [H]e said it was the most civilized and rational nation that he knew."[36]

For reasons that are complex and not altogether clear, though Kerlérec asserted that "nothing is easier than to hold [the Quapaws] in their attachment to us,"[37] the Spanish had at first found it difficult to attract and keep their allegiance. In fact, the Spanish governor Unzaga grumbled that the Quapaws were "uncivilized people, lacking reason, [and] accustomed to allowing the English traders to seduce them, offering them their merchandise at lower prices in exchange for pelts."[38] In 1768, the Quapaws, or some of them, had sent a representative to the Indian congress in Pensacola and had apparently concluded a trade agreement with the English. We know, at least, that one of the Quapaw chiefs was wearing an English medal that year,[39] and the English even promised the Quapaws to build a fort across from the mouth of the White River where they could come to trade.[40] Though the fort apparently never materialized, a trading settlement did begin to appear in that spot in 1768 at the order of John Stuart, the English Indian agent.[41] This establishment caused great alarm at the Arkansas Post because the Quapaws took their corn and furs there and to Natchez to trade for liquor. When de Clouet, the Arkansas commandant, tried to regain the affection of the Quapaws with liquor of his own, the governor scolded him and told him to lecture the Indians on the evils of drinking.[42]

It was not much later that the British grew even bolder. An Englishwoman, a merchant at the English trading settlement, not only sold liquor to the Quapaws but even ventured three leagues up the Arkansas River to the Indian villages in a trading boat with a crew of ten men. De Clouet feared that the place would "become a canteen"[43] for the Indians and the lady's activities enraged him so that he railed that she was a Magdalene,[44] that is, a whore, though it is probable that he intended this epithet figuratively. Not long afterward, however, de Clouet wrote hopefully that there was only one Englishman left across the Mississippi and predicted that even he would soon be bankrupt because he had extended credit to the Quapaws who would never repay him.[45]

In the summer of 1770, however, despite de Clouet's optimistic projection, the Englishwoman remained firmly in place across the river; more important, an Englishman had actually settled among the Quapaws near the Post on the Spanish side.[46] Though his presence was an intolerable affront to Spanish sovereignty, such was the smallness of his troop, and the ludicrous condition of his ordnance, that Commandant Demasellière was forced to tolerate the interloper. By 1773, the situation had worsened: The Quapaw great chief had adopted the English trader, and they had attended Indian congresses at Pensacola together. The chief even gave the Englishman a daughter for a wife, whereupon he had built a hut right next to the chief's and set up a store stocked by a merchant across the Mississippi. From this position of strength the Englishman spoke seditious words, ridiculed the weakness of the Spanish, and even claimed that in Virginia he had seen orders of the English king aimed at ousting the Spanish from Louisiana. Not all of the Quapaws, by any means, approved of the trespasser, and they promised the commandant to arrest him, but they failed to do so because of fear of the great chief: The chief, moreover, told them that if they killed the trader he would come back from the other world to take revenge.

Figure 34. Alexandre Chevalier de Clouet. (*Courtesy of Louisiana Room, Dupré Library, University of Southwestern Louisiana.*)

The Englishman himself was audacious enough to enter the commandant's chamber dressed and painted like an Indian.[47]

After some extensive repairs were effected to the fort, however, and new cannon and swivel guns were put in place, Commandant Leyba called the Quapaws to his house to demonstrate the might of the Spanish king. The cannon and guns roared and shook the fort's buildings with such force that dishes hung on the walls crashed to the floor. Mightily impressed, the Quapaws allowed that the British had lied in ridiculing the Spanish, drank the governor's health at the commandant's expense, and expelled the British trader.[48]

The British seem to have posed no serious threat to the essential Quapaw alliance after Leyba's triumph over this unnamed mountebank, though their trading post across the Mississippi continued in existence for a number of years. In time, it acquired the name Concordia, perhaps because an agreement with the Quapaws gave it life, though just as frequently travelers called it British Ozark. (Arkansas Post itself they sometimes called Spanish Ozark.) By 1775, the five traders and eighteen cabins of Concordia[49] would have made it perhaps as large as the Post itself. But in 1779, James Willing, who had been an unsuccessful merchant at Natchez for a time, led a pro-American expedition down the Mississippi, captured Concordia, and ordered the British out. Though they returned not long afterwards, a fire soon consumed the settlement,[50] and it does not seem to have been rebuilt. Perhaps the removal of the Post upriver to *Écores Rouges* the same year had rendered the position of British Ozark so less advantageous that its promoters thought it not worth the trouble and expense of resettling. Besides, with the capture of West Florida by the Spanish, trade competition was no longer possible.

The American Revolution soon brought a kind of prominence to the little outpost. Even before Spain declared war on Great Britain, Louisiana officials were providing clandestine aid to the colonial effort; and the Arkansas Post frequently served as a place of rest, refuge, and supply for revolutionary forces like those of Captain Willing.[51] The British, of course, were well aware of the partiality being shown by an officially neutral Spain, and the Post soon became a target for James Colbert, a Scot who had married into the Chickasaw tribe and had accumulated a great deal of wealth, including 150 black slaves. Colbert very foolishly broadcast his plans to destroy the Post of Arkansas; and in 1783, after the Spanish declared war on the English, they reacted to Colbert's posturing by increasing the garrison there to sixty-seven soldiers and two officers.

On April 17, 1783, at 2:30 A.M. James Colbert proved that he was not all bluster. With a force of Chickasaws, loyalist whites, and a few blacks, who probably totaled fewer than a hundred persons, he struck the Post of Arkansas without the alarm having been sounded: When Colbert passed the Quapaw village on the way to the Post, he had deceived the great chief Angaska, who was unfortunately drunk at the time, into believing that his whites had come to shake the hand of the Post commandant. The enemy force captured a number of the *habitants* outside the fort, as had been the case in the 1749 raid, and killed three soldiers on guard duty. The fort itself, however, held out, after a considerable battle that evidently involved as many as three hundred cannon rounds. Colbert's band beat a hasty retreat when a daring and noisy sally from the fort by ten Spanish soldiers and four Quapaws convinced them that a large Indian force had been set on foot. They pulled back downriver, pursued hotly by the Spanish and some Quapaw allies. Eventually, all of Colbert's prisoners were rescued.[52]

This battle, one of two engagements in the American Revolution fought west of the Mississippi, both of which resulted in victories for the Spanish, was remarkable in other ways as well. For one thing, it occurred after peace had been concluded in Paris though before word of it had reached Louisiana. For another, though Colbert claimed that he had been acting under a British commission, General Campbell had surrendered all the British troops in West Florida to Gálvez with the capitulation of Pensacola in 1781. Colbert, however, escaped the prosecution for piracy and sedition that would have awaited him when the old warrior died from a fall from his horse.[53]

If the Chickasaws were long-time, traditional enemies of the Quapaws, the bellicose Osages, Missouri Indians who frequently ranged southward into Arkansas, also posed a considerable threat to their safety and livelihood. As early as 1722, when La Harpe was at Law's concession preparing to press his expedition up the Arkansas River, the Quapaws attempted to prevent his departure: The Osages, they said, were sure to give him a hostile reception, for they had already killed six Frenchmen who had ventured upriver to buy horses.[54] It is probable that the Quapaws were motivated to give this warning partly by a desire to keep La Harpe from effecting a trade arrangement with the Osages; but it is nevertheless true that the Osages had practically no Indian allies and were almost universally feared and hated by their neighbors. This was because of the fierceness of their customs and their attachment to making war. On May 10, 1733, Ens. Pierre Louis de Coulange wrote to the governor that eleven hunters had failed to return from their annual trip upriver.[55] De Coulange feared that they had all perished at the hands of the Osages and even told the governor that they had; but it turned out that the Osages had killed only two persons, a slave and a Frenchman named Petit Jean. The Osages offered no reason for the attack, but they did apologize, saying that they did not mean to kill Frenchmen and had mistaken Petit Jean for an Indian.[56] Despite these protestations of good intentions, in 1740 the Osages murdered several other Frenchmen in the Arkansas region.[57]

In 1764, Pierre de Laclède Liguest founded St. Louis and was given, for a time, a monopoly over the Osage commerce, and St. Louis merchants generally thereafter insisted that they were the sole persons privileged to engage in this lucrative trade. Arkansas Post hunters and merchants, however, demanded that they be allowed to develop a share of this business,[58] and many among the Osages were equally anxious to establish this connection, partly because they were well aware of the advantages of competition. Post traders did in fact enjoy a sporadic trade with a band of the Osages in the French colonial period, but in 1766 the Osages killed and wounded two Arkansas Frenchmen and three of their Indian slaves, perhaps at the instigation of the British who were, as usual, attempting to replace Spanish influence among the Indians with their own.[59] Despite these dangers, in 1768 large numbers of merchants requested trade licenses for the upper Louisiana and Arkansas regions from the new Spanish government; Commandant de Clouet even asked for a trade monopoly with the Osages of the Arkansas region.[60] Although the Spanish officials decided to allow Osage trade only to the merchants at St. Louis, unlicensed traders in the Arkansas region supplied the Osages with liquor, guns, and ammunition with which they unfortunately attacked other Frenchmen in the area and ventured as far southward as the Natchitoches district, stealing women, children, and animals. Lieutenant Governor Athanase de Mézières of Natchitoches quite understandably condemned these renegade traders and branded the Arkansas River region "the asylum of the most wicked persons, without doubt, in all the Indies."[61]

Gov. Luis de Unzaga y Amezaga soon moved to rectify the degenerating situation at the Arkansas. In 1770 he urged the Quapaws to make war on the Osages to bring them to terms. This action very quickly brought an Osage chief, his wife, and four children to the Post in search of peace: The Quapaws and the French warily accepted the gesture and concluded an agreement.[62] A few months later, a small Osage band called at the fort to cement the arrangement, and Commandant Leyba gave them some guns and other presents.[63] Nevertheless,

Figure 35. Pierre de Laclède Liguest. (*Courtesy of Missouri Historical Society, St. Louis.*)

Osage robberies of French hunters on the Arkansas soon resumed. The Quapaws wanted in turn to reinstitute their attacks, but Commandant Leyba did not feel authorized to permit a resumption of hostilities without the governor's permission. The governor temporized: He urged Leyba to try to get the Osages to give hostages as security for their treaty.[64] The Osages refused, stepped up their depredations, and killed seven Frenchmen in two different incidents. Leyba got word that the Osages were even planning an attack on the Post itself. He had it on reliable authority that they were only sixty leagues from his fort and closing fast. Leyba believed his position hopeless: With only a handful of men, a fort so dilapidated that he described it as the weakest in the colony, and his retreat to Natchitoches blocked by flooded rivers, he reckoned desperately that his soldiers would have to resort to hand-to-hand fighting. "We can only die," he lamented, "while killing the Indians." For reasons as mysterious as the ones that gave rise to their plan to attack, the Osages evidently lost interest and pulled back upriver.[65]

Meanwhile, Governor Unzaga decided that any warfare that the Arkansas French were to wage against the Osages would have to be essentially defensive in character. Among the reasons for his caution, no doubt, was a desire to protect the nascent settlement at St. Louis from the economic disaster that would accompany a cessation of Osage trade. Then, too, there was no reason whatever to be confident of victory in a general war with the Osages. The Spanish had consented to take the part of Louisiana that lay west of the Mississippi principally to give them a clearcut border with the British: They regarded Louisiana mainly as a buffer between westering British settlers and the rich provinces of Mexico, and they had no intention of making a larger investment in government there than was necessary to carry out that mission. Therefore, after the massive show of force by O'Reilly in 1769, when he arrived in New Orleans to put down the insurrection there, Spanish troop strength was reduced dramatically and Unzaga knew that he simply did not have the muscle to overcome the mighty Osage nation. It is likely, too, that he had learned some important lessons from Bienville's humiliating defeats at the hands of the Chickasaws.

The Quapaws' sense of honor, however, was not so easily restrained. When in 1772 the Quapaws pursued a band of young Osage warriors who had stolen their horses and killed one of them, Commandant Leyba took it on himself to reward them with ammunition, liquor, and other goods. Any other course of action, he said, would have risked losing a valuable friendship.[66] Leyba wrote that the Quapaws could not comprehend the pusillanimous Spanish policy of appeasement and ridiculed him for his speeches urging peace. The Arkansas *habitants*, not surprisingly, shared and applauded the Quapaws' retributive inclination and called them their saviors when they returned from raids on the Osages.[67]

De Mézières, too, wanted a change in Spanish policy, and when the Osages ransacked a French hunting party, roasting and eating one of its members, he renewed his demand that war be initiated.[68]

The governor again hesitated. He ordered Pierre Piernas, the lieutenant governor at St. Louis, to compel the Osages to deliver up those responsible for the murders or he would wage a war of extermination against them (women and children excepted) from his forts in Illinois, Arkansas, and Natchitoches. When atrocities nevertheless continued, Unzaga rather vaguely ordered Piernas to destroy the Osages if they "could be exterminated without cost to the royal treasury." Somewhat more promising than this fey and feckless command was de Mézières's plan to join with the Caddos, Quapaws, and other Indian tribes in an effort to annihilate the Osages. Unzaga initially approved the idea, but a month later changed his mind because of unspecified "inconveniences," which included, no doubt, the expense involved and the disruption of the upper Louisiana trade.[69]

In the spring of 1773, a large party of Osages unexpectedly appeared at St. Louis and surrendered the partisan who had been responsible for the murders of the Arkansas Frenchmen the previous year. Two days later, Leyba wrote the governor that the Quapaws had only recently killed five Osages, and a month later still the Caddos revenged a raid by killing seven Osages and executing another in their village. With the Osages seemingly on the run, it looked as though peace might descend at last on the Arkansas valley. Indeed, in the summer of 1773 the Little Osages and the Spanish entered into a formal treaty of peace and extradition at St. Louis, and the Big Osages joined in it before the year was out.[70] The Quapaws, however, did not believe that the Osages were sincere and were of the opinion that "the Osages are not good nor will they ever be good." In fact, the Osages seem to have taken advantage of the Illinois peace to concentrate their fury on the hunters of the Arkansas and the Indians and *habitants* of the Natchitoches district. Vagabond traders in the Arkansas region continued to supply them with munitions. Unzaga, moreover, was eventually forced to the view that the Illinois agreement was not binding on the Osages in the Arkansas and Natchitoches districts.[71]

In the fall of 1774, the Osages resumed their depredations in the Arkansas region, this time pillaging seven groups of hunters on the White and St. Francis rivers. The Quapaws countered these forays by surprising one of the Osage camps and killing three enemy warriors. Continued attacks on the people of the Natchitoches district caused de Mézières to renew his insistence that war be undertaken against the Osages relying on Indian allies. As usual, nothing came of the demand.[72] The following spring Joseph de La Miranda and a hunting party of twenty men ventured two hundred leagues up the Arkansas and encountered a party of Osages who killed two men and seriously wounded de La Miranda's son. But this time the French party was strong enough to strike back: They killed four Osages and wounded ten others. One of the slain was the Osage partisan, whose head de La Miranda triumphantly presented to Capt. Joseph Orieta, who was commanding at Arkansas Post.[73]

In 1777 Balthazar de Villiers, a most able commandant at the Post, was able to conclude a peace agreement between the Quapaws and the Osages. As was the case when the pact with the Osages in Missouri had been effected, this peace allowed the Osages to concentrate their atrocities elsewhere, this time entirely on the Indians and Frenchmen of the Natchitoches region. Once again, Lieutenant Governor de Mézières raised the question of all-out war and wrote to Bernardo de Gálvez, the new governor, understandably full of outrage. He related gruesome tales of a young Frenchman whom the Osages had "put on a spit and roasted alive," and of a young boy whose father the Osages had beheaded before his very eyes. For Natchitoches and its dependencies, the Osage-Quapaw treaty, he said, was an "accursed peace" and "an odious and unexpected alliance."[74] De Mézières was not the only opponent of de Villiers's hard-won peace agreement. As part of the pact, de Villiers had naturally promised the Osages to provide them with a trader and, in fact, had sent Andrés López to Cadron to that end. This brought the expected and predictable loud protest from the lieutenant governor at St. Louis, who claimed that the merchants there were supposed to have a monopoly on Osage trade. Less dependence on the St. Louis traders there, he argued, would encourage the Osages to increase their horse raids and thus cause a decline in agricultural settlement in his district. The flags that de Villiers had given the Osages were, moreover, encouraging a large band of them to turn to the Arkansas to trade.[75]

Gálvez relented under the pressure of the demands from the Illinois and directed de Villiers to prohibit trade with the Osages. This alone would no doubt have been regarded as a grave breach of faith by the Osages, but in fact, even before this occurred, the Caddos had attacked an Osage party and killed four men and a woman. The Osages believed that some Arkansas hunters had connived in this act and therefore had resumed their raids on hunters. There were reports even that the British had moved into the void at Cadron and constructed a blockhouse there. Various schemes to unite Indian tribes to attack the Osages came again to naught, partly because the lieutenant governor in St. Louis had no interest in disrupting a relationship with the Osages there that was mostly peaceful and extremely profitable. This selfishness elicited from de Villiers an explosive, rhetorical question directed to Governor Gálvez: "Should [commerce]," he inquired, "be cemented by the blood of innocents . . . ?" Gálvez could furnish no adequate reply.[76] When de Villiers's moral argument fell on deaf ears, he resorted to a utilitarian one. The loss of commerce caused by Osage raids in the Arkansas country, he insisted, was greater than any loss that St. Louis would suffer by allowing trade in his district. His hunters had been robbed so often, some of them ten and eleven times, that the loss of tallow, bears' oil, and salted meats, the chief exports of the Arkansas district, was enormous. Besides, he reported, he could no longer restrain the Quapaws, who had sent out a large war party to attack the Osages and even to cut off the goods from the St. Louis merchants; and in 1780, American refugees from the Revolution who had settled briefly on the Arkansas joined the Quapaws in further attacks. De Villiers straightforwardly rewarded these excursions, when successful, with presents.[77] But Gálvez's mind was so preoccupied with war with the British that isolated skirmishes in a place that he had never been and never would be could demand little or nothing of his attention.

For a few years after 1780, the Arkansas River remained relatively free of Osage depredations. Late in 1783, Captain Dubreuil of the Arkansas Post even rewarded a friendly Osage partisan with a European outfit, a medal, a gorget, a flag, and a commission as chief. Though this act predictably angered the St. Louis establishment, Governor Miró in the next year boldly broke the St. Louis stranglehold on the Osage trade and awarded the Arkansas Osage trade to François Ménard and Jean-Baptiste Imbeau. Excluded merchants at the Arkansas protested vigorously and in the course of doing so revealed that they had in fact already been trading with the Osages. In 1785, peace talks began again at the Post between the Quapaws, Caddos, Osages, and others. Two Osage *considerados* even descended to New Orleans to parley with Governor Miró and Tinhiöouen, the Caddo great chief, and the parties concluded an agreement that the Osages could settle on the upper reaches of the St. Francis River. Not even a year later, however, the Osages attacked and killed a number of Caddo Indians. Miró then ordered all traders off the Arkansas River; only hunters with limited supplies were allowed to ascend it. He also demanded that Osage hostages be sent to New Orleans to ensure the peace. That demand having failed, Dubreuil organized a punitive expedition of 350 to 400 hunters and Quapaws, but before mounting an actual attack, he sent two Frenchmen to the Osage village for hostages. Surprisingly, the Osages supplied them; but when they arrived at the Post a mischievous Quapaw frightened them by claiming that Miró planned to burn them to death on their arrival in New Orleans. They quite understandably decamped under cover of darkness with such alacrity that a party sent in pursuit soon returned empty-handed.[78]

The Osages stepped up their attacks. In April of 1787 a hunting party led by Louis Riquet, *dit* La Verdure, was plundered sixty leagues above Arkansas Post: The Osages murdered and decapitated two Frenchmen, an Indian woman, and her five-year-old daughter. Governor Miró, finally entirely exasperated, ordered a complete suspension of trade with the Osages under penalty of death. The Osages responded by threatening to take hunters captive and burn them alive in their villages if the Spanish did not ransom them with munitions and guns.[79] In 1789, the hunters and *habitants* of the Arkansas petitioned Captain Vallière to go to war against the Osages.[80] Miró rejected the idea at least for a time until he got the St. Louis lieutenant governor's reaction to the proposal. In the meantime, Vallière sent out three separate Quapaw war parties, totaling eighty-six men, to punish the Osages.[81] In 1790, attacks continued and Delinó ordered all the hunters back to the fort.[82]

Late that year, the Osages sued again for peace, and Delinó once more asked for two hostages. When the Osages refused, Delinó seized five of them, an action that earned him a furious lecture from Governor Miró on the fine points of international law and the necessity of punctiliously observing them. In 1791 Delinó again had to evacuate the forests of hunters and outfitted a Quapaw war party of forty men to attack the Osages. That summer, two decapitated hunters were found on the White River, and early the following year the Osages killed and mutilated two more high up the Arkansas. By 1792, the hunters were again sitting idly at the Post, deeply indebted to the merchants, because they did not dare to venture out on the rivers. In short, the Osages had brought the settlement to the brink of bankruptcy. Even Michael Wolf, an industrious German farmer, and his two sons had gone missing, and Delinó feared that they had

Figure 36. Joseph Bernard Vallière d'Hauterive.
(*Courtesy of Mr. and Mrs. Howard Stebbins, Little Rock.*)

been victims of the Osages. Governor Carondolet wanted immediate action and ordered the Illinois commandant to arm the hunters, militia, and Indians of his district to go against the Osages and "finish them once and for all." Similar orders went to Delinó: He was to arm the Quapaws, Caddos, and his hunters and traders to destroy any Osages who managed to avoid the massacre planned by the force gathering at St. Louis.[83] In the spring of 1793, in an extraordinary document, the Arkansas traders and hunters agreed to go to war against the Osages and divide the spoils equally.[84]

But in the Illinois, as usual, there was no enthusiasm for such a project. Lieutenant Governor Trudeau did not even publish Carondolet's declaration of war against the Osages until his hunters had returned from the rivers, and he wrote to the governor that he simply did not have the power to strike a decisive blow against the warlike Osages. When Carondolet insisted, Trudeau belatedly published the proclamation of war, and early in May of 1793 Carondolet dispatched orders to the Arkansas commandant to unite his forces with detachments from Natchitoches and New Madrid to destroy the Osages. But coordination proved impossible, and the Arkansas forces sallied forth alone, penetrating the western country 250 leagues and diligently searching out the enemy; meanwhile, in New Madrid and Illinois the expedition had not even begun. An adamant Carondolet ordered the war to begin yet again, but before that could occur Delinó's expeditionary force returned exhausted and without having engaged the enemy.[85]

The Osages, as always, were extraordinarily adept at sensing when it was time to negotiate. They appeared suddenly in St. Louis, offered the same lame excuses for their bad behavior that they had been offering for decades, and departed. Trudeau wrote again to the governor to say that he had simply found it impossible to assemble an effective force at the Illinois because of the smallness of his white population and the reluctance of the Indians to join up without at least a promise of lavish presents. Carondolet soon thereafter abandoned his frustrated attempts to make war on the Osages because of a threat of invasion from George Rogers Clark's forces from the United States: In the spring of 1794, therefore, he informed the Arkansas commandant that the "war" with the Osages was over. Not long thereafter, he agreed to give the influential St. Louis merchant Pierre Chouteau a six-year monopoly on trade with the Osages in return for Chouteau's construction of a fort among the Osages. The Osages agreed happily to this arrangement and promised peace.[86]

This peace was, generally speaking, a lasting one for the Illinois country, and it greatly encouraged economic development there. It was not long, however, before trouble returned to the luckless French of the Arkansas. In 1797, despite Chouteau's trade monopoly, Arkansas traders had by promises of cheap goods enticed a party of the Osages to the Arkansas region to trade: The event unhappily turned into a melee in which a hunter was killed. Commandant de Vilemont admitted to the governor that he had agreed to send traders to rendezvous with the Osages at Cadron, but only because the previous summer a huge party of five or six hundred Osages had traveled to the Post to inquire whether they could exchange the product of their hunt for goods. De Vilemont had felt unable to refuse them; besides, he wanted the Osages to frequent the Post in order to drive off the Chickasaws and Choctaws who now often crossed the Mississippi to hunt in Quapaw lands. Nevertheless, the governor ordered him to cease allowing traders to go to Cadron, and he promptly promised strict obedience. Therefore in the fall of 1797 the Osages resumed their attacks on persons in de Vilemont's bailiwick, and he was obliged yet again to recall all the hunters from the forests to the Post.[87] No interruption of trade in Missouri was proposed since the safety of the few Arkansas hunters and traders was of no importance to the people of upper Louisiana. Lieutenant Governor Trudeau put it about as bluntly as he could have: The Illinois district was large and beginning to prosper in the protection afforded by the Osage peace, and the governor needed to balance this clear gain against the "slight evil suffered by the hunters and wanderers of the Arkansas River. That class of people is the scum of the posts."[88] It is no wonder that over the years the Arkansas commandants had received little satisfaction in response to their complaints.

After two years of relative peace, de Vilemont reported early in 1799 that the Osages had shot Jean d'Ortalon and stolen six horses from French hunters high up the Arkansas. In the spring of the same year the Osages commenced to raid in earnest, stealing munitions and horses, and killing an Abenaki Indian. Soon thereafter, the Osages renewed their efforts to establish trade with the Post merchants. The hunters whom the Osages had mistreated insisted that if trade were established the Osages would cease their depredations, and de Vilemont requested that Joseph Bougy be granted the Osage trade.[89] It is not clear whether Bougy himself ever engaged in this trade, but it is seems certain that some person or persons did, for the head of the American Indian Factory at the Post early in the nineteenth century told his superiors that the Arkansas commandant had granted that trade to individuals from 1799 to 1803.[90] In the summer of 1800,

Figure 37. Charles Melchior de Vilemont. (*Courtesy of Mr. and Mrs. Howard Stebbins, Little Rock.*)

however, the commandant had found it necessary again to request permission from the governor to wage war on the Osages, and as late as the summer of 1802, Capt. Francisco Caso y Luengo wrote of hunters whom the Osages had killed and wounded in his district. It therefore appears that even in the very last years of Arkansas's colonial epoch those who were licensed to trade with the Osages could have done so only intermittently. Indeed, struck by "the poverty of the hunters and traders who all owed money to either local or New Orleans merchants," Caso attempted to arrange a peace among the Osages, Quapaws, Choctaws, Chickasaws, and Cherokees in 1802 but evidently failed.[91]

Historians have long known that the Osages presented the chief obstacle to French and Spanish operations along the Arkansas River in the eighteenth century, but satisfactory explanations for their anti-European attitudes have been generally lacking.[92] Some have quite rightly looked to the Osages' barbarous mourning rite, which required the killing of the first person encountered to avenge the death of a fallen warrior, as a source of some of their atrocities. Others have guessed that the invasion of traditional hunting grounds angered the Osages. Then, too, a long-standing feud between the Osages and the Quapaws, its origin altogether lost to us and perhaps even to them, may have figured as a factor in their depredations. In the Arkansas region, however, it seems rather clear that the chief grievance that the Osages had was the refusal of the Spanish to allow them a regular trader there. It is possible that this had caused real hardship to some of the Osages, for they had come to depend on European guns and munitions for survival. There is good evidence, moreover, that among some of the indigenous peoples of North America there was a rule of behavior that a refusal to deal was equivalent to an act of war: If a tribe was not trading it was *ipso facto* an enemy.[93] This fascinating social datum, if true, is one of which economists, among others, should be able to make a great deal. In eighteenth-century Arkansas, it had evidently made for destruction and despair.

VI

GOVERNMENT, LAW, AND POLITICS

Before 1712, the colony of Louisiana, with a population of only a few hundred, had been entirely under military rule. On September 19, 1712, the Crown granted a trade monopoly to Antoine Crozat, but it gave him no governmental authority: As Henry Dart noted, the charter was "only an operating contract with the duties of government retained in the Crown."[1] The charter did, however, adopt as law for the colony *"nos Edits, Ordonnances Et Coutumes Et les usages de la Prevosté Et Vicomté de Paris"* ("our edicts, ordinances, and customs and usages of the Provostry and Viscounty of Paris").[2] The custom of Paris was a small code of some 362 titles first reduced to writing in 1510,[3] and treating both substantive and adjective law. It was itself terse, indeed epigrammatic; but by the time of its adoption in Louisiana the commentary on it was voluminous.[4] Annotated versions of the *Coutume* were therefore very popular in France, and in time they found their way to Louisiana.[5]

A separate instrument, also of 1712, created a new and important institution for the colony, the Superior Council of Louisiana.[6] Modeled on the governmental arrangements already in place in other French colonies, the Council had original and, at first, exclusive jurisdiction to decide disputes arising anywhere in Louisiana. This council consisted of the lieutenant general of New France, the intendant of the same, the governor of Louisiana, a first councilor of the king, two other councilors, the attorney general, and a clerk. Judgments in civil cases required the concurrence of at least three members, and in criminal cases of at least five. By the terms of its creation, the council was to exist for only three years, but on September 7, 1716, it became by virtue of a royal edict a permanent institution.[7]

In 1717 a fundamental change occurred in the government of Louisiana. In that year Crozat, having lost an enormous sum under his operating charter, surrendered it, and John Law's *Compagnie d'Occident* was given a monopoly over trade in the colony. Unlike Crozat's company, the *Compagnie d'Occident* was granted extensive governmental authority: It had the power to appoint the Superior Council, to name governors and military commandants, and to appoint and remove all judges. The charter also provided that "*Seront tous les juges Etablis en tous les d. Lieux tenus de juger suivant les Loix Et ordonnances du Royaume Et se Conformer a la Coutume de la Prevosté Et Vicomté de Paris*" ("all the judges established in all the said places shall be bound to judge according to the laws and ordinances of the realm, and [shall also be bound] to conform to the custom of the Provostry and Viscounty of Paris").[8] This portion of the charter obviously provided for the reception of general French legislation and the *Coutume de Paris.* In addition, it has been shown that subsequent French legislation, as soon as it was registered in the colony, and the legislation of the Superior Council itself, formed part of the body of colonial Louisiana law.[9] The subsequent French legislation was of three distinct sorts: General legislation, special colonial legislation, and colonial legislation passed specifically for Louisiana.[10]

Two years later inferior courts for outlying portions of the colony receive mention for the first time. On September 12, 1719, the king noted the need to appoint persons to act as judges "to facilitate the administration of justice in places distant from the place where the Superior Council holds its sessions."[11] The "heads or directors" of concessions along with "other of our subjects, capable and of probity" were therefore to "exercise both civil and criminal justice." The edict went on to provide that, even in these inferior courts, "three judges shall sit in civil matters and in criminal matters five judges. . . ." (The plan, evidently, was to have a kind of provincial council at each settlement.) The king further provided that an appeal from these local tribunals would lie in all cases to the Superior Council.[12] All this was being done, of course, to make ready the way for Law's colonizing schemes.

In 1720 or 1721 Louisiana was divided for the first time into districts (or counties). Arkansas was one of the nine original districts, and a local "commandant and judge" was assigned to each "to put justice with greater ease in reach of the colonists."[13] Presumably, and understandably, the plan to establish local councils outside New Orleans was abandoned at this time. The sources simply fail to say whether more than one person was expected to sit on local courts, but it would have frequently proved unworkable in remote places like Arkansas to assemble a multi-member judicial body. In May of 1722, however, the Regent did issue an order creating a provincial council for Illinois, the jurisdiction of which supposedly extended from "all places on and above the Arkansas River . . . to the boundaries of the Wabash River." The commandant of the Illinois, Lieutenant de Boisbriant, was to serve as "chief and judge" of this council, and three other persons were assigned to sit on it.[14] It thus seems to have been the plan to abolish the Arkansas district and annex its territory to its nearest northern neighbor; and the Illinois provincial council was directed "to hold its sessions at the places where the principal factories of the company shall be established."[15] This language could have been construed to require the Illinois council to sit at the Arkansas. It is, however, very much to be doubted that the council ever held such a session, and certainly it is not believable that in 1722 anyone would repair from Arkansas to Illinois to settle a grievance.

It seems probable, then, that whatever judicial power was exercised at the Arkansas while Law's company held sway there was entrusted to its resident directors who acted as civil commandants even after the creation of the council of the Illinois. The only resident director that the Arkansas ever had was Bertrand Dufresne, Sieur du Demaine, who arrived at the Post on March 22, 1722. Prior to that, Jacques Levens had been director, but as he never took up residence in Arkansas, we have to presume that if anyone exercised judicial functions it was one or more of the three subordinates to whom Levens had entrusted the management of the struggling colony: Jean-Baptiste Ménard, Martin Merrick, and Labro.[16] When Dufresne left the Arkansas around 1726, it is hard to guess the means resorted to for the settlement of disputes. Probably Father Paul du Poisson, the Jesuit missionary resident from 1727 to 1729, used his good offices to maintain order among the approximately thirty Frenchmen who had remained behind.[17]

It seems a reasonable guess, moreover, that Arkansas's first sustained exposure to European legal proceedings and principles occurred in the period during which Law's company was in authority in Louisiana. Tonty's seventeenth-century feudal seigniory no doubt carried with it the right to render justice. Though his charter from La Salle has not yet come to light,[18] other conveyances of La Salle's are extant; and in them he gave his grantees judicial power over small cases (this is called "low justice") while specifically reserving important cases ("high justice") to himself. (Cases of the latter type he directed to be heard by the judge "who shall be established at Fort St. Louis.")[19] We do not know whether Tonty's charter contained identical provisions, but it certainly would have contained similar ones. During the ten years or so that Tonty held the right to dispose of certain cases arising in his seigniory, however, it hardly seems credible that he or his deputies ever held anything resembling a court, or even executed many instruments or documents.[20]

In 1731 the Company of the Indies surrendered its charter to Louis XV, and for the rest of the period of French dominion Louisiana was a crown colony. Late that same year, as we have seen, a military garrison was reestablished in Arkansas. It was apparently during the reorganization of the colony in 1731 that civil and military authority at the Arkansas Post of Louisiana were combined in the commandant of the garrison—an arrangement that would survive into the Spanish period and even for a short time during the American regime.

Part of a post commandant's civil authority was to act as notary and judge. The exact scope of his judicial jurisdiction during the French period is obscure, there apparently being no document that describes it specifically. Francis Parkman, writing of conditions in the Illinois in 1764, says that the "military commandant whose station was at Fort de Chartres on the Mississippi, ruled the Colony with a sway as absolute as that of the Pasha of Egypt and judged civil and criminal cases without right of appeal."[21] Capt. Philip Pittman, an English engineer and Mississippi explorer who wrote about 1765, gives a slightly different version. According to him, the Illinois commandant "was absolute in authority, except in matters of life and death; capital offences were tried by the council at New Orleans."[22] Of course, the Arkansas commandant's judicial jurisdiction was not necessarily as extensive as that possessed by the commandant of the Illinois. He may very well have been subordinate to the Illinois commandant during most of the French period.

Some fitful light is thrown on the legal responsibilities of the Arkansas commandant by an interesting proceeding that took place at the Post in 1743.[23] In

October of that year, Anne Catherine Chenalenne, the widow of Jean François Lepine, petitioned Lt. Jean-François Tisserant de Montcharvaux, whom she styled "Commandant for the King at the Fort of Arkansas," asking him to cause an inventory and appraisal to be made of the community property in her possession. The widow wished to make a distribution to her son-in-law and daughter who had lost all their goods the previous May when attacked by Chickasaws on the Mississippi not far below the mouth of the Arkansas. They had narrowly escaped with their lives.[24] Widow Lepine had decided to make a distribution to "her poor children, at least to those who have run so much risk among the savages." She was preparing to marry Charles Lincto, a well-to-do resident of the Post, and she wished to partition the community which by custom had continued in her and her children after her husband's death.

The commandant informed Madame Lepine that on October 26, 1743, he would inventory the "real and personal property derived from the marital community" and would bring with him two persons to look after the widow's interest and two to represent the children. (The idea was that each side should have independent appraisers present to ensure the impartiality of the inventory and evaluation.) De Montcharvaux in the presence of these and other witnesses made the inventory on the appointed day. The estate was fairly sizeable, being valued at 14,530 *livres* and 10 *sols*, almost 5,000 dollars. It contained a great deal of personalty (movables), including four slaves, a number of animals, sixteen hundred pounds of tobacco, and notes and accounts receivable; the realty (immovables) listed was "an old house" with three small outbuildings. Interestingly, no land was mentioned.

There are two possible explanations for the absence of land in the inventory. One is that land may not have been actually granted to Arkansas settlers but only given over temporarily to their use. The other possibility is that the land on which the house was situated had belonged to Lepine before the marriage and had remained his separate property under his marriage contract or under the general provisions of the *Coutume de Paris*. The *Coutume*, which, as we saw, was in force in French Louisiana, provided that all movables belonging to a husband or wife, whenever acquired, became part of the community; but the community included immovables only if acquired after the marriage, and not even all of those.[25] These rules could be altered by contract, but in Louisiana, as in France, the *Coutume* was often specifically incorporated into marriage contracts by future spouses in defining the regime that would rule their property;[26] if there was no contract provision creating a property regime, the *Coutume* automatically applied.

The inventory is said to have been made "*Pardevant nous* Jean François Tisserent, Esquire, Sieur de Montcharvaux, commandant for the king at the fort of Arkansas." The formulaic phrase *pardevant nous* ("before us") is Parisian notarial boiler-plate and indicates that the commandant was acting in his capacity as notary. To an American common lawyer, the notary is not a member of the legal profession, not even a paralegal. But in seventeenth- and eighteenth-century France he enjoyed a much more elevated status, as indeed he still does in that country. Originally an official of the medieval European ecclesiastical courts, the notary developed into a full-blown, noncontentious secular legal professional in France. In England, partly because the canon and secular laws were not on speaking terms, "the notarial system never took deep root."[27] For one thing, an important aspect of the notary's duties, his authority to authenticate documents, was of little use to the English. The whole notion of a state-sanctioned authenticator of private acts was entirely foreign to English common law; whereas in France we see notaries making or passing contracts, the common law left that to the parties. The state was very much in the background in England and was called upon only to enforce obligations that arose by force of nature. The other aspects of the French notary's duties came to be performed by the regular legal profession in England. In sixteenth-century London a scriveners' company was organized, and it was granted a charter in the reign of James I.[28] Members were empowered to draft legal documents, especially obligations, and they gave a certain amount of low-level legal advice, particularly in commercial and banking matters.[29] The few secular notaries who practiced in London at that time were members of this company and busied themselves mainly with drafting documents relevant to international trade.[30] But in the eighteenth century the company lost its effort to keep common-law attorneys from competing, and in 1804 parliament made conveyancing the monopoly of the regular legal profession.[31] In contrast, the eighteenth-century French notary's duties had come to include the drafting of documents, conveyancing, and the giving of practical legal advice.[32] It was altogether expectable, therefore, that notaries would make an appearance in eighteenth-century Louisiana. In

New Orleans, of course, there was much work for them, but there were also provincial notaries operating in Biloxi, Mobile, Natchitoches, Pointe Coupée, and Kaskaskia.[33]

Since de Montcharvaux acted as notary for the Lepine inventory, it is reasonably clear that there was no notary resident at the Arkansas at that time. This can come as no surprise since in 1746 there were at the Post only twelve *habitant* families, ten slaves, and twenty men in the garrison,[34] hardly a sufficient population to require or attract a law-trained scrivener. When it was time to have their marriage contract made, the widow Chenalenne and her future spouse executed it in New Orleans. No doubt legal advice on which they might more comfortably rely was available there.[35] Besides, at that time there was no resident priest at the Post to perform the marriage.

After the Chickasaws destroyed the Post in 1749, it was, as we have seen, moved upriver to join the Quapaws, and in 1751 Lieutenant de La Houssaye had a full company of fifty men assigned to him. This new beginning could, in the nature of things, have given only a slight lift to the prospects for sustained settlement in the Arkansas country. Late in 1752, Governor de Vaudreuil was informed that the Osages had attempted an attack on Arkansas Post but had failed.[36] While this indicates a stability of sorts for the Post, thanks no doubt to the size of the new garrison, still the perceived danger must have been so high as to discourage all but the most intrepid from taking up residence at the Arkansas. Mentions of Arkansas in the legal records tend to emphasize the dangerousness of the place. For instance, a Pointe Coupée couple, on the verge of leaving for a hunting trip to the White River country, thought it best to deed their property to a relative, with the stipulation that the deed was to be void if they returned.[37] It is not surprising, therefore, that even as late as 1766, the last year of French dominion, only eight *habitant* families, consisting in all of forty white persons, were resident at Arkansas Post.[38]

All of these difficulties, and others, made for a place in which it might be regarded as too polite to expect the presence of much which corresponds to a legal system. In addition, political exigencies sometimes interfered to such an extent that the application of even-handed legal principle became inexpedient and thus entirely impracticable. For instance, the continued existence of the Arkansas settlement depended heavily on the loyalty of the Quapaws, and their wishes were therefore relevant to any important decision made there. Their influence could extend even to the operation of the legal system as the following incident demonstrates.

On September 12, 1756, a meeting was held in the Government House in New Orleans to hear an extraordinary request from Guedetonguay, the Medal Chief of the Quapaws.[39] His tribe had captured four deserters from the Arkansas garrison and had returned them; one of those captured, Jean-Baptiste Bernard, had killed his corporal Jean Nicolet within the precincts of the fort. The chief had nevertheless come on behalf of his nation to ask Governor Kerlérec to pardon the soldiers. Guedetonguay, obviously a great orator, began his plea by saying that he had come a long distance to plead for the soldiers' lives despite the heat and the demands of the harvest; and he remarked that his head hung low, his eyes were fixed to the ground, and his heart wept for these men. He knew, he explained, that if he had not come they would have been executed, and this was intolerable to him because he regarded them as his own children. He recited many friendly acts of the Quapaws to prove the fidelity of his people to the French. Among them was the release of six slaves (perhaps Chickasaws captured by the Quapaws) "who would have been burned" otherwise, and the recent capture of five Choctaws and two trespassing Englishmen. He himself, he related, had lost one son and had had another wounded in the wars against the Chickasaws, which he counted "a mark of affection for the French." In recompense he asked for the pardon of the soldiers. The chief added that this was the only such pardon his nation had thus far requested, and he promised never to ask again. He did not doubt that Kerlérec, "the great chief of the French, father of the red men," charged to govern them on behalf of the "great chief of all the French who lived in the great town on the other side of the great lake," would listen and do the just thing.

Guedetonguay left his best argument for last. He maintained vigorously that, under his law, any criminal who managed to reach the refuge of the *Cabanne de Valeur* where the Quapaws practiced their religious rites was absolved of his crime. It was their custom that the chief of the *Cabanne de Valeur* "would sooner lose his life than suffer the refugee to undergo punishment for his crime." The soldiers were claiming this right, and Ouyayonsas, the chief of the *Cabanne de Valeur,* was there to back them up. This last argument was an excellent one because it called upon the French to recognize an established Indian usage not dissimilar from the European custom of sanctuary. And the argument carried with it a threat of violent reaction if the custom were not allowed.

Kerlérec answered the chief that he was not unmindful of the past services of the Quapaws, nor was he ungrateful for them. "But," he said, "I cannot change the words declared by the great chief of all the French against such crimes, and . . . it would be a great abuse for the future" to pardon the soldiers. "So," he continued, "despite all the friendship that the French have for you and your nation, these men deserve death." The great chief stood for a long time with his head down and finally answered ominously that he could not be responsible for the revolutions which the chief of the privileged house might stir up—upheavals which he said "would not fail to occur." The argument continued and the governor offered to grant the chief "anything else except these four pardons." But Guedetonguay stubbornly maintained that "the sole purpose of his journey was to obtain the pardon of the four men." In the end the governor extracted from the Quapaw chiefs "publicly and formally their word . . . that they would in the future deliver up all deserting soldiers as malefactors or other guilty persons without any restriction or condition whatsoever, and that [henceforth] . . . pardons would be accorded at the sole discretion of the French."

The governor did not reach an immediate decision but later that day some of his advisors, having reflected on what they had heard, opined "that a refusal of the obstinate demands of these chiefs . . . the faithful allies of the French, would only involve the colony in troublesome upheavals on the part of the said nations who have otherwise up to the present served very faithfully." They concluded that "saving a better idea by Monsieur le Gouverneur it would be dangerous, under all the present circumstances, not to satisfy the Indians with the pardons that they demanded."

The governor took the advice but evidently did not write of the event to Berryer, the French Minister of the Marine, for some time. From the comfort of Versailles it was easy for Berryer to pick at Kerlérec's decision. In responding to Kerlérec, Berryer first made the point that Bernard's case was different from that of the other captured soldiers since he stood accused of homicide in addition to desertion. Then, too, the minister had a lot of questions: Couldn't the difference in Bernard's case have been urged on the Arkansas chiefs to get them to relent in his case? And where was the record of the legal proceedings that should have been conducted relative to the killing? If this was a willful murder, the pardon had been conceded too easily. "It would be dangerous," the minister warned, "to leave such a subject in the colony, not only because he would be an example of impunity, but also because of new crimes that he might commit." (The arguments of general and specific deterrence are not very recent inventions.) Finally, the governor was sternly admonished "not to surrender easily to demands of this sort on the part of the savages . . . If on the one hand it is necessary, considering all the present circumstances, to humor the savages, it is also necessary to be careful of letting them set a tone that accords neither with the king's authority nor the good of the colony."[40]

Nevertheless, the minister had talked with Louis XV and the king ratified the governor's decision. Writs of pardon were therefore issued under the king's name for each of the Arkansas soldiers. Because the homicide committed by Bernard was not a military crime and was cognizable therefore by the Superior Council of Louisiana, his pardon was directed to the Council. Interestingly, though Berryer had admitted knowing nothing whatever of the circumstances surrounding the killing, the pardon recited that a quarrel and fight had arisen between Bernard and Nicolet, that Bernard "had had the misfortune to kill the said Nicolet," and that the death "had occurred without premeditated murder." Thus Louis XV pardoned Jean-Baptiste Bernard for killing by mischance when there was no evidence whatever adduced as to how Nicolet had actually met his death. The decision was generated simply by a desire to accommodate an important ally. Faithful adherence to legal principle sometimes had to take a back seat to the more compelling demands of politics.

Father Louis Carette, the Jesuit missionary who came to the Post of Arkansas in 1750, nevertheless attempted to bring some order to the legal affairs of the place. As he noted in a *procuration* (power of attorney), dated at Arkansas in 1753, he was "authorized by the king to make in every post where there is not a Notary Royal all contracts and acts. . . ."[41] There is no evidence that he had any formal legal training, but he was a Jesuit, and thus a learned man, one of a handful of such who would make their residence in eighteenth-century Arkansas.

This *procuration* is itself of some interest, as it sheds light on how litigants whose cases were technically beyond the jurisdiction exercised by the Arkansas commandant (whatever that was) might have had their cases heard if they wanted to resort to regular methods of dispute settlement. As incredible as it seems, it is probable that the only court of general jurisdiction in the entire colony was the Superior Council of Louisiana. In 1769 La Harpe said that it was a two-week boat trip from the Arkansas to New Orleans, and six to eight weeks back.[42] Obviously, the *procuration* was an important device for people in remote posts like Arkansas, for it enabled them through their attorneys, in the language of the document under discussion, "to act . . . as though they were personally present."[43] Convoys or individual vessels traveled down the Mississippi frequently enough to make this means of tending to legal affairs more tolerable than it might otherwise have been. In this case, the attorney chosen was Commandant de La Houssaye, who was deputed to act in a probate matter at Pointe Coupée for Étienne de Vaugine de Nuysement and his wife Antoinette Pélagie Petit de Livilliers. An interesting feature of *procurations* which increased their utility and flexibility was that they were assignable. This feature came in handy in this instance since de La Houssaye, detained at the Arkansas due to illness, simply transferred the power of attorney to a member of the Superior Council "to act in my place as myself."[44]

Perhaps one of the reasons that Carette had acted as notary in this instance was that the commandant, the only other person in the little community so authorized, was a party to the instrument. But in the French period priests were given general notarial powers and could act even when circumstances did not prevent the commandant from doing so. For instance, Carette acted as notary, and thus probably draftsman, for a contract in which the commandant was not interested—the marriage contract of François Sarrazin and Françoise Lepine, executed at Arkansas Post on January 6, 1752.

Marriage contracts have no exact parallel in common-law practice, and thus it seems worthwhile to devote some space to their explanation and description before discussing the particulars of the Sarrazin-Lepine contract. The provisions typically found in marriage contracts executed in accordance with eighteenth-century Parisian notarial practice are well known. The first and invariable undertaking by the future spouses was a promise to celebrate their marriage in church, and the parties would then choose the regime that would govern their property during the marriage. Next would come a declaration that the antenuptial debts of the parties were to remain their separate obligations; this was followed by a disclosure of the parties' assets, a requirement for the validity of the provision regarding debts. The dowry brought to the marriage by the wife was then recited; and delineating *préciput*, the right of the spouse to specific property in the event of a dissolution of the community, frequently followed. Finally came the donation clause, usually a reciprocal grant of all or part of the predeceasing spouse's estate. In order to be valid in Louisiana, this donation had to be registered with the Superior Council in New Orleans.[45]

An inspection of the Sarrazin-Lepine marriage contract reveals that it very clearly drew on these French notarial precedents, and it reflects, moreover, an awareness of the practical requirements of the Louisiana registration provisions. It contained a promise to celebrate the marriage in regular fashion, a clause selecting the Custom of Paris to govern the couple's marital property, the amount of the wife's dowry, a mutual donation to the survivor of all property owned at death, and an undertaking to have the contract registered in New Orleans.[46] While there was no provision dealing with ante-nuptial debts and no mention of *préciput,* it is quite obvious that the good Jesuit knew more than a little about French notarial practice, and may well have had at his disposal a form book on which he could draw. For all practical purposes, it seems that he was for a time the lawyer of the Post as well as its priest.

A few months after the execution of this contract Commandant de La Houssaye wrote the governor that Mons. Étienne Vaugine, a French officer, was of a mind to marry Madame de Gouyon, the commandant's sister-in-law, and he sent along "the proposed conditions for the contract of marriage."[47] This document, probably the work of Carette, was a draft of the contract, as de La Houssaye asked the governor to pass *"l'exemplair du contrat"* along to the New Orleans notary Chantaloux if the governor decided to give his permission for the marriage. Chantaloux was "to make it as it should be."[48] Three weeks later the governor wrote to say that the contract would be sent back soon and that Chantaloux had left it intact except for one reasonably minor alteration.[49]

When in 1758 Father Carette, dismayed by the irreligious inclination of his flock, left the Arkansas, the Jesuits sent no replacement. In 1764, after Madame Sarrazin found herself widowed, Capt. Pierre Marie Cabaret Detrépi, commandant at the Arkansas, passed a second marriage contract for her which was extremely unsophisticated and rudimentary: It contained only a promise to marry regularly and a mutual donation.[50] Perhaps the good widow had tired of long-winded formalities. Just as likely, the Post was feeling the absence of Carette's drafting skills.

As tiny, remote, and inconsequential as the Arkansas settlement was during the French period, then, it is nevertheless clear that at least some of its people were part of the time adherents to French legal culture. Of course, almost everyone who lived at the Post during the period of French domination was either a native of France or French Canadian; and by the end of the French period a substantial number of native Louisianians were there. It is most interesting to find the survival of civilian legal form in so remote an outpost of empire. Obviously, not all of Arkansas's residents had lapsed into a kind of legal barbarism.

The few legal records that chance has allowed to come down to us from the French period, however, are remarkable not only for their small number, but also for the social and economic characteristics that they reveal of the people who figured in them. They were an elite, related by marriage and blood, struggling under the difficult circumstances of their situation to participate in regular legal processes. The succession proceeding of 1743 was instituted by one of the most well-to-do residents of Arkansas in the person of Anne Catherine Chenalenne, widow of Jean François Lepine. The community property inventoried included four slaves.[51] Her future husband Charles Lincto became probably the most substantial civilian resident of the Post during the French period. The 1749 census, if one excludes from it for the moment the commandant and his household, reveals that Lincto's household accounted for eight of the twenty-nine white *habitants* and seven of the eleven slaves at the Arkansas.[52] Étienne de Vaugine de Nuysement, who executed the *procuration* of 1753, was a member of one of the most distinguished French families of Louisiana;[53] and he executed the *procuration* in favor of Commandant de La Houssaye, soon to become a major of New Orleans and a knight of the Royal and Military Order of St. Louis.[54] Vaugine and de La Houssaye married sisters. The marriage contract executed at the Arkansas in 1752 was entered into by the Post's *garde magasin* and Françoise Lepine, a daughter of Anne Catherine Chenalenne, the petitioner in the probate proceeding of 1743; the bride's dowry had resulted from the partition of the community that had been the aim of that proceeding. Finally, Françoise Lepine's second marriage contract, passed by Detrépi in 1764, was prelude to her marriage to Jean Baptiste Tisserant de Montcharvaux, officer and interpreter at the Post and son of the commandant who executed the 1743 inventory. We are dealing with a propertied and interconnected gentry here, a tiny portion of what was anyway a very small population.

How the other, the major part of the Arkansas populace regulated their lives during the French period will, in the nature of things, be difficult to document. But there is some evidence on this point, and it indicates that there was a good deal of lawlessness on the Arkansas. According to Athanase de Mézières, the lieutenant governor at Natchitoches, the Arkansas River above the Post was inhabited largely by outlaws. "Most of those who live there," he claimed, "have either deserted from the troops and ships of the most Christian King or have committed robberies, rape, or homicide, that river being the asylum of the most wicked persons, without doubt, in all the Indies."[55] On another occasion, de Mézières singled out as a particularly heinous offender an Arkansas denizen named Jean du Four *dit* Brindamúr, a man "of gigantic frame and extraordinary strength." Brindamúr, de Mézières complained, "has made himself a petty king over those brigands and highwaymen, who, with contempt for law and subordination with equal insult to Christians, and to the shame of the very heathen, up to now have maintained themselves on the river."[56] Brindamúr had been resident on the Arkansas for a long time, as his name appears in the census of 1749. Interestingly, it is placed at the very head of a considerable list of "*voyageurs* who have remained up the rivers despite the orders given them."[57] All persons hunting on the rivers were supposed to return every year as passports were not issued for longer periods. But there were large numbers of hunters who lived for twenty years or more in their camps without ever reporting to the Post. They constituted a large proportion, indeed sometimes a majority, of the European population in Arkansas during the French period. The 1749 census, for instance, lists a *habitant* population of only thirty-one, including the commandant and his wife. But there were forty hunters on the Arkansas River whose passports had expired, and nine more on the White and St. Francis rivers. Sixteen hunters were said to be at the Post being outfitted to return to the hunt. Brindamúr, the bandit king, was murdered by one of his men after the end of the French period, "though tardily" de Mézières reckoned, and "by divine justice."[58] In the Spanish period, as we shall see, an effort was made to rid the river of these malefactors.

Since no records of litigation initiated at the Arkansas during the French period have survived, if indeed any were ever kept, little can be said directly on how lawsuits were conducted there. In 1747, however, François Jahan initiated a suit in the Superior Council in New Orleans against one Clermont, a resident of Arkansas Post, claiming damages for the conversion of a cask of rum at Arkansas.[59] The Superior Council had jurisdiction throughout Louisiana, and this case reveals how it exercised that jurisdiction against a defendant in the hinterlands. The summons was served on the attorney general of Louisiana; thus, as Henry Dart pointed out, "it would seem . . . that a resident of the Post of Arkansas could be sued in New Orleans by serving the citation on the Procureur [Attorney] General."[60] How the case would have proceeded from there in the ordinary instance is difficult exactly to say, but probably the Arkansas commandant would have been ordered to act as a master to gather facts and to report to the Superior Council. It seems, however, that the commandant had already ruled independently on the matter. Commandant de Montcharvaux's statement on this case, which is entered in the record a few days after the suit was initiated, indicates that he had held a hearing on the matter at the Arkansas, had taken testimony as to the rum, and had "sentenced Clermont to pay for it."[61] Apparently he had kept no record of the proceeding, as he offered none: The good lieutenant bore his own record. It is interesting to note, however, that Jahan had not brought this case to enforce the commandant's judgment; it was an entirely independent action.

How did the justice provided by the Post commandant during the French period measure up? In the absence of litigation records, this is the hardest kind of question to answer. Whatever jurisdiction the commandant exercised, he acted alone, without official advisors and without, of course, a jury. To say that rule is autocratic is not to say necessarily that it is bad. But the possibilities for arbitrary action are large in such circumstances and much of course depends on the personality and character of the autocrat.

The nineteenth-century historian Francis Parkman claimed that the Illinois commandant exercised his considerable power "in a patriarchal spirit and . . . usually commanded the respect and confidence of the people."[62] But for the most part the eighteenth-century French commandants in Louisiana had a reputation for arbitrariness. Capt. Philip Pittman had a low opinion of them, and accused the commandants in Illinois of extortion in matters of trade.[63] He once remarked generally on "the tyranny, which has been always exerted by officers of that nation commanding outposts."[64] Another commentator has written of the French post commandants as "small tyrants who were oppressing all those living under their jurisdiction."[65] At least one eighteenth-century Arkansan would have agreed with these assessments. That was Étienne Layssard, the storekeeper at the Post; except for Father Carette and the various Post commandants, he was the most visible member of the Arkansas settlement in the 1750s. He wrote long and rambling letters about conditions at the Post and complained constantly of his poverty and of his difficulties with his commandant, Captain de Gamon de La Rochette. In November of 1758 he wrote his superior in New Orleans that de Gamon claimed to be "sole master of all the commerce, of the garrison, as well as of the *voyageurs*, and is paid preferentially by virtue of his office, saying that if anything is left over the others can have it." He went on to say that "not knowing any law which establishes such authority, . . . I believe that when the commandant sells to a private person he is a merchant like me and ought to collect only his proportionate share."[66] On another occasion, according to Layssard, de Gamon had said that "no one had a right to go to the [Quapaw] village to trade but him . . . and that the trade belonged to him." Layssard lamented that this deprived him of a living, and he described his desperate circumstances: "My wife and I, four children, five slaves, a dog, a cat, and chickens live in a small house 25 feet long and 10 feet wide, with one little fireplace to warm us all . . ."[67]

While there is reason to think that Layssard was cranky and litigious (he once wrote to New Orleans demanding the prosecution of the Post surgeon for an unnamed offense),[68] there is no good reason to question his claims about the commandant's behavior. These incidents are good examples of the abuses of power that occur when civilian and military authority are combined. When Layssard wrote his letters in 1758 Arkansas Post was virtually a garrison state. There were only six houses and thus a total resident white civilian population that could not have much exceeded thirty-five.[69] On the other hand, there was a permanent garrison of fifty soldiers which was temporarily reinforced in 1756 by an additional force of sixty men because of the difficulty with the Quapaws discussed above.[70] When in August of 1758 Father Carette, discouraged by the irredeemably bad character of the Post population, gave up his post,[71] the commandant would thereafter have no one with whom to share his authority and no near equal to challenge it.

Of the ten military officers who exercised judicial authority in Arkansas during French rule we know precious little of relevance.[72] Only de La Houssaye, the commandant from 1751 to 1753, has come down to us outfitted with any kind of clear indication of character, and he does not appear to have possessed much of a judicial temperament. Governor de Vaudreuil said that he had found it necessary to relieve de La Houssaye of his position at the Alibamous Post because of "his passion for drink . . . after giving him several charitable warnings on the subject, but without effect." The governor then delivered this ominous *coup de grâce:* "In addition, his character could not be worse or more dangerous."[73]

By a secret covenant of November 3, 1762, France ceded the western part of Louisiana to Spain, but plans for transferring possession of the colony were held in abeyance for a considerable time. It was not until about two years had elapsed that word of the agreement even reached Louisiana. Two more years passed before Antonio de Ulloa, the first Spanish governor, arrived on March 5, 1766.

Not surprisingly, the treaty by which France transferred the sovereignty over Louisiana to Spain made no mention of what legal system was to be in effect under the new regime. The royal letter of April 21, 1764, by which Louis XV notified the Louisiana governor of the cession, did, however, express the hope that the king of Spain would order "the judges ordinary and the Superior Council [to] continue to render justice according to the laws, forms, and usages of the colony."[74] In fact, it seems to have been the original Spanish plan not to replace French law with Spanish, at least not immediately,[75] but in the event that was done.

Ulloa ran into considerable difficulty when he attempted to establish his authority in the province and was expelled from it late in 1768.[76] It was nine months before Gen. Alexandro O'Reilly resumed Spanish control. When he did, he did so swiftly, firmly, and (some say) cruelly. Within two months of his arrival he had held treason trials resulting in the execution of five of the principal participants in the bloodless revolution against Ulloa. Significantly, the judgment in the case recited that the Spanish court had proceeded *"segun nuestras leyes"* ("according to our laws").[77] It was a portent of things to come.

On November 25, 1769, O'Reilly abolished the Superior Council and issued two documents known today as O'Reilly's Laws. One of these documents consisted of ordinances creating the *Ayuntamiento* or Secular Cabildo of New Orleans as a replacement for the Superior Council; these ordinances also regulated the Cabildo's judicial functions.[78] The other document was a set of *Instructions* containing rules of civil and criminal procedure, the substantive law of crimes, and provisions for testate and intestate succession.[79] These two instruments left no doubt as to the sources employed to produce them, for annotations to two Spanish digests, the *Recopilación de las Indias* and the *Nueva Recopilación de Castilla,* were provided by the draftsmen. The first of these works is a digest of Spanish ultramarine law before 1680 that deals mainly with public-law matters; the second is a digest of Castilian law and concerns itself with private law.[80] Professional lawyers were at work: The preamble to these *Instructions* stated that they were digested and arranged "by the Doctor Don Manuel Joseph de Urrustia and the counsellor Don Felix Rey."

Because the *Instructions* did not cover every substantive legal area, and because their preamble contained a somewhat tentative declaration that they were to serve "until a more extensive information upon those laws [*i.e.,* Spanish law in general] may be acquired," it used to be a question much mooted whether Spanish law ever completely superseded French law in Louisiana. It is now established beyond doubt that O'Reilly deliberately annihilated French law, that he introduced Spanish law wholesale, and that he had had royal authority to do so in advance and royal approbation afterwards.[81]

Ensign Le Gros de Grandcour, the Arkansas commandant at the end of the French era, was not replaced until February of 1768 when Governor Ulloa chose Capt. Alexandre de Clouet for the post.[82] The change to Spanish sovereignty caused a considerable nervousness at the Arkansas that manifested itself in a number of ways. For instance, when the news of Ulloa's expulsion reached Arkansas, one of the Post's merchants refused, "on account of the revolution," to take the scrip money offered him in payment for the soldiers' food. De Clouet wrote that "I had to show my teeth to this man" to get him to relent.[83] Whatever misgivings the French settlers at Arkansas Post had had about the change in regime, they evidently quietly submitted to the oath of allegiance to the Spanish king, which the commandant required them all to take in the summer of 1769. The Arkansas commandant wrote the governor to report that he had administered the oath; everything had gone well enough, he thought, except that he was not sure that he had done it correctly since the law governing this kind of activity was unknown to him.[84]

Confusion about what country's law was in effect, and ignorance of its substance, caused other problems at Arkansas Post. While, as we have seen, O'Reilly formally replaced French law with Spanish in 1769, he seems not to have relayed that message to the posts, at least not to the Arkansas. In July of 1770,

Commandant Demasellière said that he had a case pending against a Lieutenant Orieta (with whom he was having all kinds of altercations) and that one of the charges was based on the fact that a search of Orieta's house had turned up firearms. The commandant, apparently believing that French law still prevailed, said that this was "against the French law which forbids anyone to have arms without the post commandant's permission." Orieta, a Spaniard, claimed not to know these laws and asked to be sent back home.[85] Yet on the other hand, an unnamed French soldier, accused of complaining overmuch about the abjectly miserable conditions at the Post, had sought to escape punishment four months earlier because "he did not know well the laws and customs of the Spanish army."[86] In another matter, the nature of which is unclear, the commandant was ambiguously instructed in August of 1770 that "the Ordinances of the kings of France and Spain must be adhered to."[87]

By the autumn of 1770, however, some order was beginning to emerge from the confusion. A letter from Arkansas dated October 4 mentions the "penal code,"[88] an evident reference to the substantive criminal provisions of O'Reilly's *Instructions* of November 25, 1769. The next month, someone, probably the governor, wrote from New Orleans to Lieutenant Orieta (who had taken over at the Arkansas) and commended him for asking for "a printed copy of the penal code."[89] Interestingly, it appears from this letter that the remote post of *Los Arcos*, as the Spaniards called the Arkansas settlement, had not been sent a copy of these laws when they were sent to the other forest posts; and it had taken a letter to New Orleans to correct the bureaucracy's forgetfulness.

Probably at the same time that he finally sent his penal code to Arkansas, O'Reilly also sent along another printed document dated February 12, 1770, and styled "Instructions to which *lieutenants particuliers* [*i.e.*, civil commandants] ought to conform . . . in all that belongs to the police and the administration of justice, civil as well as criminal."[90] These instructions gave commandants jurisdiction to judge "verbally" demands that did not exceed twenty *piastres;* cases exceeding this sum were reserved to the court of the governor general in New Orleans.[91] Commandants were also given jurisdiction over successions: In the case of a testate succession, the goods of the deceased were to be delivered for administration to his widow or, if none, to his heirs; if there were no widow or heirs, the administration was to be entrusted to some other suitable person.[92] If the value of the estate was less than one hundred *piastres,* the commandant could immediately liquidate it; having assembled the interested parties in his house, he was then to make distribution of the proceeds to the widow and heirs, "having regard to the widow's rights to nuptial gains." If there were minor heirs, the commandant was to appoint a guardian for them. Larger estates required a formal inventory, appraisal, and public auction before distribution.[93] The *Instructions* set fees that the commandant could charge for supervising successions.[94] An appeal lay to the governor's court in New Orleans in succession cases, though not in other civil causes.

In criminal matters the commandant had a vague and inconsequential authority. He could proceed to judgment only "if the criminal cause was quite light."[95] No precise jurisdictional boundary was defined, and perhaps in the nature of things that was not possible. The draftsman of the *Instructions* resorted instead to examples: "A quarrel, or injurious words of little consequence," were the kinds of criminal cases within the commandant's judicial competence. Even then he was not allowed to punish anyone; he was supposed to call the parties before him, reprimand the offender, and try to establish peace between them.[96] Obviously, no appeal could lie from such a "judgment." In serious criminal matters (again only examples are given: Killing, wounding, theft) the commandant was to take the depositions of witnesses and send a report (*information*) to the governor, keeping the prisoner under guard until the governor decided what to do.[97] In this procedure, as in others, the commandant acted both as interrogating officer and as surrogate notary; in this latter capacity he was assisted by two witnesses who were to be present throughout the entire proceeding.[98]

In French Louisiana, as we have seen, there had been a number of provincial notaries in some of the remote outposts. The Spanish, however, very severely limited the number of notaries and none was allowed outside New Orleans.[99] Therefore, the post commandants were given notarial powers in places beyond the city. "Since there are no longer any notaries [*écrivains*] established . . . who can draft and authenticate the acts and contracts of the *habitants*," the *Instructions* noted, the commandants were authorized to make *procurations*, and to sign all other necessary acts, with the assistance of two witnesses. Any instrument that created a mortgage, as, typically, a marriage contract did, was supposed to be reported to the government notary at the Cabildo in New Orleans; the date and all the particulars should be sent so that the notary could make a public record of them.[100]

The commandant's police duties also found a place in this document. A commandant was to allow no one to settle in his bailiwick who did not have the written permission of the governor.[101] Only two "cabarets" (bars) were to be allowed in each jurisdiction, and only *habitants* of good repute and conduct should be licensed. The commandant was to instruct licensees expressly not to sell any strong drink to slaves unless they had with them the written permission of a master whose signature was known. A violation of this provision would bring a fine of ten *piastres* (to be given to the church) and permanent revocation of the seller's license.[102] There was a bounty on deserters for which the commandant was eligible,[103] and he was to make sure that no one without a passport journeyed into his jurisdiction.[104] As though all this were not enough, he was to keep his *habitants* from trafficking with the English on the boats that traveled the Mississippi and in the English posts established on that river's left bank.[105] It also fell to him to oversee the building and repair of roads and enclosures (levees); they were to be built and maintained at the expense of the *habitants.*[106]

A very interesting duty of the commandant of a judicial or administrative sort deserves separate mention. In the event a runaway slave was captured and it was determined that his master was a local resident, the slave was to be interrogated to discover his reason for fleeing. If he had run away because he had not proper food or shelter, the commandant was to proceed against the master, collect costs, and impose a fine of ten *piastres* to be given to the church.[107]

Another important document of relevance, dated January 26, 1770, contained instructions that O'Reilly sent to his lieutenant governors at Natchitoches and St. Louis defining their police duties and judicial jurisdiction.[108] Their authority in civil matters extended to cases in which the demand did not exceed one hundred *piastres.*[109] In larger civil cases, the lieutenant governors were authorized to proceed up to the judgment stage, at which point they were to send the file to the governor for his determination.[110] In all civil cases the rules of civil procedure formulated in 1769 were to be adhered to. In serious criminal matters, the lieutenant governors were empowered to proceed up to the judgment stage, following the rules of criminal procedure promulgated in 1769, and they were then to pass the matter to the governor for decision.[111]

If the Arkansas commandant had followed his instructions, his jurisdiction would have been rather restricted. His criminal judicial jurisdiction was clearly trivial, although his police and investigative duties were quite considerable. Civil cases in which the demand did not exceed twenty *piastres*—that is, twenty dollars—could not have been of much importance. It follows that the people of the Arkansas who were of a mind to resort to a technically competent governmental authority for the settlement of their disputes would often have had to go elsewhere.

Even if it had occurred to some eighteenth-century Arkansan to apply to the lieutenant governor at Natchitoches for relief, that avenue was specifically closed by the *Instructions* to post commandants. Section One of those instructions provided that "as to cases which exceed [twenty *piastres*], they shall be judged by the Governor General, to which tribunal the parties shall repair either in person or by someone charged with their powers. . . ."[112] Incredibly, then, in nontrivial civil matters persons who followed these rules were expected, either personally or through an attorney, to make the trek to New Orleans for an adjudication of their difficulties. According to La Harpe, it was twelve or fifteen days by river from the mouth of the Arkansas to New Orleans, and the return trip consumed forty to fifty days.[113] Even though the use of attorneys was specifically authorized, resort to regular governmental tribunals for sorting out disputes would have been very difficult at the least. At times, and for some Arkansans most of the time, it would have been next to impossible.

The meager record evidence that survives, however, reveals a process of practical adaptation that made the system more tolerable. As noted above, post commandants were given authority to adjudicate "verbally" the civil matters within their competence. This evidently meant that there was no need for written pleadings, the taking of depositions, or even (until sometime later) a written judgment. The rules of civil procedure of 1769 did sometimes require written pleadings and depositions, but they applied only in the governor's court and the courts of the lieutenant governors. In the nature of things, then, the cases in which commandants had the power to proceed to judgment would leave no trace on the records. These cases were no doubt handled as part of the administrative routine of the post, and with respect to them the commandant was the final arbiter. Since there was no appeal from the commandant's judgment, and no trace in the Spanish judicial records of anything like a writ of prohibition, there is reason to believe that a commandant who wished to could exceed his jurisdiction without much fear of interference from the central authority. Even in the absence of record evidence, it would be a reasonable guess that this often happened at Arkansas Post.

Indeed, occasional glimpses of litigation at the Arkansas positively show that the Spanish government winked at, indeed encouraged, the exercise of unauthorized judicial power by the commandant and that the hardship which strict adherence to the rules would have produced was thus obviated in actual practice. For example, in 1770 a merchant named Tounoir took a great deal of bear oil from the boat of a hunter named Francoeur to satisfy a debt. Lambert, an *engagé* of Francoeur, petitioned the commandant in writing to order Tounoir to replace the oil; Francoeur owed him wages, he said, and he claimed preference to Tounoir because his claim was "due for hard work." Captain Demasellière, the commandant, thereupon ordered Tounoir to return the oil. When Tounoir refused, the commandant was obliged to send his sergeant to execute his order. At this point, Francoeur asked to have set off a debt of 944 *pesos* that Tounoir owed him; the note evidencing this debt, unfortunately, was in New Orleans in the hands of de Clouet, the former commandant. Demasellière wrote to the governor to ask that he order this note paid since Francoeur had nothing but his gun. The commandant then ordered Tounoir to pay court costs—that is, the sergeant's fee for taking the oil back; when Tounoir refused, Demasellière had him jailed. A short time thereafter the commandant ordered Tounoir to leave the Post, but before doing so, Tounoir got Francoeur to sign some sort of "certificate," probably a release of Tounoir's note; and, to insult the commandant and literally as a parting shot, as he was leaving at high noon, Tounoir and his company fired off a volley of thirty rounds. Francoeur thereafter signed an affidavit that he executed the release to Tounoir when he "was drunk and thus it is of no value."[114]

This case, involving a great deal more than twenty *piastres,* if we assume that it was considered a civil case, obviously did not fall within the commandant's jurisdictional limits. Yet it seems reasonably clear that Demasellière found it impossible to do nothing, so he did his best to resolve the dispute. In fact, the governor was of the view that the commandant, far from having exceeded his jurisdiction, had been too timid. When the governor received the commandant's request to collect the note from Tounoir to Francoeur, he wrote him that he should have handled the matter himself: The proper procedure, the governor scolded, was to "hear both sides, taking the testimony of reputable witnesses on both sides, and then give me the arguments on both sides."[115]

In fairness to Demasellière, there was no way that he could have known from the *Instructions* (assuming they had arrived by then, which as we saw is doubtful) that this was the proper procedure. The whole conflict was beyond his cognizance. What O'Reilly suggested that the commandant should have done corresponds more with the *Instruccion* to the lieutenant governors than with the *Instructions* to the commandants. But O'Reilly's orders in this case were in fact the only practicable way to govern a remote and mobile population like that at the Arkansas. Besides, it would have made no sense whatsoever to compel the commencement of the suit in New Orleans when the first act of the court there would probably have been to order the Arkansas commandant to take the depositions of witnesses at or in the environs of his post. The New Orleans court not infrequently asked the Arkansas commandant to act as a master to gather facts for the settlement of disputes involving Arkansas facts.

No judgment was rendered in this case. For our immediate purposes, however, the lesson is plain enough. Despite what the *Instructions* had said, when the Arkansas commandant was faced with a case that was beyond his power to adjudicate, he was expected to act as a master, gather facts, and send the file to New Orleans for decision. The procedure involved was more a matter of common administrative sense than of adherence to formal rules and was at least partly shaped by practical difficulties created by geography.

Nor did matters very soon become more formalized. A good example of the informality of legal procedure at the Arkansas in later times occurred in May of 1780.[116] At that time, François Ménard, the well-to-do merchant at the Arkansas, filed a written reply to a petition which had been directed to Capt. Balthazar de Villiers, commandant at the Post. The petition, signed by Zabulon Matheo, an Anglo-American, stated that Ménard had taken seven hundred pounds of tallow from the plaintiff's partners. By way of defense, Ménard claimed that one of the plaintiff's partners had delivered the tallow to him as payment for drinking debts; and he said that the plaintiff's complaint should therefore have been directed against the plaintiff's partner. Ménard had settled this debt out of the hunters' catch before they had returned to the Post from upriver; according to his account, he had taken this precaution because the merchants had been unable to realize anything from the hunters' catches for the last three years. Ménard's answer was quite chatty, more an irate letter than a pleading. He excoriated the plaintiff for using the phrase "make restitution" in his complaint. He did not explain why this phrase was so offensive, but he maintained that "the style of the Englishman's secretary might have been more polite," and he opined that "only a vulgar person uses these expressions."

De Villiers, in passing the case on to New Orleans for judgment, told Governor Gálvez that it was a rule at the Arkansas "that the last person to equip a hunter should, upon the latter's return, have first claim on him for repayment." Ménard had short-circuited the equipper's lien by getting the hunters to pay him first, and de Villiers therefore had caused the tallow to be withdrawn from Ménard's stores "in favor of the persons to whom the hunters are indebted." He asked the governor to approve his view that Ménard had to pay the debt owed by the petitioner's partner out of the tallow. Interestingly, de Villiers went on to say that he believed himself "authorized to do this by virtue of an ordinance, the articles of which I have sent you . . ." and he said that "the said Ménard himself invoked [the ordinance] when it was favorable to him." This ordinance, agreed to at the Post in 1778, established the rule that the last equipper of a hunter had a first lien on the hunter's catch and voided conveyances of the catch that were in fraud of creditors.[117] Though the pleadings had been in writing in this case, the good captain did not bother to take testimony in a formal way or provide a record of the proceedings. He simply reported facts that he had gathered informally. He told the governor casually that he "had first started legal proceedings in connection with what I mentioned in this letter, but I felt that in miserable posts like this one it was better to avoid pettifogging as much as possible." In other words, legal formality was an inefficient complication wholly unsuited to places like Arkansas Post.

That was not all. The commandant went on to paint the blackest possible picture of Ménard's character. "[T]he duplicity of this man is remarkable in that he knows how to claim the protection of the laws or ignore them according to his interest." He claimed that Ménard had been at odds with previous commandants and "through illegal trading had acquired some property and become arrogant. . . ." According to the captain, Ménard made a habit of receiving preferential payments "by causing the hunters to get drunk, making them gamble, and by this means getting hold of their cargos. . . ." De Villiers then stated: "He supports at his house most of the time a band of vagabonds and people of his ilk who protect him by testifying to his directions. His conversation is always evil and he disregards my orders to such an extent that last month he went so far as to induce some people who were living with him to refuse to march with a detachment that I had ordered them to join. If I am to be blamed, Sir, it is for not having sent him to you then. I fined him last year for giving brandy to the savages, and he should have been fined a hundred times." Clearly, the commandant saw the real dispute as being between Ménard and himself. The informality of the proceedings is underscored by the fact that the judgment recommended to the governor was not in favor of either of the real parties: De Villiers's view was that the tallow should have been awarded to those who had equipped the plaintiff and his partner.

In the same year, however, de Villiers proceeded in a much more regular fashion in another case involving the same ordinance. Louis Boulard, Andrés López, and François Ménard complained in writing about several hunters who were about to take their catch to town without paying their creditors, presumably the merchants who equipped them. They prayed that the hunters be deposed and that the commandant then "do right to whomever it belongs." De Villiers took the depositions and wrote on the bottom of the petition his judgment decreeing that the boats be unloaded.[118] The proceeding seems altogether remarkably craftsmanlike and professional.

Toward the end of the Spanish period, at the time that Arkansas Post was becoming a truly stable settlement, an extremely interesting criminal proceeding took place there.[119] In 1791, Anselmo Billet *dit* Lajeunesse wounded Francisco Lecler at the Post with a hatchet. On his way to New Orleans to seek medical attention, Lecler stopped at the Royal Hospital at Natchez where he expressed a desire to initiate criminal charges against Billet. Gayoso de Lemos, the governor at Natchez, took Lecler's sworn deposition, and a physician provided him with a certificate describing his wounds. He continued his journey to New Orleans where he pressed his case at the Cabildo. Governor Miró then ordered Capt. Juan Ignacio Delinó de Chalmette, the Arkansas commandant, to take the sworn depositions of relevant witnesses and send them along with his recommendations on the case to New Orleans for final decision.

Delinó first deposed four witnesses: Pedro Jardela, Luis Jardela, Gayetano Bougine (Vaugine), and Pierre Lefevre. None of the men had actually seen the incident; but they all testified that they had found Lecler sitting on the floor in François Ménard's house, wounded in the knee and in a great deal of pain. Lecler had said at that time that Billet had struck him, but he had expressed no view on whether he had done it maliciously. The captain then deposed Billet who maintained steadfastly that he had been working at Ménard's house with a hatchet and that he had wounded Lecler accidentally.

After weighing the testimony, Delinó rendered a kind of interlocutory decision. He said that "according to the said depositions [*declaraciones*] it does not seem that the said wound given by the accused Anselmo Lachenesis was effected with bad intentions." He therefore released Billet from the jail of the fort, but cautioned him to be available for the governor's questioning, should he request it. The depositions and the commandant's view of the case were sent to the governor in New Orleans: It was still pending in 1792 when the record ends.

This is the best example of a complete legal proceeding at the Arkansas in the entire eighteenth century. Delinó did an excellent job of questioning the witnesses, and the transcript of their testimony, covering about twenty pages, was nicely prepared. Second Sgt. Manuel Reyes acted as *escribano* (notary). The depositions were written in Spanish, but the interrogation was done in French; and when the testimony was read back to the deponents for their signatures, Gayetano Vaugine translated it into French for them. It can hardly be coincidental that this professional piece of legal and administrative work occurred just as Arkansas Post was beginning to achieve some respectability.

Residents of Arkansas who were temporarily in New Orleans or who had removed there could, of course, take advantage of the general, province-wide jurisdiction of the governor's court to sue an Arkansas resident. On April 8, 1771, for instance, Santiago Jacquelin and his wife, María Montcharvaux, sued François Ménard, who was then in Arkansas, for an accounting.[120] The claim was that Ménard had agreed to act as agent for Madame Montcharvaux, and a list of notes and personal belongings of hers was attached to the complaint. With the advice of his assessor, a law-trained advisor, the governor sent a dispatch to Fernando de Leyba, commandant at Arkansas, directing him to summon Ménard and to take his deposition in order to learn what he had done with Madame Montcharvaux's effects. Having received the order, Leyba first summoned his sergeant and swore him to act as *escribano pro tempore* (*ad hoc* notary). He then summoned Ménard, had him sworn, and questioned him as to the affairs entrusted to him by the plaintiff. Ménard admitted that he was supposed to collect Doña María's notes and personal effects and account for them. He accounted for the notes, but in some of the personal effects he claimed property by virtue of a gift. All of this Leyba transmitted to New Orleans for "His Lordship to determine what he may find suitable."

This case shows that the local Arkansas commandant acted as an examining magistrate or master for cases in which Post residents were sued in New Orleans.

The flexibility made possible by the civilian habit of relying on depositions taken outside the presence of the parties is exposed to view here. Had *viva voce* testimony in open court in front of the parties been required, as it usually was in common-law courts, the province-wide jurisdiction of the governor's court would not have been nearly so useful. It would not very often have been reasonable to expect witnesses and parties to travel from the forest settlements to attend hearings and give testimony. The centralized authority of the governor's court in New Orleans made it possible to collect evidence from the remotest posts and bring it together in a central point for evaluation and eventually for rendering judgment.

Once judgment was rendered against an Arkansas resident in a suit initiated in New Orleans, the Arkansas commandant was expected to execute it. For instance, in 1787 François Ménard sued Anselm Billet, a resident of the Post who had acted as surety on a note that de Villiers had executed for the purchase of a slave. De Villiers had died in 1782, and his estate was insolvent; thus a cause of action had accrued against Billet. Ménard prayed judgment on the strength of the note and asked that a writ of execution against Billet issue to the commandant of *Los Arcos*. The court complied with the request.[121] In 1791 Santiago Gaignard sued a resident of Arkansas Post, Juan Bautista Saussié, for contribution. Gaignard claimed that he had paid a note owed by both him and the defendant that had been endorsed by the original payee to de Villiers's widow; and he presented her receipt as evidence of the payment. He asked for summary judgment, as a common lawyer would say, and for a writ of execution to the commandant of Arkansas Post.[122]

Another class of case which bears on Arkansas legal history is the sort that involves occurrences at the Arkansas but does not involve Arkansas residents. These might be expected to have arisen fairly frequently in an *entrepôt* like the Post. An extremely interesting example is the case of *Pourée v. Chouteau.*[123]

In March of 1782, Eugene Pourée outfitted a *bateau* in New Orleans in which he received freight "subject to the ordinary conditions of carriage by water." One of his shippers was Auguste Chouteau, a well-known St. Louis merchant. On reaching the Yazoo River, a party of Englishmen attacked Pourée's *bateau* and compelled him to descend to Natchez. After joining a convoy there for safety, the boat resumed its voyage. On reaching the St. Francis River, Pourée encountered a *bateau* belonging to a Mr. Labaddie; its crew having informed him that English brigands had attacked and pillaged them near what is now Memphis, Pourée decided to retreat to Arkansas Post until conditions improved. After a stay of some length there, he learned that the Englishmen had retired inland and he set off again, arriving safely at St. Louis after a considerable delay. Pourée wanted to recover from his shippers the extra expenses occasioned by the delays. These included payments to Choctaw Indians for reconnoitering for the preservation of the *bateau;* payments to Quapaw Indians who accompanied Pourée to the St. Francis River; rent for a house at Arkansas Post in which the cargo was stored; payment for 150 trips of a cart for loading and unloading the *bateau* at Arkansas Post; wages of a crew sent down from St. Louis to man the vessel when it resumed its trip; payment of men at Arkansas Post for outfitting the *bateau;* payment for seventeen hundred pounds of biscuit bought at the Arkansas and eight hundred pounds of bacon; and the cost of powder and balls.

When Chouteau refused Pourée's demand, Pourée sued him in the court of the lieutenant governor in St. Louis. He recited the facts and closed his petition by noting his surprise that Mons. Chouteau would not pay his proportionate share of the increased expenses and by making known his view of the substantive law applicable to the case. He claimed that had he not completed the voyage at all due to *force majeure,* the shipper would not have been entitled under the law to a refund; likewise, "if the master makes a second equipment, the shippers are obliged to pay expenses." Pourée's complaint, in other words, doubled as a "brief" for his view of the relevant legal principles.[124] Mons. Chouteau answered simply that he had paid in advance, and he added his own view of the applicable rule: ". . . it would be a great wrong to shippers to have to pay a second time the freight upon a venture embarked in a *bateau,* upon which the freight had already been paid before it left port."[125]

The lieutenant governor, rather than decide the case himself, referred it to arbitration. Each party named one arbitrator, and these arbitrators elected a third. The record noted that "this tribunal shall finally decide and determine this cause according to the rights of each party." The arbitrators were all well-known and well-respected merchants of St. Louis. Though the record does not say so, the parties presumably agreed to this mode of settling their differences. The arbitrators decided that Chouteau was obligated to pay for some of the extra expenses occasioned by the layover at Arkansas Post, but not nearly as much as Pourée was claiming.

The manner of proceeding in civil cases in the lieutenant governor's court in St. Louis, as at the Arkansas, was a model of simplicity. Some cases were heard on oral plaint. If written pleadings were used, an informal petition initiated the action. The petition told the plaintiff's story simply, reciting the facts in a straightforward, though sometimes discursive way. No particular form was prescribed; as in common-law bill procedure, all the plaintiff had to do was to set out the salient features of his case.[126] The defendant then replied with his version of the facts. Occasionally a defendant replied with an answer containing a counterclaim to which the plaintiff answers; but only rarely will the plaintiff otherwise file a responsive pleading.

As was the case during the French period, one of the Arkansas commandant's chief duties during the Spanish regime was to attract and hold the loyalty of the Quapaw Indians. Very soon after Capt. Alexandre de Clouet took command of the Post in 1768, he wrote that supplying the Indians with liquor was absolutely necessary to an amicable relationship with them. Otherwise, he claimed, they simply could not be relied on.[127] Besides, he said a few months later, they would get liquor whether the French supplied it or not: In 1768 the English had begun building the settlement that would come to be called Concordia on the left bank of the Mississippi across from the upper mouth of the Arkansas, and the Quapaws were quite happy with this development "since it is to be expected that they will get more food and drink."[128] To make matters worse, de Clouet reported the same year that for the last four years "because of the fear of floods [the inhabitants] have not made any crop." As a result, the French were completely dependent on the Indians for food, and the Quapaws threatened that in the future they would take only liquor in exchange for their corn.[129]

Despite de Clouet's animadversions, the governor chided the commandant for using liquor to buy the Indians' friendship. His duty, the governor said, was to keep the Quapaws away from the English "by persuasion."[130] Later he suggested to de Clouet that he call the Indians together and "make a speech to them on the evils of drinking." If that was in fact done, it accomplished little: A year later a drunken Quapaw became so rowdy that the commandant was obliged to make an inquiry and confiscate the remaining stock of the person who had supplied it.[131] Again we see that the Arkansas commandants exercised judicial power beyond that technically delegated to them by their formal instructions.

The English continued to put pressure on the French by trading liquor to the

Quapaws. De Clouet claimed in 1769 that "the English make canteens [saloons] for the red men out of their posts."[132] When late in 1769 Capt. François Demasellière took command at the Post he said that the Quapaws complained to him of de Clouet's policy of not allowing them to trade for liquor. This caused them to take their corn to the English to trade. "What they miss is liquor," the captain bluntly noted, "and I need more."[133] A few months later, the captain renewed his demand.[134] In 1770 a Quapaw chief named Long Thin One gave him a good deal of trouble because he was refused liquor and tried to strike the commandant in the head. "I threw him out of my house," Demasellière noted laconically, "and I told him that I did not want to see him any more."[135]

In 1772 Capt. Fernando de Leyba, the Arkansas commandant, was faced with a very alarming situation. The Quapaw head chief had flatly told General O'Reilly that he believed Leyba did not like the Quapaws,[136] and he wanted him replaced. Part of the difficulty was that the Spanish were not paying the Indians as well as the French had for their goods;[137] part of the difficulty was that Leyba was a Spaniard. The Quapaws quite frankly expressed their preference for a Frenchman,[138] and Leyba could not even speak French.[139]

On June 13, 1772, Leyba arrested Nicholas Labussière, the trader stationed among the Quapaws, for selling liquor to the Indians and for other trade violations. This action so enraged the Quapaws that one of their chiefs threatened to raze the Post and kill all the civilians there unless Labussière was released. Some time was bought for sixty *pesos;* but if the white man was not returned within three months, the Quapaw chief promised "to cut every throat on the post." Even after striking this bargain, the chief, according to Leyba, sent an Indian "back for a barrel of whiskey or my head."[140] A few days later representatives from the three villages came to humiliate the captain: They brought him a dead horse and demanded whiskey in exchange for it. They threatened to kill everyone unless they got it, and so menaced the women that the commandant's wife fainted and all the rest were crying.[141] The governor finally wrote the Quapaw chief demanding that he behave himself "or else."[142]

The regulation of the liquor trade with the Indians remained of grave concern throughout the Spanish period.[143] In 1779 de Villiers wrote to Governor Gálvez and said that when he arrived at the Post he had found a regulation in effect that he had followed since it seemed to him "wise and necessary." Under it, no one was to trade liquor to the Quapaws without a license from the commandant, and sales had to be made at a place designated by custom. The Quapaw chiefs complained that every other sort of trade was free and that it was an irritating discrimination that the Indian liquor trade was not. De Villiers, who wrote eloquently on the virtues of, and his devotion to, the ideals of free trade, had decided to open the Indian liquor trade to everyone. The *habitants* and merchants reacted strongly to this deregulation. They wrote: "Today, the thirteenth of the month of September, 1779, we, the *habitants* and merchants of the Post of Arkansas, on the decision that Mons. de Villiers our commandant has told us was taken, that to content the savages he would permit them the full liberty to trade for *eau de vie* wherever they want, are assembled; and of one common accord we declare that such a liberty would expose the *habitants* to the continual insults of the said savages . . . [and we ask] whether the commandant would not make a wiser decision than this, namely, that a single place be established where drink would be distributed to them with order and propriety [*avec ordre et mesure*]." De Villiers evidently acceded to this request: He could not very well have done otherwise.

It was not long before the Indian chiefs' complaints would be stood on their heads. In 1786 the three great chiefs of the Quapaws asked the governor to forbid all liquor trade to the tribe because of widespread drunkenness and addiction to alcohol among the members of the tribe.[144] The governor did not do so immediately, and within the first three months of Vallière's command five Quapaws died in drunken brawls. Finally, after a minor Quapaw chief had been murdered and his mutilated body thrown into the river during a drunken altercation, Governor Miró issued an order that the liquor trade to the Indians at Arkansas Post be entirely prohibited. Vallière published the order at the Post on October 17, 1787.[145]

Though Indian relations demanded much of the Post commandants' attention, controlling the activities of the European hunters on the Arkansas and the other nearby rivers also gave them considerable grief. "[These hunters] lead a pretty fast life," Capt. Josef Orieta complained; "They claim that, being on the river, they owe obeisance to no one."[146] They were thus self-proclaimed outlaws in the technical sense. To hear some tell it, many of them were also outlaws in the popular sense.

In 1770, as we noted before, Athanase de Mézières, the lieutenant governor at Natchitoches, wrote to Governor Unzaga about some of the hunters of

Arkansas.[147] "On the Akansa River," he said, "there live, under the name of hunters, some men of whose pernicious customs I must give your Lordship a brief account." He painted these people with a broad brush: "Most of those who live there," he claimed, "have either deserted from the troops and ships of the most Christian King or have committed robberies, rape or homicide, that river being the asylum of the most wicked persons, without doubt, in all the Indies." He went on to assess their morality and, in particular, their attitude toward law. "They live so forgetful of the laws," he complained, "that it is easy to find persons who have not returned to Christian lands for ten, twenty, or thirty years, and who pass their scandalous lives in public concubinage with the captive Indian women whom for this purpose they purchase among the heathen, loaning those of whom they tire to others of less power, that they may labor in their service, giving them no other wage than the promise of quieting their lascivious passions; in short they have no other rule than their own caprice, and the respect which they pay the boldest and most daring, who control them." The outraged lieutenant governor revealed that these hunters supplied the Osages with guns and ammunition and encouraged them to attack the people in his district and steal women, children, and horses. He suggested to the governor that he "order that this race, through despairing of all supplies, may be forced to abandon the river on which they reside." In this way, the lieutenant governor hoped that the Osages would be deprived of a market for their human contraband and would pull back farther north. The same day that he suggested this plan to the governor, de Mézières wrote him to say that François Beaudoin, "one of the hunters and magnates of the Arkansas River," had arrived at Natchitoches with his family and a captive Indian girl. The lieutenant governor had arrested him immediately, he reported, and was sending him to New Orleans.[148]

In another letter, de Mézières gives some information about an Arkansas denizen nicknamed Brindamúr, to whom we alluded briefly before, "whose sole employment was to roam the forests and entertain himself in hunting—an occupation very conducive to laziness and to all other vices as well."[149] It seems that this man had seduced a married lady of Pointe Coupée and had taken her to his camp in Arkansas. When Brindamúr and his paramour learned of the death of the good lady's husband (which de Mézières attributed to "the unexpected rashness of his wife"), they descended the Arkansas River, "famous asylum of evildoers," to the Post where they got married. The lieutenant governor continued his tale: "They then returned at once to their haunts, because the groom, who was of gigantic frame and extraordinary strength, had made himself a petty king over those vagabonds and highwaymen, who, with contempt for law and subordination, with equal insult to Christians, and to the shame of the very heathen, up to now have maintained themselves on that river. But a short time after this new journey inland, it happened that one of his subjects, not only angered at the ill treatment which Brindamúr gave him, but frightened as well of the threats which he made that he would kill him (which he would have done on three different occasions had not the rest prevented it), killed Brindamúr, though tardily, by divine justice for the punishment of the misdeeds chargeable to the said Brindamúr." It needs no saying after this that at least in lower Louisiana the reputation of some of the Arkansas hunters could hardly have been worse.

It seems likely that de Mézières's account of the Arkansas population alarmed Unzaga. Whether he thought the reports were completely accurate we cannot tell, but very soon we hear of a scheme aimed at civilizing the hunters of the various Arkansas rivers. In 1770 Demasellière ordered all the hunters to return to the Post "under penalty of having to pay all the damages caused by Indian raids."[150] Evidently it was thought, at the very least, that their presence on the rivers was aggravating the Osages and that their removal might relieve tensions some. Perhaps also the governor had believed de Mézières's claim that some of them were instigating the Osage attacks in his district.

In May of 1770, seven separate war parties of Osages ransacked many of the hunting camps along the Arkansas taking weapons and ammunition; the Arkansas commandant suspected the English, not any of the French hunters, of fomenting the attacks.[151] A few days later a number of hunters sent word that they were returning to the fort with their families,[152] and some in fact soon began trickling in. The Francoeur brothers, for instance, arrived from the White River in June of 1770 with women and children; the children did not even have shirts.[153] The Francoeurs had lived on the river for twenty-five years, had taken up with Indian women, and had had a large number of children by them.[154] A man named Sasemission showed up soon thereafter with a family in the same general shape.[155] A month later, a hunter named Bartolmieu arrived with an Indian wife and six children: They were so ragged that the *habitants* had to take up a collection for them that brought sixty *piastres* worth of clothing.[156] The commandant's plan was to make all the hunters "go to town"—that is, to New Orleans—to get married and get their children baptized. Better yet, he suggested to the governor, why not send a priest or a monk to the Arkansas for a few days to take care of all of this at once?[157]

One of the reasons that some of the hunters had so readily complied with the order to come down to the Post was that, as we noted, the Osages had relieved them of most of their guns and ammunition. Demasellière had ordered the merchants of the Post not to resupply the hunters in order to force their obedience to this order, but this plan proved difficult to effect.[158] On July 15, 1770, the commandant wrote to O'Reilly that while some hunters had returned from the river, "others supplied by [the merchant] Tounoir, against my orders, have remained."[159] The scheme to clear the river of hunters nevertheless continued to meet with some success. The next month the commandant renewed his request for a priest as there had by now arrived at the Post seventy children in need of baptism.[160] When some of the hunters requested permission to return to their camps for their things, Demasellière allowed them to do so but kept back all their women to ensure their return.[161]

By 1786 the general reputation of the Arkansas hunters had not markedly improved. In that year Jean Filhiol, commandant at Ouachita Post, wrote a most informative description of his bailiwick, much of which lay within the present-day boundaries of Arkansas.[162] The inhabitants of the Ouachita, like most of the Arkansas population, were subsistence hunters. "These men," Filhiol said, "are composed of the scum of all sorts of nations, several fugitives from their native countries, and who have become fixed here through their attachment to their idleness and their independence, perhaps even to escape from the pursuit of justice before there was a command."[163] As for their morals, Filhiol stated: "Hardly do they know whether they are Christians."[164] At the slightest provocation they would abandon any settlement as "their rifle and their powder horn comprise their entire property, and every country is good to them"; and "if they hunt a little," he said, "it is only to satisfy their first needs of nature."[165] Filhiol tried to coax them into forming an agricultural community, "hoping to have them close together to bring them more easily into social life by counsels and example." His attempt met with little success.

Whether the Spanish government grew bored with its efforts to rid the Arkansas of undesirables, or whether the task was simply beyond its power, it nevertheless is the case that hunters continued for a long time to compose the major portion of Arkansas's small eighteenth-century population. The census of Arkansas Post for 1768 reported a total of only twelve *habitant* families, including those of Commandant de Clouet and La Vigne the *garde magasin*. The total number of Europeans was seventy-eight, of whom fifty were children; there were thirty slaves living with them.[166] Two years later a census of the white population reported a total of seventy-five persons at the Arkansas.[167] The bulk of the residents of Arkansas were hunters or merchants: *Habitants* of a more or less permanent sort with a stake in making a true and lasting settlement of the Post were extremely difficult to attract, partly because engaging in agriculture at its downstream location was almost impossible.

Proof of this is provided by a lengthy and interesting report that Captain de Villiers submitted to the governor in August of 1777, in which he gave a short account of the history of the Post and recounted the extreme difficulties that the few *habitants* there had experienced.[168] "This settlement was moved about 1756," he said, "during the governorship of Kerlérec when Monsieur de Reggio was commandant, from the place called *Écore Rouge* to the place where it is presently situated, eleven leagues down the river [on the right bank in descending] and four leagues from its mouth." When the Post was moved, the commandant claimed, its new situation was flooded only every eight or nine years. "Today," however, he went on to say, "it is regularly underwater every year." De Villiers complained that the "water rises and destroys the fruits of the labor of the *habitants* and the savages, and they are all discouraged." He argued vigorously that the Post should be moved back to *Écores Rouges*. It was true that this might cause some inconvenience to the Illinois convoys, but river traffic was slight anyway: "The king no longer sends boats on his own account," he argued, "and the four or five which ascend to the Illinois on behalf of private parties can just as well (and a good deal more securely) obtain supplies eleven leagues higher up the river where livestock and other produce could be produced without any obstacle." More important, he said, one could attract respectable *habitants* to such a place.

As expected, de Villiers was much concerned about the character of the people who lived in Arkansas. More than once in his letters he referred to his desire to establish a "respectable settlement" on his river. The census included in his 1777 report had listed only seven *habitant* families of fifty whites and eleven slaves; and at least four of these families were headed by merchants. De Villiers described the Post as being "a place of residence for merchants and a supply point for the hunters who come here to equip themselves . . . paying their debts and then equipping themselves anew or taking their catch to town."[169] He regarded the hunters as altogether undesirable people. "You would not believe," he wrote the governor in January of 1777, "the brigandage, the insubordination, and the libertinage which have reigned for so long on this river."[170] In March of 1779 he was much more pointed: "The hunters [are] for the most part people of bad behavior who could soon be replaced by more useful colonists"[171] if only a more suitable settling place were provided. "Farmers without the embarrassment of the families of hunters" were what, in de Villiers's view, was needed; and that required moving the Post to a place where agriculture was possible.

The *habitants* were, however, quite skeptical about de Villiers's scheme. They were at first "all determined to descend to the coast of the colony rather than [move upriver and] expose themselves to the incursions of the savage Chickasaws."[172] Thus, not "being assured of being protected by a fort," and given the reluctance of his *habitants,* de Villiers for a time suspended his plan for relocation. But the ravages of the spring flood of 1779 convinced his residents that their position was no longer tenable. Even the most-elevated houses faced ruin, almost all the livestock had drowned, the fort was open in several places, and the well had caved in.[173] Somehow the good captain persuaded the *habitants* to make the twenty-seven-mile journey up the river despite the lack of a fort there, rather than abandon the Arkansas entirely.

On March 2, the commandant wrote that in a few days he was going to lead a first contingent to the new establishment at *Écores Rouges.*[174] These were the families of some hunters from the St. Francis and the families of Anglo-American refugees that had been granted asylum the year before when they had found Concordia (British Ozark) deserted.[175] Their arrival had more than doubled the white population of Arkansas Post. They were to make some temporary huts at the new site. "The savages," de Villiers claimed, "strongly approve the steps that I am taking, and so much the more since there are eight inches of water on the place where they planted their crops—the which are lost."[176]

Less than two weeks later the commandant wrote proudly that "this new post finds itself completely established." The captain now remembered to be concerned about the settlers' title to their land. "The *habitants* have built on the assurance that I have given them that you will not change anything in the dispositions that I have made in the arrangement of their lands," he wrote, and he asked the governor's approval of what he had done. "Please authorize me," he requested, "to guarantee them their property."[177] The governor replied that de Villiers should send the *habitants'* papers to him so that he could execute grants in proper form in order to avoid the titles being put in question in the future.[178] This was in accord with the regulations, promulgated in 1770 by General O'Reilly, that required all grants to be made by the governor.[179] In fact, those same regulations required that the governor send a surveyor to fix the bounds of all grants in the presence of the commandant of the district and two adjoining landowners.[180] There is no indication that de Villiers ever provided the governor with the papers requested, and there is no evidence that any Spanish surveyor was at work in Arkansas until very late in the century. Still, it seemed that de Villiers was on the very verge of making a success of his settlement.

In 1782, however, the commandant reported only fifteen *habitant* families at the Arkansas; and five of these abandoned the river later that year.[181] The smallness of the population is almost certainly attributable to the cataclysmic events that occurred at the Post in the 1780s. Only a very few months after the Post was moved, Spain sided with the American colonists and declared war on Great Britain.[182] Arkansas Post was the most vulnerable of all the Spanish forts in the Mississippi Valley because of its isolation and the small number of troops stationed there. Until it was reinforced by twelve soldiers in 1781, the garrison at full strength boasted only a captain and twenty soldiers. The possibility of a British attack on the Post was therefore very much on the minds of its soldiers and *habitants.* In this tense atmosphere, two German soldiers (members of the Spanish detachment) and several American settlers at the Post were accused early in 1782 of plotting to betray it. They had planned to open the gates of the fort to British sympathizers who would then butcher the garrison. De Villiers took depositions from various people, including those accused, and sent the record and the defendants to New Orleans where a special tribunal sentenced two of the Americans and the two German soldiers to death.[183]

Most unfortunately, the records of de Villiers's proceedings cannot be located. But when Governor Miró wrote to the captain general in Havana for confirmation of the sentence, though his letter was short, he revealed a great deal in it.[184] He described Arkansas Post as being very vulnerable since it was 250 leagues [*sic*] from its nearest northern neighbor. Arkansas was an immense country, he said, inhabited by innumerable Indians among whom lived many wandering Englishmen, the one group influencing the other; the British were "as hard to get rid of as a hydra-headed monster." The governor then went on sheepishly to admit that the record he was sending would reveal an error: The accused had not been confronted by the two witnesses against them. But since it would take too long to get the witnesses to New Orleans, Miró asked that the captain general overlook *esta pequeña falta* ("this small error"). Time was of the essence, and Miró closed by saying that allowing such acts as these to go unpunished leads to occurrences like the Natchez rebellion of the previous year—"fatal consequences" Miró termed them. The short reply from Cuba followed three and a half weeks later: The captain general let the convictions stand, and the sentence was carried out.[185] This case provides another example of legal norms yielding to political exigency and reveals again the highly subjective character of the process of adjudication in eighteenth-century Arkansas.

Arkansas Post long remained a place where it was well, whatever your nationality or status, to keep your political opinions to yourself. In 1788 François Ménard, by now surely the richest man at the Post, confided to the Abenaki medal chief that it would not be long until the Americans took over Louisiana; and he allowed that the tribe had better look to taking the right side in the event of a struggle. So at least Joseph Tessié, in his deposition, accused Ménard of saying; no one else had heard it, but three sergeants of the garrison swore that they were in the room when the words were alleged to have been spoken. Tessié had turned to them and repeated what he claimed Ménard had said. Capt. Josef Vallière sent the depositions and Ménard to New Orleans. He apologized for not sending a pre-trial examination of the defendant, but the Post had no jail, a defect that he was hoping soon to supply.[186]

The procedure for obtaining and perfecting a land grant from the Spanish government of Louisiana can be reconstructed with remarkable ease from printed sources. That is partly because the number of unadjudicated claims based on Spanish land grants remained large well into the nineteenth century.[187] Since ultimate resolution of these claims depended on their validity under Spanish law, many people were drawn to ransacking the old books for ordinances and regulations dealing with grants from the Spanish royal domain; and many of these laws found their way into print at various times after the American takeover.[188]

As soon as O'Reilly had established himself in authority in New Orleans, he made an extensive trip into the interior of what is now the state of Louisiana to make inspections, hear complaints, and generally inform himself on the state of governmental affairs in some of the more remote posts in lower Louisiana. Of course, he did not journey as far north as the Arkansas. Upon his return, he issued a set of regulations bearing on the concession of land. Under them, each newly arrived family was entitled to a plot of six or eight arpents in front by forty in depth. The grantees as *quid pro quo* were expected to build levees and ditches during the first three years of their possession and were obligated to keep the roads in repair. Within the same three-year period, moreover, they were "bound . . . to clear the whole front of their land to the depth of two arpents." If grantees did not fulfill these conditions, the regulations provided, "their land shall revert to the king's domain and be granted anew." During the initial three years of possession, which had the aura of a probationary period, written permission from the governor to make an alienation was required; and he was not to give it unless, "on strict inquiry, it shall be found that the conditions above explained have been duly executed."[189] There was also a requirement that the entire front of each concession be enclosed during the three-year period, but it was not made an express condition of the grant.[190] All grants were to be made by the governor, and the government surveyor was to fix the bounds in the presence of the local commandant and two settlers. These last four were to sign a *procès-verbal* reciting the events, and three copies of it were to be made: One for the archives of the Cabildo, one for the governor, and one for the proprietor "to be annexed to the titles of his grant." Though these regulations were clearly generated by local conditions encountered by O'Reilly on his visits, and while they specifically mention Opelousas, Attakapas, and Natchitoches more than once, it seems that the general intended these rules to be observed everywhere in Louisiana: They close with his injunction to the "governor, judges, Cabildo, and all the inhabitants of this province, to perform punctually to all that is required by this regulation."[191]

Not until 1797 was further regulation of land concessions made. In that year Governor Gayoso laid down some rules on who was qualified to receive grants. A stranger who was not a farmer or artisan, and who was unmarried and propertyless, was ineligible for a concession until he had been a resident for four years. Unmarried artisans, on the other hand, were privileged, and could qualify after having exercised their art or profession for three years. Married persons could immediately receive two hundred arpents plus fifty arpents for each child. The regulations specifically stated that a new settler would "lose [his lands] without recovery, if, in the term of one year, he shall not begin to establish himself upon them, or if in the third year he shall not have put under labor ten arpents in every hundred." Grants were, moreover, to be made contiguously, as to do otherwise "would offer a greater exposure to the attacks of the Indians, and render more difficult the administration of justice, and the regulation of the police. . . ."[192]

When in 1798 the power to regulate land concessions passed to the intendancy, Juan Ventura Morales issued an extensive set of regulations on the subject. No grant was to exceed eight hundred arpents. Grantees "on the river" were under the duty to build levees and canals, make and maintain roads, and construct necessary bridges. All settlers were to clear and put in cultivation within three years the whole front of their concessions to a depth of at least two arpents; if they did not, the rules provided, "the land granted [will be] remitted to the domain. . . ." O'Reilly's restraint on alienations during the "probationary" period was repeated, as was Gayoso's instruction on the necessity for contiguous grants.[193]

An interesting feature of Morales's rules was that, for the first time, they fixed the point at which title passed to the grantee. O'Reilly's regulations had not directly spoken to that point. Morales's regulations noted that some people had thought that title passed when their petition for a grant was filed, others when the order of survey was given, and still others when the survey was made. None of these people was right according to Morales: "Real titles" were required before the grant was perfected. These were to be issued when the surveyor's *procès-verbal* and a certified copy of it were sent to the intendant. At that point, the intendant, with the consent of the king's attorney, would deliver "the necessary title paper." Those occupying lands without such titles, unless they perfected their titles within six months, were "to be driven therefrom as from property belonging to the crown," except that those who had been in possession ten years or longer would be allowed to stay after paying "a just and moderate retribution."

There is no evidence whatever that any of this vast array of regulation had the slightest impact in Arkansas. Only 29 claims totaling just over eight thousand acres were confirmed in the entire state of Arkansas by the first American land board which reported in 1812. (By contrast, 1,311 claims in Missouri were confirmed.)[194] Among the Arkansas claims, 14 were confirmed on the basis of settlement rights, 7 on the ground of ten years' possession, and only 8 on the strength of a "concession." Even these last were not complete titles under Spanish law. Four were "concessions" from commandants—1 from Vallière and 3 from de Vilemont. Even under the most liberal construction of O'Reilly's laws, as we have seen, a local commandant had no power to grant lands from the royal domain. The other 4 concessions were from governors, 3 from Miró and 1 from Gayoso; but none of these was supported by a real title and thus would have failed under Morales's regulations. There was not a single regular Spanish land title ever made out in the entire state of Arkansas. Capt. Amos Stoddard estimated that 95 percent of the land claims in upper Louisiana were incomplete,[195] but this estimate turned out to be low since only 13 complete titles were ever proved up in the whole Missouri Territory.[196] The lack of anxiety among Arkansas residents about complying with the land law was, according to Lafon, a New Orleans engineer, easily explained. "Land situated so remote from population and commerce," he said, speaking of Arkansas Post, "was held in very little estimation, scarcely worth paying the fees of office for the file papers."[197]

The conveyancing practices of commandants and settlers at the Arkansas are illustrated by an instructive pair of documents available in the Archives of the Secretary of State of Missouri in Jefferson City. The first is Joseph Bougy's petition (in French) requesting permission to settle at Arkansas Post: "To Monsieur de Valliere, captain of infantry, civil and military commandant of the Post of Arkansas: Joseph Bougy, *habitant* of the Post of Kaskaskia, saying that he would like to come to settle in this place of the Arkansas with his family, humbly prays that it would please you to grant him eight arpents of the ordinary depth on the bank of this river. The applicant will pray for the saving of your days *etc.* Arkansas, 24 September, 1787. Mark X of Joseph Bougy." The only other document in this chain of title was the following (in Spanish): "I certify the said land [as] belonging to the royal domain. Arkansas, 25 September, 1787. Josef Valliere."

This last document was the only semblance of a grant that Bougy had. It was actually only a statement by the commandant that the land was vacant. Beginning in the 1790s, the commandant who endorsed a petition for a land grant almost always prefaced his certificate of vacancy with a statement such as, "I consider the petitioner worthy of the favor that he asks." But during the Spanish period the commandants at the Arkansas never actually purported in writing to make grants from the royal domain. A new formula introduced at the Post just before the American takeover, however, adopts a tone that stops just short of purporting to make a grant. Caso y Luengo, the last Spanish commandant at the Arkansas, seems responsible for the new language. A good example of it comes from February 26, 1803, when Pierre Lefevre petitioned for an addition to one of his tracts so that he could cut enough trees to build a sawmill. He asked that Caso y Luengo "deign to accord [*acordar*] him an extension of the depth of his land, which he believes, far from prejudicing anyone, would be much to the advantage of the settlement." The commandant replied that since the "proposal would redound much to the benefit of this settlement, I find no objection to me granting him what he asks. . . ." This artful reply comes about as close to using words of grant as one can without actually doing so. Caso y Luengo used these and similar words in many of his endorsements.

It is abundantly clear, however, despite the law, that the settlers at the Arkansas regarded their land as having been granted to them as soon as the commandant endorsed their petitions. For instance, on May 7, 1799, Charles Drouot, *habitant* of the Post, petitioned Capt. Carlos de Vilemont for 240 arpents of land. De Vilemont endorsed the request by replying: "I consider the petitioner worthy of the favor that he requests and it appears to me that the land he wants is vacant and belongs to the royal domain." The next instrument in this chain of title is one signed by Drouot which states: "I certify that I have ceded the above-mentioned concession to Monsieur Pierre Lefevre, in faith of which I have subscribed [this instrument] at the Arkansas. . . ." Clearly, though erroneously, Drouot believed that the commandant's endorsement was a concession that he had given him an alienable interest in realty. Indeed, petitioners for land in Arkansas often revealed a belief that commandants had the power to give some kind of title, for they almost invariably asked the commandant *accorder une concession* or *conseder la . . . tierra*—to grant a concession or concede land. After the American takeover Arkansas commandants were actually bold enough to claim that they had possessed a power that in fact the land regulations had clearly denied them. For instance, when in October of 1804 Henry Cassidy became anxious about the title to land that he claimed on the St. Francis, he obtained an affidavit from Caso y Luengo stating that, when he was commandant, he "had conceded him a portion of land in the place called the little prairie."

The commandants and *habitants* of the Arkansas thus very clearly ignored the extensive set of land regulations promulgated by various eighteenth-century governors and others. It was simply too costly and too complicated to comply, especially when the benefits of conforming seemed in any case not very great. An interesting contrast to this insouciance, on the other hand, is provided by the few eighteenth-century wills executed at the Arkansas that have survived. The stakes were higher in the case of wills than in the case of land grants since very often a great deal of personalty, especially receivables and slaves, would purport to pass under them. For instance, in 1791 François Ménard executed a will and codicil at the Post shortly before he died, leaving to his wife his fourteen slaves (three of whom were runaways), his desk (bureau) full of notes and bonds, and his liquor and other merchandise, subject to a trust in favor of his illegitimate daughter Constance.[198] Ménard also declared his ownership of a house in New Orleans situated in the *Rue de la Madame Boisclare.*

Capt. Juan Ignacio Delinó de Chalmette, called to Ménard's bedside at four o'clock one morning, did quite a serviceable job of drafting this will and codicil. He caused them to be executed, moreover, in accordance with the formal requirements prevailing in Louisiana. O'Reilly's *Instructions* of 1770 to the post commandants had indicated that wills ought to be signed by the testator, surrogate notary, and five witnesses—two to aid the commandant's attestation and three others.[199] But O'Reilly's Laws of 1769 specifically said that "if there be no notary [attesting], there must be present five witnesses, residents of the place in which the will shall be made; if, however, it be impossible to procure the last-mentioned number, three may suffice." The *Nueva Recopilación de Castilla* was cited in support of this proposition.[200] Delinó had only three witnesses to the will and codicil, but this, as just demonstrated, was evidently authorized by O'Reilly's Laws. It is likely that this was in any event the custom at the Arkansas since the only other complete specimen of a will executed there in the eighteenth century is executed precisely the same way—indeed, with the same witnesses.[201]

The Spanish archives of Arkansas Post had grown quite large when, on March 23, 1804, they were delivered to Lt. James B. Many of the United States Army. There were over two hundred items, dating at least to 1780, listed in the inventory that Many signed by way of receipt for their delivery by Capt. Francisco Caso y Luengo.[202] The archives themselves have, unfortunately, been lost, but the inventory reveals a good deal of instructive data.

The commandant's notarial duties consumed a significant portion of his time. There were recorded in the archives eight wills, seven marriage contracts, five other contracts (*acuerdos* and *convenios*), a large number of bonds and receipts, numerous deeds (of land, houses, slaves, and livestock), and three deeds of emancipation. The commandant's judicial duties were also considerable. There were almost thirty successions, and this kind of case presumably accounted for a great deal of the commandant's judicial work. It could be rather remunerative as well, especially if the estate was large and thus required some time to inventory and settle. For instance, on May 27, 1778, de Villiers had to travel two leagues downriver from the Post to inventory the goods of Pierre de Laclède Liguest, the founder of St. Louis, who had died in his trading boat near the mouth of the Arkansas.[203] It took three days and fifteen pages to list all his goods. De Villiers also acted as coroner in this instance, for he noted that, having inspected the body, Laclède's "death had occurred naturally."

Adversarial litigation at the Arkansas may have been rare, but the condition of the evidence is such that statements on this subject are exceedingly hazardous. The inventory of the Post archives records the presence of five petitions (*instancias*), probably written complaints whose function was the initiation of litigation. The existence of six *procesos* is also mentioned, and these are probably case files that had been advanced at least to the deposition stage. This seems a rather small number of cases, but probably both the *instancias* and *procesos* have to do with litigation that would eventually be decided in New Orleans. It is well to recall that matters within the commandant's power to decide could be initiated and determined "verbally" according to O'Reilly's *Instructions* of 1770, so the number of suits adjudicated by the commandant may have been rather larger than the archives at first seem to indicate. In 1792 commandants were ordered to begin keeping a written book of judgments,[204] and the mention in the inventory of a "book which contains various *determinaciones*" may be evidence that the Arkansas commandants conformed to that requirement. But without such a book it is impossible to tell what the litigation rate in eighteenth-century Arkansas was.

Still, some interesting conclusions can be drawn from even so meager a record as this. For instance, four of the five *instancias* and three of the six *procesos* involved merchants on one side or the other; François Ménard alone was a party to five of these eleven cases. Marriage contracts seem to have been employed by relatively few people: Seven within a space of twenty-five years is not a very large number. The social status of the parties to them, moreover, tended clearly toward the *bourgeoisie:* Luis Dianna, Joseph Lambert, Juan Larquier, Luisa Jardela, and Joseph Bartolomé, parties to marriage contracts, were all probably of this class. Likewise, those who executed wills were either propertied or of old French families. François Ménard, Andrés López, Jean Baptiste Duchassin, and René Soumand were all merchants; Luis Lefevre, though hardly well off, was a member of an important Post family. Not much is known of the social and economic status of Pedro Burel, but it is a reasonable guess that he was among the more well-to-do residents of Arkansas.

As was the case in the French period, therefore, it appears that the social and economic class of those persons who adhered to European legal traditions and resorted to regular modes of dispute settlement was quite narrow and their number very small: They were, for the most part, the merchants and *habitants* of the Post. The hunters, the *coureurs de bois,* the bulk of the Arkansas population of roughly 450 at the end of the Spanish period, simply regulated their lives by whatever light nature could provide. Many claimed to owe obeisance to no state and steadfastly refused to take part in the ordered, agrarian community that de Villiers and others had so desperately wished to create. They preferred instead to pass their lives in silent beauty and in danger.

EPILOGUE

FIN DE SIÈCLE/FIN DEL SIGLO

Thirty years and more before the founding of New Orleans, Frenchmen came to Arkansas to hunt and to trade with the Indians. During the period of French domination, and well into the Spanish epoch as well, the tenacious little Post community barely managed to survive the Indian attacks, floods, famines, and epidemics that constantly threatened its very existence. But its position on the Arkansas River, guarding the way to Santa Fe and maintaining the essential Quapaw alliance, rendered it too important strategically for the government, French or Spanish, ever to abandon it for very long. The garrison, as small as it was most of the time, and the fort, though often makeshift and ruinous, guaranteed that a number of hunters and merchants, and even a few farmers, would continue to gather there. When the Post moved for the final time to the high ground at *Écores Rouges* in 1779, there was reason to be optimistic that it would in time acquire a kind of agrarian respectability. Indeed, Captain de Villiers exuded that at his new location he could expect to produce *toutes les douceurs de la vie*—all the pleasures of life. If his goal remained for the most part unattained, that was in large measure due to forces over which he could never have realistically hoped to gain an ascendancy.

What, then, shall we finally say about so extraordinary a place as this? The datum that must come to mind most prominently is the rather low opinion that most eighteenth-century observers had of the Arkansas region. Some of these expressions of distaste can be laid to old-fashioned class bias: Most observers were quite naturally from the upper orders and could not therefore be expected to hold in very high esteem the *coureurs de bois* that they found in the Arkansas and Ouachita valleys. It is true that the social structure at the Post could boast some representatives of all the classes in the province as a whole: Knights, gentry, merchants, farmers, *voyageurs,* hunters, laborers, and slaves were all there in some numbers. But the distribution of the population was undeniably skewed toward the lower end of the social scale, and this would have created a dominant impression of poverty and lawlessness in the minds of the *hauts bourgeois* who traveled through and recorded what they saw. Indeed, their impressions were frequently shared even by the few gentry who resided at the Arkansas.

It is nevertheless true that a great deal of progress was made at the Post in the 1790s under the capable leadership of commandants Vallière, Delinó, and de Vilemont. They all worked to elevate the level of commercial and cultural activity there: They tried to attract population, teachers, priests, farmers, and people with business acumen, and in this effort they had the help of Governors Miró and Carondolet. Indeed, Carondolet, ever the politician, assured de Vilemont in 1796 that his "settlement was going to become very considerable." The population of the Post did in fact triple to about 400 souls, white and black, in the last decade of the eighteenth century. Many of those who immigrated came from the American Illinois country, doubtless fleeing the Northwest Ordinance which had abolished slavery; German families, perhaps from Indiana, also became solid and productive citizens. A few others were even Americans: For instance, in 1796 Governor Carondolet made a huge grant of almost one million acres in Arkansas to Joseph Stilwell, Gabriel Winters, and others, who he hoped would establish a cattle ranch on the prairies to supply the colony with meat. Some of these new settlers built horse-drawn grist mills, a sawmill, and, early in the American period, even a cotton gin. But Arkansas Post nevertheless continued to be among the very smallest settlements in the entire province. A census published in 1807, for instance, purporting to record the population of Louisiana at the time of its cession to the United States, reports 397 persons at the Arkansas in a total for the province that approached 50,000. Only Galveztown, at 247 souls, was smaller.[1]

Though the reasons for the inability of the Spanish government to attract settlers to the Arkansas are complex, chief among them had to be the dangerousness of the place. The Osages were especially bellicose, and although a sporadic trade was carried on with them, their savage attacks on the hunters, though these were usually well upriver, must have given the Arkansas an unenviable reputation. We have it on good authority that even at and near the Post wandering Indian bands, probably Chickasaws and Choctaws driven by the expanding American frontier across the Mississippi to hunt, frequently stole horses and even crops. Consequently, as Victor Collot noted, the population was "generally poor and miserable."[2]

While the poverty of the Arkansas region may be directly laid to marauding Indians, it was, at bottom, the Spanish commercial policy of not allowing Arkansas denizens to compete with St. Louis merchants that caused much of the violence there. Not all of the Osages were content with this arrangement; they viewed the refusal to deal as a kind of embargo or quarantine, and they ransacked Arkansas hunting camps in retaliation. Spanish commercial policy may be far from excusing the Osages, but the Spanish government surely knew the views of the Osages on this point. Yet, for most of the eighteenth century, colonial officials bowed to pressure from the St. Louis mercantile establishment and the Arkansas hunters became expendable, their deaths, injuries, and loss of property mere costs attendant on maintaining an oligopoly. It was here that class bias is perhaps most apparent: The hunters of Arkansas were simply "scum" whose interests did not bear consulting. De Villiers's memorable rhetorical question—"Must commerce be cemented with the blood of innocents?"—was answered with a silence beyond the reach and power of words. The hunters, as a social matter, were much condescended to by the upper classes, and it is likely that Don Carlos de Gran Pré, speaking of the Ouachita Post, expressed the prevailing opinion of them: "Having observed the ruinous passion of a part of the habitants for the hunt," he said, "the absence of 65 of them who would not return until March or April of next year explains the reason that lands so anciently settled are still in standing timber, with hardly any buildings: . . . they are in general raised in indolence [and] in the carelessness of their mothers and fathers."[3] Their bad reputation even extended to doubting their loyalty to the government. In 1792 Carondolet, fearing an American invasion, feared, too, that the hunters of the colony, including those of Arkansas and Ouachita, might well join the enemy. "They are a hardy people who live only on maize," he said, and, moreover, they were "all people who have nothing to lose."[4]

A noticeable improvement in the building methods and the administration of the law at the Post did occur during the 1790s. A decade earlier, de Villiers, perhaps partly moved by a cynicism that his financial woes had created, shrugged off due process as "pettifogging" unsuited for miserable places like the Post of Arkansas. But, when he wanted to, he could do quite a professional job of managing litigation; and Ignacio Delinó, one of his successors, was punctilious in his observance of the rules of legal procedure. Still, there was always a major obstacle in the way of achieving an even-handed legal system at the Post, for the commandants were engaged in trade in competition with the merchant-capitalists there, and this must surely have often led to a conflict of interests. This conflict would have created an invitation to corruption that not every commandant could have resisted, and in any event it must have given the appearance of partiality in many cases. The Spanish no doubt saved a lot of money operating the forest posts of Louisiana in this way, but the costs in terms of popular confidence in government must have been large.

Stable settlers, persons with an attachment to making a serious settlement of their village, would have frequently desired the presence of the civilizing influence of the church. In the last decade of the eighteenth century, Fathers Flavien, Gibault, and Janin did manage to effect a Christianizing presence for about five years all told; but the little parish of St. Stephen failed late in 1799, and it never revived. This loss could have done little to encourage immigration. Nor did the gentry who sojourned at the Post contribute positively to its reputation. In 1797, after little Victoire Delinó de Chalmette had moved with her family from Arkansas to New Orleans, Joseph de Pontalba confided that she was "very pretty and gay" with "a natural wit and great sprightliness"; but, he added, her mother "congratulates herself upon getting back from the Post so that she can give [her daughters] what teachers we have here for music and dancing."[5]

On March 23, 1804, Lt. James B. Many of the American army, bearing a commission from the colonial prefect Pierre Laussat to act for the French Republic, received the dilapidated Fort St. Estevan from Capt. Francisco Caso y Luengo who commanded there for Spain. After the manner of the civil law, the parties to the transaction had each chosen two Post merchants to value the trifles transferred: Joseph Bougy and Jean-Baptiste Desruisseaux performed this duty for

Figure 38. Victoire Delinó de Chalmette.
(*Courtesy of Mrs. Marie Reinecke, New Orleans.*)

His Catholic Majesty; François Vaugine and Pierre Lefevre acted on behalf of Napoleon's republic. After examining the buildings and sentry-boxes, and conferring briefly with each other, the appraisers reckoned that the property of the Spanish king at his Louisiana post of *Los Arcos* was worth no more than 631 dollars—a small enough sum for five generations of effort. The imagist Arkansas poet John Gould Fletcher has quite rightly invented a drama for this portentous day: "The fierce tricolour snapped and vividly flared from the jackstaff," he wrote; and it remained there overnight, until, at dawn, "the star-flown flag that the lilies had once come to aid, rose in the air, storming westward."[6] Though events like these indeed occurred on the days that sovereignty changed hands at St. Louis and Natchitoches,[7] no record that has survived allows us to relate what actually happened at the *Poste aux Arcs* on that gray March day. We cannot even say who was there: The appraisers, all merchants, may have been virtually the only white male civilians at the village, for the hunters sometimes did not come back from upriver until April. Perhaps a dozen soldiers on each side were present, and curious house servants and field hands, those who were not indifferent or cynical, may have paused briefly to wonder about the meaning, if any, of it all. Perhaps, too, as at Ouachita Post,[8] there was no ceremony whatever: The people of Arkansas Post had never been much for pomp and politics.

The thoughts of the principal participants do not, however, require much effort to divine, even at a distance of almost two centuries. No doubt Many and Caso y Luengo were cordial enough, the one to the other, at least in a formal way; but their differences must have seemed to them nearly as large as those revealed more than 130 years before, when the baroque French cleric Jacques Marquette had gazed unsympathetically on a Quapaw shaman, and the uncompromising eyes of the stone age had stared back. It may be that some of those who passed by that day—hunter, widow, slave, Indian, merchant—had harbored a patriotic or sentimental thought for the country that had abandoned them to Spain 40 years before and had just recently and narrowly missed making amends. If such there were, they must have passed at least some few uncomforted moments with a little secret, and a lot of apprehension, in their hearts.

APPENDIX I

JUDGES OF THE ARKANSAS, 1686–1804[1]

I. FRENCH DOMINATION

1.	1686–1699	Henri de Tonty[2]
2.	August 1721 to March 1722	Jean-Baptiste Ménard, Martin Merrick, and Labro[3]
3.	March 1722 to 1726	Bertrand Dufresne, Sieur du Demaine[4]
4.	1726 to 1731	Unknown

[Note: From 20 September 1721 to March 1725, Lieutenant La Boulaye was commandant of the French garrison at Arkansas. It is not clear what part, if any, he played in the resolution of civil disputes. In 1731 civil and military authority were probably combined in the commandant of the garrison.]

5.	Late in 1731 to 1734	First Ensign Pierre de Coulange
6.	1734	First Ensign Jean Ste. Thérèse de Langloiserie
7.	1734–1739	Lieutenant Joseph Louis Boucher de Grandpré
8.	1739 to Autumn 1748	Lieutenant Jean-François Tisserant de Montcharvaux
9.	Autumn 1748 to 1751	First Ensign Louis-Xavier-Martin Delinó de Chalmette
10.	1751 to August 1753	Lieutenant Paul Augustin le Pelletier de La Houssaye
11.	August 1753 to 1757	Captain Charles Marie de Reggio
12.	1757 to 1763	Captain de Gamon de La Rochette
13.	1763 (temporary)	First Ensign de Brichet
14.	27 September 1763 to Spring 1764	Captain Pierre Marie Caberet de Trépi
15.	Spring 1764 to 1766	Ensign Le Gros de Grandcour

II. SPANISH DOMINATION

1. 1766 to February 1768	Ensign Le Gros de Grandcour
2. February 1768 to 13 December 1769	Captain Alexandre de Clouet
3. 13 December 1769 to 10 December 1770	Captain François Demasellière
4. 10 December 1770 to 29 April 1771	Lieutenant Josef Orieta
5. 29 April 1771 to 18 April 1774	Captain Fernando de Leyba
6. 18 April 1774 to 16 June 1776	Captain Josef Orieta
7. 16 June 1776 to 7 September 1776	Sergeant Garcia (*ad interim*)
8. 7 September 1776 to 19 June 1782	Captain Balthazar de Villiers
9. 19 June 1782 to 7 January 1783	Lieutenant Luis de Villars
10. 7 January 1783 to March 1787	Captain Jacobo Dubreuil Saint-Cyr
11. March 1787 to July 1790	Captain Josef Bernard Valliére d'Hauterive
12. July 1790 to 11 July 1794	Captain Juan Ignacio Delinó de Chalmette
13. 11 July 1794 to Summer 1802	Captain Carlos Melchior de Vilemont
14. Summer 1802 to 23 March 1804	Captain Francisco Caso y Luengo

APPENDIX II

POPULATION OF THE ARKANSAS, 1686–1798

(Numbers above bars refer to notes.)

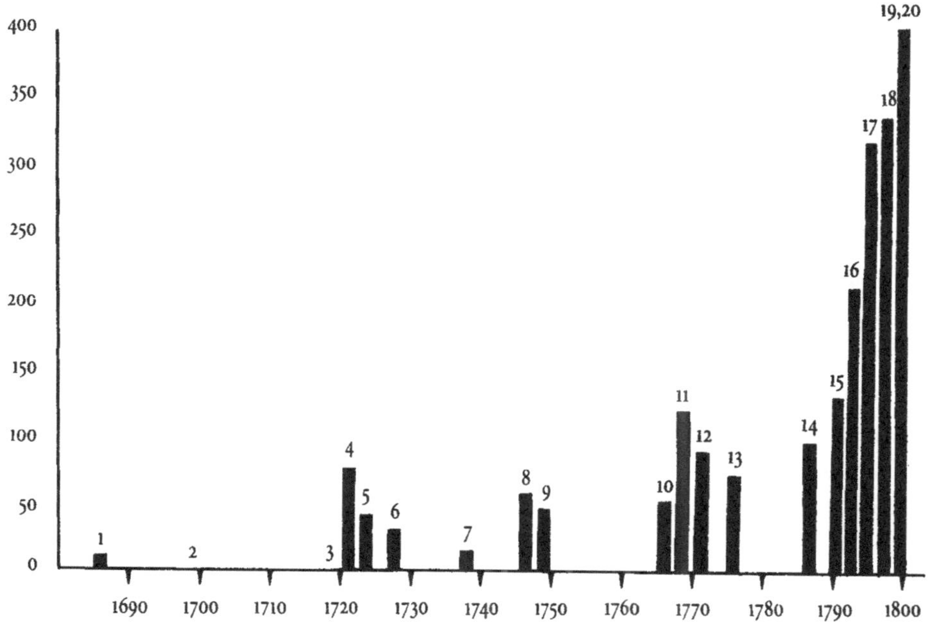

1. **1686.** Six Frenchmen first occupied Tonty's post in 1686; only two of them were left when Joutel visited there in 1687. Faye, "The Arkansas Post of Louisiana: French Domination," 26 *LHQ* 633 at 635 (1943).
2. **1699.** Tonty's post was abandoned by 1699. *See* 18 *Collections of the Wisconsin Historical Society* 427, n.37 (1908); 1 M. Giraud, *History of French Louisiana* 8 (J. Lambert trans., 1974).
3. **1721.** There were no French settlers in Arkansas in 1721 before the arrival of Law's colonists in August of that year. *See* J. Delanglez, *The French Jesuits in Lower Louisiana* 434 (1935).

4. **1721.** There were about eighty Frenchmen in the party which landed at the Arkansas in August of 1721. ANC, G[1], 464.
5. **18 February 1723.** Forty-one whites and six slaves occupied the Arkansas at this time. They were divided into two groups: Fifteen whites and six slaves at Law's concession; twenty-six whites (including four bondsmen) two leagues up the river where the troops were. *Les Arkansas du 18. Fever 1724. Recensement.*, Louisiana History Center, Louisiana State Museum, New Orleans; 4 M. Giraud, *Histoire de la Louisiane Française* 274 (1974). The version of this census appearing in C. Maduell, *The Census Tables for the French Colony of Louisiana from 1688 through 1732* at 30 (1972) is misleading and contains erroneous information. A census of 1 January 1726 reported only fifteen *habitants*, but this was probably just at Law's concession proper. The census included Sieur Dufresne and one Indian slave. *Recencement, Les Arkansas, sur la droitte en descendant, Jan. 1, 1726,* Louisiana History Center, Louisiana State Museum, New Orleans.
6. **1727.** In this year Father du Poisson estimated the European population at the Arkansas at thirty. J. Delanglez, *supra* note 3 at 436.
7. **1739.** Governor Bienville writes in this year that "our fort of the Arkansas is falling into ruins; there are only a missionary and three *habitans* there who do nothing." *See* "Journal of Father Vitry of the Society of Jesus, Army Chaplain during the War against the Chickasaw,"28 *Mid-America* 30 at 34, n.25 (1941). Assuming that each *habitant* had a family and that the average family size was four, there would have been only twelve white persons resident at the Arkansas.
8. **1746.** In this year there were said to be a dozen male *habitants* and ten black slaves at the Post. Assuming an average family size of four, the total population at this time would have been fifty-eight. *See Mémoire sur l'État de la Colonie de la Louisiane en 1746*, ANC, C^{13A} 30:242 at 249.
9. **1749.** Arkansas Post contained at this time thirty-one whites, fourteen slaves, three horses, twenty-nine bulls and steers, sixty cows, and twenty-nine pigs. *See Resancement General des habitants, voyageurs, femmes, enfans, esclaves, chevaux, beufs, vaches, cochons, etc. de Post des Akansa, 1749.* Vaudreuil Papers, LO 200, Huntington Library, San Marino, California.
10. **22 May 1766.** There were forty whites and ten slaves at the Arkansas at this time according to the census of 22 May 1766. *See* J. Voorhies, *Some Late Eighteenth-Century Louisianians, Census Records of the Colony, 1758-1796* 157 (1973). Capt. Harry

Gordon in October of 1766 said that "the few Banditti of Arkansas don't deserve the name of settlement"; and two months later George Morgan remarked of the Post as he passed through that it contained "about 10 Families in the neighborhood of the Indian Village, which has near 200 Families." *The New Regime, 1765-1767,* 11 *Illinois Historical Collections* 303, 442 (1916).

11. **2 December 1768.** A census taken at this time claimed a population of sixty-eight whites and thirty-one slaves for Arkansas Post *Recensement des habitants, femmes, enfants, et esclaves du Poste des Arkansas,* AGI PC *leg.* 107. A census of 5 January 1770 showed seventy-nine whites; the slave population was not given. *See Estada presente de todo los inhabitantes del puesto de los Arkancas . . . ,* AGI, PC, *leg.* 107.
12. **2 September 1771.** The Louisiana census of this date showed sixty-two whites and sixteen slaves at the Arkansas. 1 L. Kinnaird, *Spain in the Mississippi Valley, 1765-1794* 196 (1949).
13. **1777.** On 3 August 1777, de Villiers reported fifty whites and eleven slaves at Arkansas Post. *See Dénombremant du Poste des Arkansas et de la Nation Sauvage de ce Nom . . . ,* AGI, PC, *leg.* 190.
14. **1788.** The general Louisiana census for this year gave Arkansas a population of seventy-five free persons and forty-four slaves.
15. **1791.** One hundred and fourteen free persons and thirty-seven slaves were reported at the Post for this year. *Rescencement du Poste des Arkansas de l'Anée 1791,* AGI, PC, *leg.* 2365.
16. **1793.** There were 171 free persons and 49 slaves reported at Arkansas this year. *Padron del Puesto de Arkansas,* AGI, PC, *leg.* 123.
17. **1794.** A large jump in population occurred in the year 1794. At the end of that year there were 283 free persons and 53 slaves listed in the census. *See Padron del Puesto de Arkanzas,* AGI, PC, *leg.* 2364.
18. **1796.** Two hundred and eighty-two free persons and forty-two slaves were reported resident at the Post in this year. *See Padron del Puesto de Arkanzas,* AGI, PC, *leg.* 2364.
19. **1797.** According to 2 C. Robin, *Voyages dans l'Intérieur de la Louisiane* 206 (1807), Arkansas Post had a population of 340 whites, 3 free people of color, and 47 slaves in this year.
20. **1798.** The last census surviving from the Spanish period gave Arkansas Post a free population of 337 and a slave population of 56 *See Padron de Puesto de Arkancas,* AGI, PC, *leg.* 2365.

NOTES

CHAPTER I

1. W. Eccles, *The Canadian Frontier, 1534-1760* 85 (rev. ed., 1983).

2. Quoted in *id.* at 104.

3. One close student of this voyage reckons that it ended very near the town of Ratio in Phillips County. *See* J. Delanglez, *Life and Voyages of Louis Joliet (1645-1700)* 117–18 (1940).

4. 2 P. Margry, *Découvertes et établissements des Français dans l'ouest et dans le sud de l'Amérique septentrionale (1614-1754)* 183 (1877).

5. 1 M. Giraud, *Histoire de la Louisiane Française* 8 (1953).

6. A land grant to Jacques Cardinal from Tonty is transcribed and translated in *The French Foundations, 1680-1693* 396 (T. Pease & R. Werner eds., 1934).

7. The French text of these grants is in Delanglez, "Tonti Letters," 21 *Mid-America* 209, 236–37 (1939). Tonty granted the Jesuits about six acres for a chapel and priest's house and about twenty-five hundred acres for agricultural purposes.

8. J. Shea, *Discovery and Exploration of the Mississippi Valley* 219–20 (1852); 3 P. Margry, *supra* note 4 at 442 (1880).

9. W. Eccles, *supra* note 1 at 110–13.

10. *Id.* at 128.

11. Crane, "The Tennessee River and the Road to Carolina: The Beginnings of Exploration and Trade," 3 *Mississippi Valley Hist. Rev.* 3 (1916).

12. *Id.*

13. *Journal* of Pierre-Charles Le Sueur, ANP, Delisles ms. 115x, 9, f.7; *cf.* Father Gravier's account in *Early Voyages up and down the Mississippi* 126–27 (J. Shea ed., 1861).

14. W. Eccles, *supra* note 1 at 131.

15. *Id.* at 8.

16. According to Commandant Orieta, Natchitoches was normally a ten- or eleven-day journey by land from Arkansas Post, but in flood times the trip could take as long as seven weeks. Orieta to Governor, 31 March 1771, AGI, PC, *leg.* 107. In 1803 it was estimated that the Post of Ouachita was a four days' journey by land from Arkansas Post. *Mémoire sur le District de Ouachita dans la Province de la Louisianne par citoyen Paulmier Dannemours,* American Philosophical Society, Philadelphia.

17. In 1769, Pierre-Joseph Favrot was sent to the Illinois with service packets; he

went on horseback with an Indian escort. *See* de Clouet to the General, 19 October 1769, AGI, PC, *leg.* 107; 1 *Favrot Family Papers* 140 (G. Falcon ed., 1988). An American soldier at the Post reported in 1809 that his French sweetheart was going on foot to New Madrid "to partake of the Holy Sacrament . . . 300 miles through the wilderness, God bless her." A. Stewart to Thomas Moulton, 27 February 1809, Missouri Historical Society, St. Louis.

18. In 1797, the commandant advised the Marquis de Maison Rouge, from whom he had bought wheat for the Post, to ship it by water from Poste du Ouachita because of the difficulty of overland travel. Vilemont to Carondelet, 28 August 1797, *VLB* 64.

19. K. Pyeatt, *The Pyeatt Genealogy* 11 (W. Lemke ed., 1955).

20. For a discussion of the various water crafts employed in eighteenth-century Louisiana, *see* N. Surrey, *The Commerce of Louisiana during the French Régime, 1699–1763* 55–81 (1916).

21. La Harpe to Duc de Choiseul, Minister of the Marine, 8 August 1763 (transcript in Little Rock Public Library).

22. The story of Louisiana during the epoch of John Law is admirably told in 3 M. Giraud, *supra* note 5.

23. *See*, for example, F. Hempstead, *A Pictorial History of Arkansas: From Earliest Times to the Year 1890 . . .* 85–86 (1890); 1 F. Hempstead, *Historical Review of Arkansas: Its Commerce, Industry and Modern Affairs* 17–18 (1911); 1 D. Herndon, *Centennial History of Arkansas*, 94 (1922); 1 D. Thomas, *Arkansas and Its People: A History, 1541–1930* 23–24 (1930); 1 D. Herndon, *Annals of Arkansas, 1947 . . .*, 34 (1947).

24. 4 M. Giraud, *supra* note 5 at 248, 273.

25. *See* H. Ashmore, *Arkansas: A Bicentennial History* 7 (1978); C. Williams, *Arkansas, An Illustrated History of the Land of Opportunity* 23–24 (1986).

26. 4 M. Giraud, *supra* note 5 at 199.

27. M. Giraud, *A History of French Louisiana* 49 (J. Lambert trans., 1974).

28. *Fleur de Lys and Calumet, Being the Penicaut Narrative of French Adventure in Louisiana* 241–42 (R. McWilliams trans., 1953).

29. *See* McCann, "Pénigaut and His Chronicle of Early Louisiana," 23 *Mid-America* 288 (1941), where the author demonstrates that Pénigaut's chronicle is riddled with errors and warns strongly against accepting anything that Pénigaut reports without "checking his statements with other available contemporary materials."

30. Pénigaut also wrongly asserts that Louis-Elias Stutheus caused the establishment of Law's colony. Stutheus did not even arrive in Louisiana with the first group of *engagés* bound for the Arkansas Post until early April 1721, and he died on April 12. Jacques Levens succeeded him as director, and it was he who organized the expedition to Arkansas. *See* 4 M. Giraud, *supra* note 5 at 199, 207, 217.

31. *Fleur de Lys and Calumet, supra* note 28 at 242. Father du Poisson, resident at

the Arkansas from 1727 to 1729, wrote that there were only five boats in the convoy that established Law's concession, and this seems much more likely. *See 68 Jesuit Relations and Allied Documents* 259 (R. Thwaites ed., 1900).

32. 4 M. Giraud, *supra* note 5 at 273.

33. 6 P. de Charlevoix, *Journal d'un voyage fait par ordre du roi dans l'Amérique septentrionnale* 164 (1744). In Le Conte, "The Germans in Louisiana in the Eighteenth Century," 8 *La. Hist.* 67, 77 (1967), the author claims that Father Charlevoix asserts that Law's Germans abandoned the Arkansas for English Turn. Charlevoix in fact offers not a word to that effect.

34. Smith, "Exploration of the Arkansas River by Benard de La Harpe, 1721–1722: Extracts from His Journal and Instructions," 10 *AHQ* 340, 349 (1951).

35. *Id.* at 362.

36. Ayer Manuscript 257, Newberry Library, Chicago, Illinois.

37. *Id.* at f. 121.

38. *Id.*

39. Delanglez, "A Louisiana Poet-Historian: Dumont *dit* Montigny," 19 *Mid-America* 31 (1937).

40. *Mémoires historiques sur la Louisiane* (Paris, 1753). This book carries the name of Abbé Le Mascrier on the title page, but this is merely Dumont's fictitious *nom de plume.*

41. P. Pittman, *The Present State of the European Settlements on the Mississippi* 41 (1770). Pittman states: "It was here that the famous Mr. Law had his Concession . . . ; when he failed, the Germans, whom he settled in this country, left it, being too remote. They, on their petition, had lands granted them ten leagues above New Orleans, and which their posterity at present possess." Le Page du Pratz, whose *Histoire de la Louisiane contenant la découverte de ce vaste pays . . .* was published in Paris in 1758, in discussing Law's Arkansas concession, states (on p. 171) that after Law's fall "almost all the Germans settled eight leagues above and to the west of the capital." Du Pratz does not expressly state that the Germans were ever at the Arkansas, though his words can certainly be made to bear that meaning. But even if that is what he meant to indicate, it seems likely that he was merely following Dumont here as he did elsewhere. Dumont's story continued to be repeated in the literature. *See, e.g.,* Champigny, *La Louisiane ensanglantée* vi (1773).

42. N. Mereness, ed., *Travels in the American Colonies* 56 (1916).

43. *Id.*

44. *Id.* at 86. Diron d'Artaguiette's censuses are reproduced in *Arkansas Colonials* 2 (M. Arnold & D. Core eds., 1986).

45. *See* 4 M. Giraud, *supra* note 5 at 248. Nor, so far as the censuses reveal, were

there any Germans among the *engagés* who reached the Arkansas. *See* the censuses cited above in note 44.

46. Personal communication to the author, 5 December 1988. I am much indebted to Professor Giraud for numerous, detailed letters on the subject of Law's Arkansas colony.

47. McCarty to de Vaudreuil, 27 March 1752, in B. Barron, *The Vaudreuil Papers* 118 (1975).

48. In 1766, Aubry and Ulloa stated that this relocation occurred in 1756. AGI, SD, *leg.* 2585. A few years later, de Villiers said that it occurred "about 1756." De Villiers to Gálvez, 3 August 1777, AGI, PC, *leg.* 190.

49. The various locations of the Post are documented in detail in M. Arnold, *Unequal Laws unto a Savage Race* 212–17 (1985) and in Arnold, "The Relocation of Arkansas Post to *Écores Rouges* in 1779," 42 *AHQ* 317 (1983). *See also* T. Hutchins, *An Historical Narrative and Topographical Description of Louisiana and West Florida* 56 (1784) where the author remarks of Arkansas Post that "[t]he inundation of the Mississippi, about three years ago, occasioned the evacuation of the above post, and the establishment of another on the northern bank of the river 36 miles higher up."

50. The name appears as early as 1799 on a map of northern Louisiana and southern Arkansas contained in a letter written by Juan Filhiol, commandant at Poste du Ouachita. The map is reproduced in this book as Figure 6 on page 19. Numerous early nineteenth-century documents attest to this as the French name for Little Rock. *See, e.g.*, Bizzell, "A Report on the Quapaw: The Letters of Governor George Izard to the American Philosophical Society, 1825–1827," 29 *Pulaski County Hist. Rev.* 67 (1981): At page 78 of this article, in a French-Quapaw vocabulary prepared about 1827, the phrase "Petit Rocher" appears, and it is plain that the reference is to Little Rock. *See also* Holweck, "The Arkansas Mission under Rosati," 1 *St. Louis Catholic Hist. Rev.* 243, 244 (1919), where Father Odin, an 1824 visitor, refers to Little Rock as Petit Rocher. For the view that the place was called Petite Roche, *see* Dickinson, "Colonial Arkansas Place Names," 48 *AHQ* 137, 165 (1989) and Mr. Dickinson's letter to the editor in 31 *Pulaski County Hist. Rev.* 17 (1983).

51. For a discussion of the early settlers of Little Rock, some of whom may have established themselves near there as early as the 1760s, *see* Ross, "Squatters' Rights: Some Pulaski County Settlers Prior to 1814," 4 *Pulaski County Hist. Rev.* 17 (1956).

52. *See* Ross, "Cadron: An Early Town That Failed," 16 *AHQ* 3 (1957) for an interesting account of this settlement.

53. For the murder of Petit Jean, *see* G. Din & A. Nasatir, *The Imperial Osages* 43 (1983); 1 *BLC* 25–26. He is described in these sources as a *bohème* (tramp). The legend of Petit Jean, already current in the nineteenth century, transformed this *bohème* into a

young woman who disguised herself as a cabin boy in order to follow her lover from France to Louisiana. For the legend, *see* F. Allsopp, *Arkansia* (n.d.); F. Allsopp, 1 *Folklore of Romantic Arkansas* 193 (1931); M. Turner, *Petit Jean* (1955). Of course, Petit Jean was a common nickname in eighteenth-century Louisiana. For instance, one Jean Chabot *dit* Petit Jean was living in the Illinois country in 1737. *See The Village of Chartres in Colonial Illinois, 1720-1765* 420–21 (M. Brown & L. Dean eds., 1977).

54. "According to tradition, *coureurs de bois* from their fur stations on the Nescatenga, Illinois, Verdigris, and Grand rivers rendezvoused here [Belle Point] before advancing on Post of Arkansas and New Orleans for the annual exchange and frolic." E. Bearss & A. Gibson, *Fort Smith: Little Gibraltar on the Arkansas* 8 (1969).

55. For the founding of Natchitoches, *see* M. Giraud, *supra* note 27 at 366–67; 2 M. Giraud, *supra* note 5 at 181–83 (1958); R. Phares, *Cavalier in the Wilderness* 43–44 (1952).

56. Miroir, Harris, *et al.*, "Bénard de La Harpe and the Nassonite Post," 44 *Bulletin of the Texas Archaeological Society* 113 (1973).

57. *See Natchitoches, 1729-1803: Abstracts of the Catholic Church Registers of the French and Spanish Post of St. Jean Baptiste des Natchitoches in Louisiana* 407 (no. 3410) and 416 (no. 3456) (1977) for references to soldiers "living at the Post of Caddodoche" in 1795.

58. Dickinson, "Don Juan Filhiol at *Écore à Fabri*," 46 *AHQ* 133, 139 (1987); Blaine, "French Efforts to Reach Santa Fe: André Fabry de la Bruyère's Voyage up the Canadian River in 1740–41," 20 *La. Hist.* 133 (1979); Hardin, "Don Juan Filhiol and the Founding of Fort Miro: The Modern Monroe, Louisiana," 20 *LHQ* 463–64 (1937).

59. E. Williams, *Spanish Law, Justice, and the Church in the Colonial Ouachita Valley* 26 (1983).

60. Brothers Francoeur to Demasellière, 17 June 1770, AGI, PC, *leg.* 107.

61. There is an informative account of the White River country and the settlements on it in the early nineteenth century by Samuel Treat in *APLB* 92–102. Almost all of the settlers on the White River were removed by order of General Wilkinson in 1806 because they had no title. *See id.* and F. Cuming, *Sketches of a Tour to the Western Country* 272, 273 (1810).

62. *See* Holmes, "Louisiana in 1795: The Earliest Extant Issue of the *Moniteur de la Louisiane*," 7 *La. Hist.* 133 (1966).

63. Phillips settled there about 1797. *See VLB* 19. A boatman named Joseph Egg deposed in 1835 that in 1804 there was no settlement on the Mississippi at all from the mouth of the St. Francis to the Yazoo River (Vicksburg, Mississippi). *Id.* at 43. As late as 1806, Phillips was evidently the only settler at or near what was frequently called Big Prairie, for in that year Thomas Ashe records that a few miles below the St. Francis "he came to a beautiful prairie . . . ," on which he "found one solitary dwelling, inhabited by

a family who traded with the Indians up the river and occasionally dealt with the boats which descended the Mississippi." There he purchased "some dried venison, and a few fowls, at half a dollar a piece, from the solitary settler at the prairie. . . ." T. Ashe, *Travels in America Performed in 1806* . . . 301–2 (1808). In 1808, Fortescue Cuming noted Phillips's "fine well opened farm . . . where a handsome two-story cabin with a piazza, seemed to promise plenty and comfort." F. Cuming, *supra* note 61 at 270. Evidently quite a number of families had settled near Phillips by about 1810, for it is said that the St. Francis settlement, "formerly considerable," was destroyed by the New Madrid earthquake late in 1811. *See* J. Penick, Jr., *The New Madrid Earthquakes* 65 (rev. ed., 1981), quoting Z. Cramer, *The Navigator* 191 (1814). About ten years later the missionary Thomas Flint stayed with "an opulent family of the name of Phillips" who lived at "the St. Francis settlement." T. Flint, *Recollections of the Last Ten Years* 283 (1826).

64. For the founding of Esperanza, *see* Roper, "Benjamin Fooy and the Spanish Forts of San Fernando and Campo de la Esperanza," 36 *West Tenn. Hist. Soc. Papers* 41 (1982). The later history of this settlement is described in Demuth, "The Burning of Hopefield," 36 *AHQ* 123 (1977).

65. References to these sailors are fairly numerous in the surviving records. *See, e.g.*, Grande to Governor (?), 3 February 1800, AGI, PC, *leg.* 702:771.

66. A list of the twenty grants made at Esperanza in the fall of 1802 is in AGI, PC, *leg.* 138B.

67. For this oft-told tale, *see, e.g.*, J. Davis, *History of Memphis* 163 (1873); J. Shinn, *Pioneers and Makers of Arkansas* 118 (1908). One historian has pointed out that this story is plainly false since Volney never got any closer to Esperanza than Vincennes, Indiana. Roper, *supra* note 64 at 63. Another authority claims that Fooy had projected a colony of Dutchmen for Arkansas. *See* 1 L. Houck, *The Spanish Regime in Missouri* 114n. (1909). But I have seen no hint of any such plan in the hundreds of pages of documents, including many long letters from Fooy himself, that pertain to the settlement and fort at Esperanza.

68. For the surviving Arkansas Post censuses of the 1790s, *see Arkansas Colonials*, *supra* note 44 at 42–91.

69. This is the figure given in H. Brackenridge, *Views of Louisiana* 130 (1814). An estimate of six hundred for the population of Arkansas Post in 1803 "made by a gentleman of great respectability and correct information, residing at Natchez" is too high; indeed, his figure of about ninety thousand for the population of Louisiana at the time of the cession to the United States exaggerates by almost a factor of two the true number. For these figures, *see* 1 *American State Papers, Misc.* 384 (Gales & Seaton eds., 1834).

70. For interesting explanations of the Spanish government's vacillating attitudes toward American immigration into Louisiana, *see* Din, "The Immigration Policy of Governor Esteban Miró in Spanish Louisiana," 78 *Southwestern Hist. Q.* 155 (1969); Din,

"Spain's Immigration Policy in Louisiana and the American Penetration, 1792–1803," 76 *Southwestern Hist. Q.* 255 (1973).

71. M. Savelle, *George Morgan, Colony Builder* 204–26 (1932).

72. M. López-Briones, *Spain in the Mississippi Valley: Spanish Arkansas 1762-1804* 91–92 (Ph.D. diss., Purdue University, 1983).

CHAPTER II

1. For a detailed account of one such move, *see* Arnold, "The Relocation of Arkansas Post to *Écores Rouges* in 1779," 42 *AHQ* 317 (1983). For a documented discussion of the various locations of the Post, *see* M. Arnold, *Unequal Laws unto a Savage Race: European Legal Traditions in Arkansas, 1686–1836* 212 *et seq.* (1985).

2. Delanglez, "Journal of Father Vitry of the Society of Jesus, Army Chaplain during the War against the Chickasaw," 28 *Mid-America* 30 at 34, n.25 (1941).

3. *The New Regime, 1765-1767,* 11 *Illinois Historical Collections* 303 (1916).

4. De Villiers to Gálvez, 11 June 1778, AGI, PC, *leg.* 191. The phrase in French is *"le réduit le plus désagréable de l'univers."*

5. 2 V. Collot, *A Journey in North America* 40 (1826).

6. The most stinging nineteenth-century denunciation of Arkansas Post is contained in T. Nuttall, *A Journal of Travels into the Arkansas Territory during the Year 1819* 83–88 (S. Lottinville ed., 1980). One needs to remember, however, when reading Nuttall that he was an extraordinary cultural imperialist and had a hatred of the French that bordered on the irrational.

7. M. Arnold, *Unequal Laws, supra* note 1.

8. P. Margry, *Relations et mémoires inédits* 24 (1867). This letter, frequently referred to as "Tonty II" and often misattributed to 1694, was used by a literary jobber in 1697 as a partial basis for a book spuriously attributed to Tonty. The letter has been translated many times. *See, e.g.,* T. Falconer, *On the Discovery of the Mississippi* 78 (1844), reprinted in 1 *Collections of the Illinois State Historical Library* 128 (1903). A much better translation is L. Kellogg, *Early Narratives of the Northwest* 286 (1917).

9. J. Shea, *Discovery and Exploration of the Mississippi Valley* 219–20 (1852).

10. 3 P. Margry, *Découvertes et établissements des Français dans l'ouest et dans le sud de l'Amérique septentrionale (1614-1754)* 442 (1880). There is a rather loose translation of this passage in H. Stiles, *Joutel's Journal of La Salle's Last Voyage, 1684-87* 178 (1906).

11. J. Edwards, *Louisiana's Remarkable French Vernacular Architecture* 5–6 (1988).

12. *Id.* at 5.

13. Wilson, "Colonial Fortifications and Military Architecture in the Mississippi Valley," in *The Architecture of Colonial Louisiana* 43 (1987).

14. *See* M. Giraud, *The History of French Louisiana* 8 (J. Lambert trans., 1974).

15. Tonty granted Cardinal "twenty-two square feet in the fort which he constructed there [*dans le fort qui y construit*]." *The French Foundations, 1680-1693, 23 Collections of the Illinois State Historical Library* 396 (T. Pease & R. Werner eds., 1934). Stanley Faye evidently misunderstood the language of this grant, for he opined that Tonty expressed only a future intention to build a fort. Faye, "The Arkansas Post of Louisiana: French Domination," 26 *LHQ* 635, n.6 (1943).

16. In 1765 Capt. Philip Pittman visited Cahokia, Illinois, and he states: "What is called the fort is a small house . . . ; it was formerly enclosed with high pallisades, but these were torn down and burnt." P. Pittman, *The Present State of the European Settlements on the Mississippi* 48 (1770).

17. 2 P. Margry, *supra* note 10 at 181.

18. M. Giraud, *supra* note 14 at 8.

19. For an excellent account of Law's colony on the Arkansas, *see* 4 M. Giraud, *Histoire de la Louisiane Française* 271–75 (1974).

20. 6 P. de Charlevoix, *Journal d'un voyage fait par ordre du roi dans l'Amérique septentrionnale* 164 (1744). I have seen two eighteenth-century English translations of this work. In 2 *Journal of a Voyage to North America Undertaken by Order of the French King* . . . 247 (1761), the phrase *tristes débris* is rendered "melancholy ruins"; and in *Letters to the Dutchess of Lesdiguieres* . . . 307 (1763), the phrase becomes "sad ruins." Perhaps these translators thought that Father Charlevoix was referring to the physical appearance of the buildings at the concession.

21. Bénard de La Harpe, *Journal du voyage de la Louisiane*, BNP, Ms. Fr. 8989, f. 70. The crudeness and makeshift nature of a *cabane*, translated as "hut" here, can be gathered by the following description of one in H. Joutel, *Remarques sur l'ouvrage de Tonty relatif à la Louisiane* (1703), Archives du Service Hydrographique v. 115–19, n.12: "*font avec des perches quils plient les unes contre les autres en forme de dôme et couvrent avec des écores d'arbres.*" ["They make (cabanes) with branches which they bend over on each other in the shape of a dome and cover with the bark from trees."] There is a translation of relevant parts of this journal in Smith, "Exploration of the Arkansas River by Benard de La Harpe, 1721–1722: Extracts from His Journal and Instructions," 10 *AHQ* 339 (1951).

According to the *Journal historique de l'établissement des Français à la Louisiane* 314 (1831), the colonists at Law's concession had cleared four acres of land and had sown them with wheat. An annotated English translation of this work is *The Historical Journal of the Establishment of the French in Louisiana* (J. Cain & V. Koenig trans., G. Conrad ed., 1971). Jean de Beaurain, King's geographer, is sometimes said to be the compiler of this book (*see, e.g.*, 3 M. Giraud, *supra* note 19 at 399), but it has been established beyond cavil that La Harpe wrote it. *See* Wedel, "The Bénard de La Harpe Historiography on French Colonial Louisiana," 13 *La. Studies* (1974).

22. "Journal of Diron Dartaguiette," in *Travels in the American Colonies* 56, 86

(N. Mereness ed., 1916). The census is reproduced in *Arkansas Colonials* 2 (M. Arnold & D. Core eds., 1986).

23. *Mémoires historiques sur la Louisiane 68, 69* (1753). Mr. Samuel D. Dickinson has very kindly suggested to me that *pavillon* might be more properly translated as "tent" in this context. But *pavillon,* when used as a description of officers' quarters, frequently meant a substantial building. *See, e.g.,* AN, Dépôt des Fortifications des Colonies, Louisiana, Item 122c, for a plan, section, and elevation of the *casernes et pavillons* (barracks and pavilions) of Fort Condé at Mobile.

24. Faye, *supra* note 15 at 668, n.34.

25. "Letter from Father du Poisson, Missionary to the Arkansas, to Father———," in 67 *The Jesuit Relations and Allied Documents* 277, 321 (R. Thwaites ed., 1900). In this translation the letter is dated at the Arkansas, 3 December 1727. There is another translation by W. A. Falconer in 4 *Publications of the Ark. Hist. Assoc.* 353 (1917), where the date is given as 9 October 1727.

26. *See* M. Arnold, *Unequal Laws, supra* note 1 at 212–14. In the early nineteenth-century records of Arkansas Post, this lake was known as the "bayou of the Old Fort." *See, e.g., Arkansas County Record Book A,* Arkansas County Courthouse, De Witt, Arkansas, p. 60 for a grant of land *"située au Bayou du vieux fort. . . ."* The "old fort" referred to is the one described in the paragraph that follows in the text. Nuttall refers to the fact that there was once a fort "on the borders of the lagoon near Madame Gordon's," another reference to what is today called Lake Dumond. *See* T. Nuttall, *supra* note 6 at 87. This lake was also called the Bay of Arkansas in early records.

27. The French foot was equal to about 12.8 inches.

28. ANC, C^{13A} 18:84–v. There is a translation of this document in 3 *MPA* 665–66. I have departed from this translation in some particulars. Faye, *supra* note 15 at 674, has misunderstood the phrase *bois sur solles* and has therefore transformed the house and powder magazine into buildings of horizontal logs raised above the ground.

29. *See* J. Edwards, *supra* note 11 at 3, where the author remarks that *poteaux sur solles* construction "was used as early as 1704 in the construction of Fort Louis in Mobile."

30. ANC, C^{13A} 18:85.

31. Faye, *supra* note 15 at 684. *See also* Delanglez, "Journal of Father Vitry," *supra* note 2 at 34, where a 1738 visitor describes Arkansas Post as follows: "The fort is small; a larger one is not needed for the twelve men who are commanded by an officer."

32. Faye, *supra* note 15 at 684.

33. *Id.* at 712. This claim needs investigation since the total cost was 15,500 *livres.*

34. *See Toisé des ouvrages du fort et des bâstiments ou logements qui ont esté faits à neuf, à quinze lieues du fleuve dans la rivière des Akançs, par Mr. Delahoussaye suivant le devis du 17 8bre et le marché du 21 même mois 1751.* [Survey of the works of the fort and

the buildings or lodgings that have been newly constructed at fifteen leagues from the Mississippi River on the River of the Arkansas by Mr. de La Houssaye, according to the specifications of 17 October and the contract of the twenty-first day of the same month, 1751.] This most interesting document is among the documents styled "Fort Papers" at the Missouri Historical Society in St. Louis. It is lengthy (eight large manuscript pages) and written in a most legible hand and reasonably good French. It is extremely detailed, including such items as the number of posts, rafters, and so forth in each building, and, therefore, while there is no plan with it, it would be possible to reconstruct the fort from it to a tolerable degree of accuracy. There is a translation of this document appended to Mattison, "Report on the Historical Investigations of Arkansas Post, Arkansas," unpublished papers, National Park Service, Omaha, Nebraska (1957), but it is not entirely reliable.

The descriptions of the fort and its buildings that follow in the next paragraphs are taken from this manuscript. This document, incidentally, demonstrates that the parties to the building of this fort conformed to eighteenth-century legal customs in ordering their affairs. The *toisé* (survey), *devis* (specifications), and *marché* (contract) referred to in it were all regular steps in the making and execution of construction contracts in eighteenth-century France and Canada. *See generally*, P. Moogk, *Building a House in New France* 89 *et seq.*, 110 (1977).

35. J. Edwards, *supra* note 11 at 7. In the Illinois country, where stone was plentiful, *pierrotage* (rubble stone and clay) served as a nogging material in half-timber houses; indeed, houses entirely made of stone (*pierre sur pierre*) were quite common there. *See* N. Belting, *Kaskaskia under the French Regime* 30, 36–37 (1948). But there were no stones near to hand in the region of the Arkansas occupied by the French in the eighteenth century, so all nogging material was *bousillage* and chimneys and fireplaces were of necessity made of mud and wood. There is, moreover, no evidence of any brick being used for building at the Arkansas Post until the nineteenth century.

36. *See* M. Arnold, *Unequal Laws, supra* note 1 at 214–15.

37. The mistaken omission of a comma caused this misnomer. The caption to a sketch of the remains of this fort published in 1893 says "Old French Fort Desha, Arkansas"; it should have said "Old French Fort, Desha, Arkansas." *See* 10 *Miscellaneous Documents of the House of Representatives for the Second Session of the Fifty-third Congress, 1893–94* 241 (1893). This site is described in McClurkan, "Fort Desha, The Location of Arkansas Post, *ca.* 1735–1750," 6 *Conference on Historic Site Archaeology Papers, 1971* 32 (1972). The author there gives the wrong dates for the occupation of this fort.

38. P. Pittman, *The Present State of the European Settlements on the Mississippi* 40 (1770). This remarkable book is available in three reprint editions: F. Hodder ed., 1906; R. Rea ed., 1973; and J. McDermott ed., 1977. The latter two editions are facsimile

reprints with extensive scholarly introductions. The best edition for students of the Arkansas is Professor McDermott's, because in his introduction he reprints letters and extracts from letters that make it clear that Pittman was, indeed, at Arkansas Post in 1765; and these letters and extracts give more details about the Post and its situation than found their way into the book.

39. Pittman's letter to Gage is set out in P. Pittman, *The Present State of the European Settlements on the Mississippi* liv (J. McDermott ed., 1977).

40. Faye, *supra* note 15 at 681, n.46.

41. M. Arnold, *Unequal Laws, supra* note 1 at 116–17. Father Carette had only a one-room building at the new Post which served both as his house and chapel. *See id.* at 117–18.

42. Pittman's measurements, moreover, correspond almost exactly with those appearing in the field notes of Edward Palmer, an archaeologist who visited the site of this fort in 1883. Palmer's notes say that "on the Arkansas River in Desha County there are the outlines of an old fortification; . . . there are three-quarters of an acre within its boundary." Palmer, "Arkansas Mounds," 4 *Publications of the Ark. Hist. Assoc.* 401 (1917). Three-fourths of an acre is not a bad approximation of an arpent; indeed, if Pittman meant that the fort was 180 *English* feet square, as he presumably did, then the discrepancy between Pittman and Palmer disappears almost entirely. When, however, Palmer's observations were published by Dr. Cyrus Thomas, the fort somehow became a "square, measuring 150 yards from side to side." *See Miscellaneous Documents, supra* note 37 at 328. A square of 150 yards is huge: It contains almost five acres. Someone, in calculating the sides of a square containing three-fourths of an acre, has simply made a mistake.

43. ANC, C^{13A} 40:349–50, dated 24 June 1766. The descriptions of the repairs that follow are taken from this document.

44. Professor Din doubted that the *habitants* would have moved downriver before the fort was completed. *See* Din, "The Spanish Fort on the Arkansas," 42 *AHQ* 271, 272 n.1 (1983). But the document cited in note 43, *supra,* makes it clear that they did. Indeed, when the settlement was relocated in 1779, the *habitants* again moved before a fort was provided. *See* Arnold, "Relocation of Arkansas Post," *supra* note 1 at 324.

45. Alexandre de Batz, an engineer-architect in the employ of the colonial French government, was at the Arkansas in the summer of 1757 supervising the building of the fort there, and he had "plans and papers" pertaining to it, for on 14 August 1757, he was ordered to turn them over to the Sieur de Champigny who was to replace him. *See* Wilson, "Louisiana Drawings by Alexandre De Batz," in *The Architecture of Colonial Louisiana* 261 at 271–72 (1987). I have not been able to locate these drawings.

46. *See, e.g.,* the comments of de Villiers concerning the flooding of even the most elevated houses at the Post in Arnold, "Relocation of Arkansas Post," *supra* note 1 at 324.

47. Inventory, AGI, PC, *leg.* 107.

48. J. Edwards, *supra* note 11 at 6. Remote African origins for the gallery are posited in Edwards, "The Complex Origins of the American Domestic Piazza-Veranda-Gallery," 21 *Material Culture* 3 (1990).

49. *Id.*

50. *See* de Villiers's complaints about his population in Arnold, "Relocation of Arkansas Post," *supra* note 1 *passim.*

51. The full story is told in *id.*

52. The map is reproduced here as Figure 5.

53. The new fort, called Fort St. Esteban (St. Stephen), was not completed until 1791. In the meantime, "Fort Charles III consisted largely of ruins and most of the soldiers were then quartered outside the fort." Din *supra* note 44 at 282. The Spanish government finally approved a payment to the *habitants* for this work, but only begrudgingly, and with the warning that in the future the residents would have to bear all expenses for maintaining the fort, as was the case with Poste du Ouachita. AGI, SD, *leg.* 2556, No. 43.

54. 2 V. Collot, *supra* note 5 at 40. Governor Carondolet did not think much more highly of his Arkansas fort than Collot did, for in 1793 he dismissed it as only a "circle of stakes." *See* Din, *supra* note 44 at 287.

55. The inventory is translated in 2 *The Spanish Regime in Missouri* 341–42 (L. Houck ed., 1909). The assertion in Din, *supra* note 44 at 291, that "[i]n the last years of Spanish Louisiana, Fort St. Stephen seems to have been kept in a good state of repair" does not find support in the sources. Indeed, Captain Caso y Luengo had already complained in 1802 that the "habitation or house of the commandant is such that no one could occupy it except one who had no other place to put himself, because of its lack of comfort, the threat of ruin, and its leaky roof." The kitchen and storehouse were in worse shape, he said; the one entirely useless, the other only a shell. The best building was the barracks and jail. AGI, SD, *leg.* 2619, No. 163. Juan Perchet, a Spanish engineer, had some repairs to Fort San Esteban in 1796, but the buildings that Caso described were built in 1797 under the direction of Francisco Rivas, superintendent of works for Louisiana, and by order of Governor Carondolet. Jean-Baptiste Desruisseaux acted as contractor for the project, which involved transporting timber through the wilderness by water or ox-drawn carts (*carretas*). *VLB* 59, 60, 61–62, 66, 81, 83; AGI, SD, *leg.* 2614, No. 70.

56. *See* J. Edwards, *supra* note 11 at 23 (fig. 47, floor plans M2b and M2j).

57. This plan was probably made by John B. Treat, factor at the Arkansas Post Trading House.

58. J. Edwards, *supra* note 11 at 2.

59. *See* the 1791–1798 censuses in *Arkansas Colonials, supra* note 22 at 46–91.

60. A. Nasatir, *Spanish War Vessels on the Mississippi* 165–66 (1968). The village proper was evidently quite compact, for in 1805 Samuel Treat decided not to rent a house there, though it was cheaper than the one he did rent, because it was "surrounded with many others, and very combustible buildings, without adjoining ground. . . ." Treat instead chose a house closer to the fort which had a garden and pasture. *APLB* 12.

61. *See* Core, "Colombage," 21 *GPHSB* 34 (1978). The original record cited there is in French, and the portion quoted in the text above reads: "*une maison à colombage de la longueur de trente pieds sur vingt de largeur evec galleries tout en tour, le tout couvert en bardeaux.*" Likewise, the 1810 inventory of Pierre Lefevre, a prominent Post resident, records that he owned "*une maison principale de trente cinq pieds de long sur vingt deux de largeur, avec galleries, le tout couvert en bardeaux*" (a main house thirty-five feet long by twenty-two feet wide, with galleries, the whole covered with shingles).

62. W. Pope, *Early Days in Arkansas* 67 (1895).

63. *The Western Journals of Washington Irving* 169 (J. McDermott ed., 1944).

64. *Id.* at 177–78.

65. *Id.* at 178.

66. W. Halliburton, *A Topographical Description and History of Arkansas County, Arkansas from 1541 to 1875* 105 (1901?).

67. W. Pope, *supra* note 62 at 35. This hotel is probably the one called, variously, the Arkansas Hotel or the Tavern of Messrs. Long & Scantland. It was on lot sixty-two of the ill-fated Town (not Post) of Arkansas. On 8 January 1821, a deed recited that there was situated on that lot a "house called the garrison house." *See* E. Bearss & L. Brown, *Structural History, Post of Arkansas, 1804-1863 and Civil War Troop Movement Maps, January, 1863* 158 (1971). This seems to imply that the hotel was once one of the buildings of Fort San Esteban, perhaps the commandant's house refurbished. Further evidence that this hotel was at one time a building of the old fort is provided by John James Audubon, the great ornithologist, who visited the Post in 1820. He applied at Montgomery's tavern for lodging, and Mrs. Montgomery showed him to his quarters in "a large Building that formerly perhaps saw the great Councils of Spanish Dons." D. Peattie, *Audubon's America* 145–46 (1940). This would seem to indicate that the building where Audubon lodged himself was visibly of Louisiana colonial architecture and had the look of a government building.

68. There is a floor plan similar to that described above in J. Edwards, *supra* note 11 at 23 (fig. 47, floor plan M3i2).

69. Scull Papers, Arkansas History Commission, Little Rock.

70. W. Pope, *supra* note 62 at 62.

71. For the date of Montgomery's removal, *see* E. Bearss, *supra* note 67 at 3.

72. W. Halliburton, *supra* note 66 at 105. *See also id.* at 150, where the author says

that "after having destroyed the fortifications [at the Post] and all the houses in the village of Arkansas Post the whole [Union] Army departed down the River."

73. On 20 November 1819, the first number of the *Arkansas Gazette,* seeking to acquaint its readers with the Post of Arkansas, ran an article signed *"A Citizen,"* which states: "There are at present but few buildings [at the Post], and those principally in the French style. . . ." Similarly, "Philolaos" in a letter in the 2 December 1820 edition of the *Arkansas Gazette* said that the Post "contains about thirty houses, chiefly built in the French style. . . ." William Woodruff, who moved to the Post in 1819 to establish the *Arkansas Gazette,* asserted in 1876 that when he arrived there the houses were built "with rived planks set on end." Woodruff to Trimble, Trimble Papers, Arkansas History Commission, Little Rock.

74. For an excellent account of Ste. Genevieve in the eighteenth century, *see* C. Ekberg, *Colonial Ste. Genevieve* (1985). There is a lucid discussion of colonial building techniques and house styles in this work at 284–98, 440–51, with pictures of surviving colonial houses in Ste. Genevieve. These have survived at Ste. Genevieve to a greater extent than in any other place in upper Louisiana. *See also* Porterfield, "Ste. Genevieve, Missouri," in *Frenchmen and French Ways in the Mississippi Valley* 141 (J. McDermott ed., 1969), which contains a large number of pictures of the French houses of Ste. Genevieve, mostly before restoration.

75. For St. Louis colonial architecture, *see* Peterson, "The Houses of French St. Louis," in *The French in the Mississippi Valley* 17 (J. McDermott ed., 1965), and C. Peterson, *Colonial St. Louis: Building a Creole Capital* (1949).

76. The collected essays of Samuel Wilson, Jr., are available in *The Architecture of Colonial Louisiana* (1987). These excellent essays, written over a period of forty years, are a treasure trove of information on Louisiana architectural history and especially of building in New Orleans. For the galleried houses of New Orleans, *see* P. Pittman, *supra* note 39 at 11; P. Laussat, *Memoirs of My Life* 20 (A. Pastwa & R. Bush trans. & eds., 1978).

77. *See* M. Arnold, *Unequal Laws, supra* note 1 at 59–61, 97–98, 119.

78. Delanglez, *supra* note 2 at 34–35.

79. 2 G. Featherstonhaugh, *Excursions through the Slave States* 234 (1844). For more about the village of Carondolet, *see* W. Foley, *The Genesis of Missouri: From Wilderness Outpost to Statehood* 85–86 (1989).

80. 2 G. Featherstonhaugh, *supra* note 79 at 260–61. *Cf.* N. Finiels, *An Account of Upper Louisiana* 55–56 (C. Eckberg & W. Foley eds., 1989): "The population of Carondolet is composed of [French] Canadians and Creoles from Illinois. Paltry wooden cabins serve as their dwellings. In general they are poor. . . ."

81. For Ménard's will, *see* M. Arnold, *Unequal Laws, supra* note 1 at 109, where Ménard declares himself the owner of such a house. In 1773, Ménard already had a house

measuring fifteen by forty-two feet at Arkansas Post, for in that year he mortgaged it to the New Orleans merchant Oliver Pollock. Acts of Andrés Almonester y Roxas, p. 45, 4 March 1773, New Orleans Notarial Archives.

82. For this census, *see Arkansas Colonials, supra* note 22 at 42–45.

83. *See* the contract cited *supra* note 69.

84. For Governor Miller's letter to his wife, dated 20 March 1820, *see A Documentary History of Arkansas* 17 (C. Williams *et al.* eds., 1984). In 1875, Judge Daniel T. Witter wrote that when he arrived at the Post in 1819, he found W. E. Woodruff, publisher of the *Arkansas Gazette,* occupying "a small French built house of two rooms, the larger of which was probably eighteen or twenty feet square." One room Woodruff used as an office and bedroom, the other for the printing press. Witter to Trimble, Trimble Papers, Arkansas History Commission, Little Rock. This sounds like a simple *salle* and *chambre* arrangement. *See also* 2 G. Featherstonhaugh, *supra* note 79 at 229 (1844), where the author describes Antoine Barraque's family dwelling at New Gascony as ". . . a house containing two large and very comfortable rooms, neatly and sufficiently furnished."

85. *See* Witter to Trimble, *supra* note 84. According, however, to William E. Woodruff, publisher of the *Gazette,* the house in which he first established his newspaper was built of horizontal logs in the American style. For a sketch which Woodruff said gave a fair representation of this house, *see* M. Ross, *Arkansas Gazette: The Early Years 1819-1866* 8 (1969).

86. *APLB* 259.

87. 2 *The Spanish Regime in Missouri* 341–42 (L. Houck ed., 1909).

88. AGI, SD, *leg.* 2616, No. 295 (1799).

89. *Arkansas County Record Book A* 131, Arkansas County Courthouse, De Witt, Arkansas. The kitchen, however, may not have had a well. In 1805, Samuel Treat reported that there were so many salt springs around the Post that "at this Post the waters are not to be drunk, which makes it very inconvenient to the inhabitants, who entirely depend on the river for culinary and every other use: not from preference, but they being too indolent to sink wells, one of which alone is in [the] whole town, although those residents from the bank being provided are fully supplied at all seasons with excellent water, at the depth of from thirty to forty feet." *APLB* 28. Joseph Bougy dug a well for the fort in 1794, but in 1802 Captain Caso y Luengo noted "the vestiges of a well . . . built in the time of my predecessor, but worthless because it was badly built." The soldiers therefore had to haul water from the river about one hundred yards away. *VLB* 51, 52; AGI, SD, *leg.* 2619, No. 163.

90. C. Ekberg, *supra* note 74 at 292.

91. F. Billon, *Annals of St. Louis.* Another authority asserts that eighteenth-century St. Louis houses ranged "from twenty by twenty feet to twenty by forty feet in floor

area." Smelser, "Housing in Creole St. Louis, 1764–1821: An Example of Cultural Change," 2 *LHQ* 337 (1938).

92. I have arrived at this figure by averaging the dimensions of individual houses that are reported in N. Belting, *supra* note 35 at 33–37.

93. For whitewashing in eighteenth-century St. Louis and Kaskaskia, *see* C. Peterson, *supra* note 75 at 23 and N. Belting, *supra* note 35 at 31.

94. A. Stoddard, *Sketches, Historical and Descriptive of Louisiana* 328 (1812).

95. Spanish Judicial Records, 8 April 1771, Louisiana State Museum, New Orleans. Synopsis in 8 *LHQ* 314 (1925).

96. For a discussion of Louisiana armoires, *see* Van Ravensway, "The Creole Arts and Crafts of Upper Louisiana," 12 *Bulletin of the Missouri Historical Society* 213, 226–27 (1956); J. Poesch, *Early Furniture of Louisiana* 2–3 (1971); J. Poesch, *The Art of the Old South* 104–7 (1983).

97. Van Ravensway, *supra* note 96 at 232.

98. *Id.* at 228.

99. Core, "First Bankruptcy in Arkansas County Records," 16 *GPHSB* 8, 9–10 (1973).

100. 68 *Jesuit Relations and Allied Documents* 323 (R. Thwaites ed., 1900).

101. T. Nuttall, *supra* note 6 at 88. It is impossible to believe, as Nuttall at least intimates, that there were no glass windows at all at the Post. In fact, Samuel Treat reported in 1810 that most of the windows in his house were "glazed with blinds," by which he probably meant casement windows. *See APLB* 259. Casement windows were common in Kaskaskia by the middle of the eighteenth century. *See* N. Belting, *supra* note 35 at 31.

102. D. Peattie, *supra* note 65 at 147.

103. W. Halliburton, *supra* note 66 at 120.

CHAPTER III

1. Core, "Arkansas through the Looking Glass of 1743 Documents," 22 *GPHSB* 16 at 22 (1979).

2. 1 *The Favrot Family Papers: A Documentary Chronicle of Early Louisiana* 80 (G. Falcon ed., 1988).

3. *Id.* at 136.

4. *Id.* at 135.

5. De Clouet to Commandant, 20 September 1769, AGI, PC, *leg.* 107; Inhabitants of the Arkansas Post to de Clouet, AGI, PC, *leg.* 107.

6. Dart, "A Louisiana Indigo Plantation on Bayou Teche," 9 *LHQ* 565, 574, 579 (1926).

7. ANC, C[13A] 40:328–29.

8. De Villiers to Gálvez, 11 June 1778, AGI, PC, *leg.* 191.

9. 2 *Favrot Papers, supra* note 2 at 127, 129, 243.

10. B. Roselli, *Vigo: A Forgotten Builder of the American Republic* 54–55 (1933) erroneously states that Vigo and Leyba met in St. Louis and became partners. In fact, they were acquainted at least as early as 1774 at the Arkansas.

11. For Vigo's business affairs at the Arkansas, *see* Unzaga to Orieta, 9 August 1774, AGI, PC, *leg.* 107; Orieta to Unzaga, 17 October 1774, *id.*; *id.* to *id.*, 14 December 1774, *id.*; Governor to Orieta, 23 February 1775, *id.*

12. J. Holmes, *Honor and Fidelity* 77 (1965); G. King, *Creole Families of New Orleans* 320 (1921). According to Pontalba, in 1795 Delinó's fortune amounted to forty thousand dollars. G. King, *supra* at 94.

13. Core, "André Fagot," 17 *GPHSB* 3 (1974).

14. *See, e.g.*, the militia lists in *Arkansas Colonials, 1686-1804* 25–38 (M. Arnold & D. Core eds., 1985).

15. Spanish Judicial Records, 14 February 1793, Louisiana State Museum, New Orleans.

16. *Arkansas Colonials, supra* note 14 at 42.

17. *Id.* at 77.

18. *Id.* at 47.

19. T. Nuttall, *A Journal of Travels into the Arkansa Territory* 72 (1821).

20. *See* p. 52, *supra*, for a list of these furnishings.

21. Journal of La Harpe, BNP, Ms. Fr. 8989, ff. 78–79.

22. Quoted in Delanglez, "Journal of Father Vitry of the Society of Jesus, Army Chaplain during the War against the Chickasaw," 28 *Mid-America* 30 at 34, n.25 (1941).

23. *See* Core, *supra* note 1 at 22.

24. De Clouet to the Governor, 6 October 1768, AGI, PC, *leg.* 107.

25. *Id.*

26. ANC, C[13A] 4:119.

27. N. Belting, *Kaskaskia under the French Regime* 17 (1948).

28. *Id.* at 54.

29. N. Surrey, *The Commerce of Louisiana during the French Régime, 1699-1763* 291 (1916); N. Belting, *supra* note 27 at 54.

30. In 1772, François Ménard of Arkansas Post delivered three thousand pounds of flour from the Illinois country to the Post on board his barge, and Daniel Fagot of Ste. Genevieve dropped off two thousand pounds from his *batteau* called *San Daniel* on its way downriver. 1 L. Houck, *The Spanish Regime in Missouri* 55, 57 (1909). François Ménard evidently made the trip to Illinois for flour on a regular basis. *See*

C. Lopez-Briones, *Spain in the Mississippi Valley: Spanish Arkansas, 1762–1804* 174 (Ph.D. diss., Purdue University, 1983). In 1773, François Vallé of Ste. Genevieve sent ten thousand pounds of flour to Arkansas Post aboard his *batteau* called *San Francisco*. L. Houck, *supra* at 87, 89. In 1774, Louis Bolduc of Ste. Genevieve had his barge drop three hundred pounds of flour off at Arkansas Post on the way to New Orleans, and one Esteban Barre delivered forty-five hundred pounds on his *batteau* named *Principe Negro* (Black Prince). *Id.* at 93, 95.

31. Dubreuil to Miró, 26 March 1783, AGI, PC, *leg.* 107.

32. Dubreuil to Miró, 9 June 1783, AGI, PC *leg.* 107. *See also id.* to *id.*, 26 August 1783, AGI, PC, *leg.* 107.

33. *Id.* to *id.*, 26 August 1783, AGI, PC, *leg.* 107; *id.* to *id.*, 2 September 1784, AGI, PC, *leg.* 107.

34. Vallière to Miró, 14 January 1789, AGI, PC, *leg.* 15A:63–64.

35. *Arkansas Colonials, supra* note 14 at 42–46.

36. 2 V. Collot, *A Journey in North America* 40 (1826).

37. *See* C. Robin, *Voyage to Louisiana* 139 (S. Landry trans., 1956).

38. *Arkansas Colonials, supra* note 14 at 47–52.

39. *Id.* at 53–64.

40. *Id.* at 65–76.

41. *Id.* at 77–91.

42. John B. Treat to William Davy, 6 October 1805, *APLB* 23.

43. 1 L. Houck, *supra* note 30 at 326.

44. John B. Treat to the Hon. Henry Dearborn, 27 March 1806, *APLB* 57.

45. John B. Treat to William Davy, 11 February 1806, *id.* at 53.

46. *Resancement General des habitants, voyageurs, femmes, enfans, esclaves, chevaux, beufs, vaches, cochons, etc. de poste des Akansa, 1749.* Vaudreuil Papers, LO 100, Huntington Library, San Marino, California.

47. ANC, G[1], 464.

48. *Mémoire sur l'état de la colonie de la Louisiane en 1746*, ANC, C[13A] 30:242, 249.

49. P. Pittman, *The Present State of the European Settlements on the Mississippi* 40 (1770).

50. De Villiers to Gálvez, 3 August 1777, AGI, PC, *leg.* 190.

51. *Id.* to *id.*, 2 March 1779, AGI, PC, *leg.* 192.

52. *VLB* 55.

53. Leyba to Governor, 22 November 1771, AGI, PC, *leg.* 107.

54. *Probate Record Book AA* 14–15, Arkansas County Courthouse, De Witt, Arkansas. Lefevre's will was executed on 13 October 1793.

55. Natchitoches, Louisiana Archives, 11 May 1770.

56. Ordinances in AGI, PC, *leg.* 191 (1778) and in de Vilemont to Gayoso, 15 November 1798, AGI, PC, *leg.* 215A:281–82.

57. *See* C. Ekberg, *Colonial Ste. Genevieve: An Adventure on the Mississippi Frontier* 130–32 (1985); N. Belting, *supra* note 27 at 21–22.

58. *Arkansas Colonials, supra* note 14 at 45, 51.

59. *Id.* at 74.

60. *Abstract of Catholic Register of Arkansas (1764-1858)* 12 (D. Core ed., N. Hatfield trans., 1976).

61. *Arkansas Colonials, supra* note 14 at 91.

62. De Clouet to Commandant, 4 August 1769, AGI, PC, *leg.* 107.

63. *Arkansas Colonials, supra* note 14 at 42.

64. *Journal of John Halley, 1789* 3–4, Durrett Collection, University of Chicago.

65. 3 *SMV* 117.

66. *Arkansas Colonials, supra* note 14 at 43. Two years previous, however, the census listed her as a farmer, and she had produced two hundred barrels of corn and six barrels of wheat.

67. Amos Stoddard, commandant of upper Louisiana in the early American period, went so far as to say that "[m]ost of the inhabitants of that village [Arkansas Post], are of mixed blood, and the same mixture is observable among the Indians . . . ," though this is something of an overstatement. A. Stoddard, *Sketches, Historical and Descriptive, of Louisiana* 206 (1812).

68. *See, e.g.*, Dubroca, *L'Itinéraire des Français dans la Louisiane* 78–79 (1802).

69. *Register, supra* note 68 at 17–36.

70. Core, "Vizzier: On the Way to Arkansas," 31 *GPHSB* 45 (1988); Core, "Vizzier: Arkansas Residence Established," 32 *GPHSB* 7 (1989).

71. Halley, *supra* note 64 at 3–4.

72. 68 *Jesuit Relations and Allied Documents* 291–93 (R. Thwaites ed., 1900).

73. *Id.* at 313–15.

74. Halley, *supra* note 64 at 4.

75. *Id.*

76. References to Arkansas buffalo tongues are numerous in the records. *See, e.g.*, the letter of 17 February 1797, in which Governor Carondolet thanks Captain de Vilemont for "the tongues that you have sent me, and which have already left for Madrid." *VLB* 83.

77. S. Le Page du Pratz, *The History of Louisiana* 24 (1774).

78. 1 P. de Pages, *Voyages autour du monde* 48 (1782).

79. *Cf.* C. Robin, *supra* note 37 at 4, where the author notes of early nineteenth-century Pensacola: "A billiard room is the general meeting place of everyone from the

Governor down to the laborer and the humblest clerk. Here the shoemaker considers himself as good as the highest military officer. Here, in short, equality reigns."

80. Dubreuil to Miró, 17 January 1784, AGI, PC, *leg.* 107; Miró to Dubreuil, 17 February 1784, AGI, PC, *leg.* 107; Miró to Dubreuil, 29 October 1785, AGI, PC, *leg.* 107.

81. For a reference to this billiard room in 1809, *see* Core, "Marie Longuedoc," 16 *GPHSB* 10, 12 (1973).

82. Leyba to Unzaga, 19 January 1773, AGI, PC, *leg.* 107.

83. F. Perrin du Lac, *Voyage dans les Deux Louisianes . . . en 1801, 1802 et 1803 . . .* 360 (1805).

84. A. Stewart to Thomas Moulton, 27 February 1809, Missouri Historical Society, St. Louis.

85. Worley, "A Letter of Governor Miller to his Wife," 13 *AHQ* 389–90 (1954), reprinted in *A Documentary History of Arkansas* 17 (C. Williams *et al.* eds., 1984).

86. T. Flint, *Recollections of the Last Ten Years* 263, 264 (C. Grattan ed., 1932).

87. Holweck, "The Arkansas Mission under Rosati," 1 *St. Louis Catholic Hist. Rev.* 243, 258 (1919).

88. T. Nuttall, *A Journal of Travels into the Arkansas Territory during the Year 1819* 88 (S. Lottinville ed., 1980).

89. *The Western Journals of Washington Irving* 166 (J. McDermott ed., 1944).

90. *Id.* at 172.

CHAPTER IV

1. *A Baptismal Record of the Parishes along the Arkansas* 1–14 (1982). Between 1796 and 1799 only twenty-nine godparents signed the baptismal records: Nineteen were men and ten were women, indicating, perhaps, lower literacy among females generally. It is interesting to compare these figures with those at the settlement of St. Phillipe in Illinois. Between 1761 and 1765, seventeen baptisms were performed there. All but six godparents indicated that they could not sign their names, and all six who could were men. This reflects a literacy rate of about 17 percent. *See* Bovey, "Some Notes on Arkansas Post and St. Phillipe in the Mississippi Valley," *Transactions of the Royal Historical Society of Canada* 29 (1939).

2. *Pierre-Joseph Favrot's Education Manual for His Sons* 13 (G. Falcon ed., M. Gruming trans., 1988).

3. G. King, *Creole Families of New Orleans* 321 (1921).

4. De La Houssaye to Vaudreuil, 1 December 1752, LO 410, Huntington Library, San Marino, California.

5. B. Barron, *Calendar of the Vaudreuil Papers* 152 (1975).

6. Delinó to Baron de Carondolet, AGI, PC, *leg.* 25A.

7. For education in colonial Louisiana generally, *see* Riley, "The Development of Education in Louisiana Prior to Statehood," 19 *LHQ* 595 (1936); Noble & Nuhrah, "Education in Colonial Louisiana," 32 *LHQ* 759 (1949); Liljegren, "Frontier Education in Spanish Louisiana," 35 *Missouri Hist. Rev.* 345 (1941).

8. Spanish Judicial Documents, Succession of Ménard, 14 February 1793, Louisiana State Museum, New Orleans.

9. M. Carroll, *The Ursulines in Louisiana 1727-1824* 18 (1886). But *see Le Chevalier de Pradel, Vie d'un colon Français en Louisiane au xviii*[e] *siècle d'après sa correspondence et celle de sa famille* 145 (A. Baillardel & A. Prioult eds., 1928), for the assertion that Pradel sent his daughters to France in 1749 to be educated there in preference to the Ursulines' New Orleans establishment. The Ursulines also instructed poor students, Indians, and blacks. For more about this school, *see* H. Semple, *The Ursulines in New Orleans, 1727-1925* (1925). The curriculum there at first consisted of the catechism, reading, writing, and needlework, but it later expanded to include French, English, geography, arithmetic, history, music, sewing, and housework. Riley, "The Development of Education in Louisiana Prior to Statehood," 19 *LHQ* 595, 605 (1936).

10. These numbers are based on the burials recorded in *Abstract of Catholic Register of Arkansas* (1764–1858) *passim* (D. Core ed., N. Hatfield trans., 1976).

11. Books were not numerous in Ste. Genevieve, but they do occasionally appear in estate inventories. *See* C. Ekberg, *Colonial Ste. Genevieve: An Adventure on the Mississippi Frontier* 274–76 (1985), where the author estimates that in the 1790s the town may have contained five hundred to one thousand volumes. For books in Kaskaskia, *see* N. Belting, *Kaskaskia under the French Regime* 37 (1900). John Francis McDermott's remarkable study of eighteenth-century St. Louis turned up a surprising number of books there, probably as many as two thousand to three thousand volumes. J. McDermott, *Private Libraries in Creole St. Louis* 21 (1938). Of course, in New Orleans there were some rather large libraries. An inventory taken there in 1784 of the house and belongings of Gilbert Antoine de St. Maxent revealed an astonishing forty-seven hundred books in his library. J. Coleman, *Gilbert Antoine de St. Maxent: The Spanish Frenchman of New Orleans* 50 (1968). For some discussion of colonial New Orleans libraries, *see* J. Goudeau, *Early Libraries in New Orleans: A Study of the Creole Influence* (1965) (Ph.D. diss., Western Reserve University); McCutcheon, "Libraries in New Orleans, 1771–1833," 20 *LHQ* 152 (1937); McCutcheon, "Books and Booksellers in New Orleans, 1730–1830," 20 *LHQ* 607 (1937).

12. J. McDermott, *supra* note 11 at 49 (1938).

13. *Pierre-Joseph Favrot's Education Manual, supra* note 2 at ix.

14. *See* F. Jumonville, *Bibliography of New Orleans Imprints, 1764–1864* (1989).

15. *Id.*, nos. 33 & 34. *See generally*, E. Tinker, *Louisiana's Earliest Poet, Julian Poydras and the Paeans to Galvez* (1933).

16. D. McMurtrie, *Early Printing in New Orleans* 53 *et seq.* (1929).

17. Berquin-Duvallon, *Vue de la colonie Espagnole du Mississippi, ou des provinces de Louisiane et Florida occidentale . . .* 207 (1803). Another late colonial account cites the same statistic, but this may simply be derived from Berquin-Duvallon. *See* C. Robin, *Voyage to Louisiana* 160 (S. Landry ed., 1966).

18. *The Western Journals of Washington Irving* 168 (J. McDermott ed., 1944).

19. *APLB* 12–13.

20. It is published in Villiers, "L'Établissement de la province de la Louisiane, poème composé de 1728 à 1742, par Dumont de Montigny," 23 *Journal de la Société des Américanistes* 273 (1931). For an interesting biography, *see* Delanglez, "A Louisiana Poet-Historian: Dumont *dit* Montigny," 19 *Mid-America* 31 (1937).

21. *Id.* at 275.

22. *Id.* at 335–36.

23. J.-B. Bossu, *New Travels in North America* 107 (S. Dickinson ed. & trans., 1982). I have deviated from this translation somewhat, but not because it is not an excellent one. There is another translation in J. Masterson, *Tall Tales of Arkansas* 19 (1943). J.-B. Bossu, *supra* at 101, also puts a collection of couplets in the mouth of an Arkansas chief who is made to address Ferdinand de Soto during his voyage through Arkansas in 1541–42.

24. 1 J. Duffy, *The Rudolph Matas History of Medicine in Louisiana* 48 (1958). For a translation and partial reproduction of this decree, *see* McMurtrie, "A Louisiana Decree of 1770 Relative to the Practice of Medicine and Surgery," 86 *New Orleans Medical and Surgical Journal* 7 (1933).

25. The surgeon's name was Jean Michel. *See* B. French, *Historical Collections of Louisiana and Florida* 27 (1875).

26. 4 M. Giraud, *Histoire de la Louisiane Française* 272 (1974). In 1727, Father du Poisson wrote that a general sickness had prostrated the people of the Arkansas and that he had provided them with the few medicines that he had brought with him. 68 *Jesuit Relations and Related Documents* 261 (R. Thwaites ed., 1900).

27. *See, e.g.*, the 1758 list of customers at the Arkansas Post store in *Arkansas Colonials* 12 (M. Arnold & D. Core eds., 1986).

28. Bolton, "French Intrusions into New Mexico," in *The Pacific Ocean in History* 394, 396 (H. Stephens & H. Bolton eds., 1917).

29. *Toisé des ouvrages du fort et des bâstiments . . . dans la rivière des Akanças . . . 1751*, in Missouri Historical Society, St. Louis. One student of colonial Louisiana medicine has written that, during the Spanish period, the colonial hospitals, except for

those at New Orleans and Natchez, "in most cases were merely shacks containing a cot or two." Holmes, "Medical Practice in the Lower Mississippi Valley during the Spanish Period, 1769-1803," 1 *Alabama Journal Medical Science* 332, 337 (1964).

30. *Arkansas Colonials, supra* note 27 at 18.

31. *Declaraciones tomadas sobre el herido que vaso de Arkanzas nombrado Francisco LeCler, August 19, 1791* 4v. Spanish Judicial Records, Louisiana State Museum, New Orleans.

32. J. Holmes, *Gayoso: The Life of a Spanish Governor in the Mississippi Valley, 1789–1799* 134 (1965); Holmes, *supra* note 29 at 336.

33. T. Nuttall, *A Journal of Travels into the Arkansas Territory during the Year 1819* 86 (S. Lottinville ed., 1980).

34. J.-B. Bossu, *supra* note 23 at 68. This was quite common throughout colonial North America. *See* V. Vogel, *American Indian Medicine* 111 *et seq.* (1970).

35. J.-B. Bossu, *supra* note 23 at 64–69.

36. *Id.* at 39.

37. *Id.* at 71.

38. *Id.* at 70.

39. *État des médicaments que j'ay laissé aux Poste des Arkanças,* 4 January 1770, AGI, PC, *leg.* 107.

40. ANC, C^{13A} 39:209 (15 April 1756). Perhaps the offending medicine was mercurous chloride, called calomel, which was a popular eighteenth-century purgative frequently used in the treatment of venereal disease.

41. *VLB* 66. For similar incidents, *see id.* at 49, 56. There are numerous references in this source to the death of soldiers at the Post, doubtless an indication of its unhealthiness.

42. *Medicamens, Et précis de la méthode de Mr. Masdevall Docteur Médecin du Roi d'Espagne Charles IV, pour guérir toutes les maladies Epidémiques, putrides and malignes, fiévres de différents genres etc. and pour en préserver* (1796). A copy of this book, evidently unique, is in the W. S. Hoole Special Collections Library of the University of Alabama. This work also quotes from a medical book by Dr. Martin Rodon-Bell on the subject of epidemics that was published in 1787. *See id.* at 37. Some notice of the book appears in J. Duffy, *supra* note 24 at 160–62.

Medical books seem to have been generally scarce in the colony. One observer claimed that colonial Louisiana doctors were "so convinced of the uselessness of books that all of their books together would not make a good enough one for an apprentice." C. Robin, *supra* note 17 at 41.

43. Carrigan, "Impact of Epidemic Yellow Fever on Life in New Orleans," 4 *La. Hist.* 5 (1963) states that yellow fever first occurred in New Orleans in 1796.

44. C. Robin, *supra* note 17 at 2.

45. *Id.* at 5.

46. *Id.* at 17.

47. *Id.* at 3. *See id.* at 31 for similar comments about the air in unventilated ballrooms, churches, and other gathering places.

48. Letter of Father Paul du Poisson from Arkansas, 3 October 1727, in 67 *The Jesuit Relations and Allied Documents* 293 (R. Thwaites ed., 1900).

49. *Journal of John Halley, 1789 and 1791,* Durrett Collection, University of Chicago.

50. Du Poisson, *supra* note 48 at 295. Another observer advises that "the best way of driving [mosquitoes] out of the houses is to burn a little brimstone in the mornings and evenings. The smoke of this infallibly kills them, and the smell keeps others away for several days. An hour after the brimstone has been burnt, the apartments may be safely entered into by men." S. Le Page du Pratz, *The History of Louisiana* 285 (1774).

51. T. Flint, *Recollections of the Last Ten Years* 262–63 (C. Grattan ed., 1932).

52. *Arkansas County Record Book A,* Arkansas County Courthouse, De Witt, Arkansas, 131–37. The inventory is translated in Core, "First Bankruptcy in Arkansas County Records," 16 *GPHSB* 8 (1973).

53. T. Flint, *supra* note 51 at 256.

54. A. Stewart to Thomas Moulton, 27 February 1809, Missouri Historical Society, St. Louis.

55. 1 B. des Lozières, *Second Voyage à la Louisiane* 271 (1803). This was a commonplace of eighteenth- and nineteenth-century political theory.

56. *Some Considerations on the Consequences of the French Settling Colonies on the Mississippi, with Respect to the Trade and Safety of the English Plantations in America and the West-Indies* 26 (1720) (repr. 1928). Professor Beverley W. Bond, Jr., in his introduction to the reprint of 1928, says that "the author was from New England, a conclusion that is confirmed by the extensive acquaintance that is shown with the difficulties of a solicitor in the New England admiralty courts." *Id.* at 8.

57. *Id.* at 26.

58. *Id.* at 28.

59. *Id.* at 38.

60. *Id.* at 41. For some discussion of the political and commercial motives that lay behind the French government's desire to establish the Jesuits in Arkansas, *see* J. Delanglez, *The French Jesuits in Lower Louisiana* 54, 75–76, 434 (1935). *See also* C. O'Neil, *Church and State in French Colonial Louisiana* 29 (1966), where Iberville is quoted as saying of the Indians of Louisiana: "We would then promptly put our missionaries among them, who will keep them on our side, and will draw a great number of people to religion." O'Neil concludes, *id.* at 30, that if "for a moment the missionary

societies hesitated before Iberville's frankly political role for the missionary, they soon resolved the doubt in his favor."

61. Guy, "The Catholic Church in Arkansas, 1541–1803" 34 (n.d.). This unpublished manuscript is among the Guy Papers in the Arkansas History Commission, Little Rock. It is a much-expanded version of a thesis submitted by Father Guy in 1932 for the M.A. degree at the Catholic University of America.

62. *Id.* at 35. Foucault had complained that the Quapaws had mistreated him in unspecified ways, and he had therefore resolved to leave them. *See* J. Delanglez, *supra* note 60 at 454.

63. C. Vogel, *The Capuchins in French Louisiana (1722–1766)* 86 (1928). *Cf.* J. Delanglez, *supra* note 60 at 437.

64. 4 M. Giraud, *supra* note 26 at 217.

65. Guy, *supra* note 61 at 37. Father Guy there documents visits from Father Charlevoix in 1722 and Father Le Boullenger in 1723.

66. *Id.* at 44.

67. *Id.*

68. *Id.* at 47. Father de Guyenne may have been resident for a brief time around 1732, and Father Avond was at Arkansas from about 1737 to 1740. *See* J. Delanglez, *supra* note 60 at 437–39; S. Faye, *The Arkansas Post of Louisiana: French Dominion*, 26 *LHQ* 633, 675–76 (1943). The 1744 visit of the missionary Father Laurat is documented in Bovey, *supra* note 1. The record of the four baptisms he performed at the Post on 10 July 1744 may be found in *id.* at 39, 40 and in *Abstract of Catholic Register of Arkansas (1764–1858)* 74 (D. Core ed., N. Hatfield trans., 1976).

69. J. Delanglez, *supra* note 60 at 444, quoting P. Watrin's *Banishment of the Jesuits.*

70. Quoted in *id.*

71. *Id.*

72. *Id.*

73. *Nombre des Religieux que nous croyons necessaires dans la colonie* . . . 14 February 1770, AGI, PC, *leg.* 2357.

74. Demasellière to General, 20 May 1770, AGI, PC, *leg.* 107.

75. Inhabitants of Arkansas Post to de Clouet, no date, 1770(?), AGI, PC, *leg.* 107. Visiting priests also evidently considered the building in question a chapel. *See Register*, *supra* note 68 at 26, where the missionary Sebastien Louis Meurin attests to baptisms in 1764 "in the chapel of the fort of Arkansas." In 1768 the commandant recounts burial dues being paid to the chapel, and five years later another commandant allowed a merchant to work off a fine of ten pesos by making repairs to the chapel. De Clouet to Governor, 6 October 1768, AGI, PC, *leg.* 107; Leyba to Unzaga, 25 March 1773, *id.*

76. Guy, *supra* note 61 at 53–54. The town of New Madrid was not founded until 1789.

77. *See Register, supra* note 68 at 14–26 for Gibault's acts while ministering to the *habitants* and Indians of the Arkansas.

78. For further information on Flavien, *see* AGI, PC, *leg.* 107; R. Baudier, *The Catholic Church in Louisiana* 224 (1939). For a record of some of the pastoral acts that Flavien performed at the Arkansas, *see Register, supra* note 10 at 26, 28. He soon became the pastor of St. Charles on the German Coast. *See* note 92, *infra.*

79. *Diligencias obradas sobre la ereccion y provision de un Parrocha para el Puesto de Arkanzaz,* in *Records of the Diocese of Louisiana and the Floridas,* 1 June 1796. In 1797, the intendant sent Father Janin more ornaments, this time from the abandoned parish of San Estevan de Tombecbé in Alabama. The intendant retrieved them from storage in Mobile and transmitted them to Arkansas so that the priest "could execute the duties of his holy ministry." AGI, SD, *leg.* 2613, No. 127.

80. *VLB* 57.

81. *Id.* at 82.

82. AGI, SD, *leg.* 2616, No. 295.

83. In 1800, St. Louis proper had a population of about one thousand, and the district of St. Louis probably contained around twenty-five hundred souls. *See* L. Primm, *Lion of the Valley: St. Louis, Missouri* 65, 67 (1981). Arkansas Post's population, by contrast, was only about four hundred at that time.

84. *Diligencias para la provicion del Curato de San Luis en los Ylinueses en el Presbitero Don Pedro Janin* in *Records, supra* note 79, : May 1799.

85. Guy, "The Catholic Church in Arkansas, 1541–1803" 25 (M.A. thesis, Catholic University of America, 1932). In 1802, Father Juan Brady, a Carmelite monk and priest of the Parish of Our Lady of Carmen at the settlements of the Red and Ouachita rivers, visited the Post for a short time. The record of the baptisms that he performed there is printed in *Record, supra* note 1 at 80–81.

86. *See Calendar of the Microfilm Edition of the Records of the Diocese of Louisiana and the Floridas at the University of Notre Dame* (1967) for 22 December 1795.

87. *See id.*

88. *Id.*

89. *Id.*

90. *Id.* for 21 December 1795.

91. *Id.*

92. Bishop Peñalver so instructed Father Sébastien Flavien, pastor of St. Charles (German Coast) in a letter of 8 January 1796. *Id.* for 8 January 1796.

93. *Id.* for 1 October 1796.

94. Maxwell to Didier, *id.* for 21 December 1795.

95. Peñalver's instructions to parish priests in *id.*

96. *See generally Register, supra* note 68 and *Record, supra* note 1. When Father

Carette left Arkansas for New Orleans in August of 1758, he took the church registers of the Post with him. *See* J. Delanglez, *supra* note 60 at 446.

97. *Register, supra* note 68 at 20, 21.

98. *Id.* at 11.

99. *Id.* at 41. *See also id.* at 25, where a marriage record of 15 October 1792 notes that the couple had previously contracted before "Mr. DeValliere, commandant."

100. *See generally,* Baade, "The Form of Marriage in Spanish North America," 61 *Cornell L. Rev.* 1 (1975).

101. What follows is based on *Calendar, supra* note 86, for 19 August 1801.

102. *See, e.g., Register, supra* note 68 at 20.

103. *See, e.g., id.* at 19.

104. J.-B. Bossu, *supra* note 23 at 63–64.

105. *Calendar, supra* note 86, for 27 December 1795.

106. *Id.* for 7 January 1796.

107. *Id.* for 7 August 1801.

108. In 1798 there were fifty-six slaves at Arkansas Post. *Arkansas Colonials* 91 (M. Arnold & D. Core eds., 1986).

CHAPTER V

1. *View of the Spanish Colony of the Mississippi 1802, by a Resident Observer on the Premises* 60 (1802).

2. 4 M. Giraud, *Histoire de la Louisiane Française* 273. The garrison may have been reduced to eight men in 1725. ANC, C^{13A} 9:40; 3 *MPA* 513. In R. Chartrand, *The French Soldier in Colonial America* 17 (1984), the size of the Arkansas garrison at this time is given as thirty-four, but no source is cited and the number seems high.

3. *See* the facsimile of Marquette's 1673 map in J. Shea, *Discovery and Exploration of the Mississippi Valley* (1852).

4. On the destruction of Natchez, *see generally* Delanglez, "The Natchez Massacre and Governor Perrier," 17 *LHQ* 631 (1934).

5. 4 *MPA* 76.

6. Périer wrote that without this precaution the Chickasaws would have seduced the Quapaws into an alliance against the French. *See* ANC, C^{13A} 13:233.

7. 3 *MPA* 656.

8. 1 *MPA* 168.

9. ANC, C^{13A} 15:177.

10. ANC, C^{13A} 21:269.

11. F. Martin, *A History of the Bouligny Family and Allied Families* 30 (1990).

12. For general accounts of the First Chickasaw War, *see* P. Woods, *French-Indian Relations on the Southern Frontier, 1699-1762* 111–27 (1980); C. Alvord, *The Illinois Country, 1673-1818* 176–80 (repr. 1987).

13. ANC, C^{13A} 23:212; 1 *MPA* 390–91.

14. 1 *MPA* 391.

15. *Journal de la guerre du Micissippi contre les Chicachas, en 1739 et finie en 1740, le Ier d'Avril, par un officier de l'armee du M. de Nouaille* 37 (J. Shea ed., 1859).

16. Delanglez, "Journal of Father Vitry of the Society of Jesus, Army Chaplain during the War against the Chickasaw," 28 *Mid-America* 30, 37 (1941).

17. *Id.* at 40.

18. P. Woods, *supra* note 12 at 141.

19. Delanglez, *supra* note 16 at 41.

20. *Journal de la guerre, supra* note 15 at 62, 63; 1 *MPA* 428–30.

21. P. Woods, *supra* note 12 at 141–46.

22. ANC, C^{13A} 26:190; 26:192.

23. 4 *MPA* 250.

24. ANC, C^{13A} 28:251; 4 *MPA* 307.

25. 5 *MPA* 30; 5 *MPA* 41; 69 *Jesuit Relations and Allied Documents* 217 (R. Thwaites ed., 1900); J. Adair, *The History of the American Indians* 344 (S. Williams ed., 1930).

26. J. Adair, *supra* note 25 at 344.

27. ANC, C^{13A} 30:242, 249.

28. 5 *MPA* 35.

29. Faye, "The Arkansas Post of Louisiana: French Domination," 26 *LHQ* 633, 715 (1943). But *cf.* M. Villiers, *The Last Years of French Louisiana* 77 (H. Phillips trans., C. Brasseaux & G. Conrad eds., 1982), where the claim is made that this reinforcement came in 1754. A list of troops in Louisiana as of 10 December 1754 puts the Arkansas troop strength at fifty with an additional fifty present as a "supplementary garrison." M. Villiers, *supra* at 74.

30. Din, "Arkansas Post in the American Revolution," 40 *AHQ* 3, 10 (1981).

31. P. Pittman, *The Present State of the European Settlements on the Mississippi* (J. McDermott ed., 1977).

32. C. Howard, *The British Development of West Florida, 1763-1769* 20, 36, 41, 44 (1947).

33. C. Johnson, *British West Florida, 1763-1783* 73 (1942); D. James, *Antebellum Natchez* 15–16 (1968).

34. Demasellière to the General, 15 January 1770, AGI, PC, *leg.* 107.

35. 1 *BLC* 53, 54.

36. *Estado veridico de la Louisiana, 1762. See also Descripcion historico de la*

Louisiana por Don Josef Gabriel y Esternoz . . . 1806, Archives Nationales, Archives du Service Hydrographique, Ms. 5.1.9.14, f.51: "The Arkansas inhabiting the mouths of the river of that name are brave, and excellent hunters . . . and have many times emerged victorious in the wars with the Chickasaws."

37. *Instruccion particular que deve observar el Capitan Don Joseph Orieta commandante del Puesto de Arcansas,* 11 March 1771, AGI, PC, *leg.* 131.

38. 1 *BLC* 54.

39. General to de Clouet, no date, AGI, PC, *leg.* 107.

40. De Clouet to General, 8 July 1768, AGI, PC, *leg.* 107.

41. *Id.* to *id.*, 26 July 1768, AGI, PC, *leg.* 107.

42. General to de Clouet, *supra* note 39.

43. De Clouet to Commandant, 14 February 1769, AGI, PC, *leg.* 107.

44. *Id.* to *id.*, 25 February 1769, AGI, PC, *leg.* 107.

45. *Id.* to *id.*, 20 September 1768, AGI, PC, *leg.* 107.

46. Virzaga to Governor, 1 June 1770, AGI, PC, *leg.* 107.

47. Leyba to Governor, 22 November 1771, AGI, PC, *leg.* 107; Leyba to Unzaga, 26 October 1773, AGI, PC, *leg.* 107.

48. Orieta to Unzaga, 14 July 1774, AGI, PC, *leg.* 107.

49. Orieta to Governor, 31 May 1775, AGI, PC, *leg.* 107.

50. Din, *supra* note 30 at 7 and 11, n.22.

51. *Id.* at 7.

52. *See generally id.*

53. *Id.* at 29.

54. J.-B. de La Harpe, *The Historical Journal of the Establishment of the French in Louisiana* 147 (J. Cain & V. Koenig trans., G. Conrad ed., 1971).

55. ANC, C^{13A} 17:256; 1 *MPA* 201–2; 1 *MPA* 206.

56. 1 *BLC* 25.

57. 1 *BLC* 27.

58. G. Din & A. Nasatir, *The Imperial Osages* 58 (1983).

59. *Id.* at 59.

60. *Id.* at 67.

61. *Id.* at 70.

62. *Id.* at 75.

63. *Id.*

64. *Id.* at 76.

65. Leyba to Governor, 4 January 1772, AGI, PC, *leg.* 107; *id.* to *id.*, 26 January 1772, AGI, PC, *leg.* 107.

66. *Id.* to *id.*, 27 April 1772, AGI, PC, *leg.* 107.

67. *Id.* to *id.*, 30 April 1773, AGI, PC, *leg.* 107.
68. G. Din & A. Nasatir, *supra* note 58 at 78.
69. *Id.* at 83, 84.
70. *Id.* at 85, 89.
71. *Id.* at 91.
72. *Id.* at 95, 97.
73. *Id.* at 98.
74. *Id.* at 100, 102–3.
75. *Id.* at 103–7.
76. *Id.* at 108.
77. *Id.* at 122, 123–24, 125.
78. *Id.* at 149–56.
79. *Id.* at 170, 171, 180.
80. 2 *SMV* 273–74.
81. G. Din & A. Nasatir, *supra* note 58 at 193.
82. *Id.* at 204.
83. *Id.* at 205–6, 207, 213, 223, 227, 228.
84. 3 *SMV* 145–46.
85. G. Din & A. Nasatir, *supra* note 58 at 239, 240, 241, 244, 246.
86. *Id.* at 248, 252, 258–61.
87. *Id.* at 275, 282, 283, 295.
88. *Id.* at 297.
89. *Id.* at 303, 305.
90. *APLB* 53.
91. G. Din & A. Nasatir, *supra* note 58 at 303, 341, 343.
92. For a review of these explanations, *see* M. López-Briones, *Spain in the Mississippi Valley: Spanish Arkansas, 1762-1804* 112–14 (Ph.D. diss., Purdue University, 1983).
93. Usner, "The Frontier Exchange Economy of the Lower Mississippi Valley in the Eighteenth Century," 44 *The William and Mary Quarterly*, 3d Series, 165, 171 (1987).

CHAPTER VI

1. Dart, "The Legal Institutions of Louisiana," 3 *Southern Law Quarterly* 247 (1918). This article also appears in 2 *LHQ* 72 (1919).
2. The charter is printed in 4 *Publications La. Hist. Soc.* 13 at 17 (1908).

3. For a *précis* of its provisions, title by title, *see* Schmidt, "History of the Jurisprudence of Louisiana," 1 *La. Law Journal,* No. 1, 1 (1841).

4. The most useful eighteenth-century commentary is C. Ferrière, *Commentaire sur la Coutume de la Prevoté et Vicomté de Paris.* It is available in several editions.

5. Dart, "The Law Library of a Louisiana Lawyer in the Eighteenth Century," 25 *Reports of the Louisiana Bar Association* 12 at 22 *et seq.* (1942).

6. *See* Dart, *supra* note 1 at 249 *et seq. See also,* for some discussion of the work of this body, Hardy, "The Superior Council in Colonial Louisiana," in *Frenchmen and French Ways in the Mississippi Valley* 87 (J. McDermott ed., 1969); Micelle, "From Law Court to Local Government: Metamorphosis of the Superior Council of French Louisiana," 9 *La. Hist.* 85 (1968).

7. The edict is printed in 4 *Publications La. Hist. Soc.* 21–23 (1908).

8. *Id.* at 48.

9. Baade, "Marriage Contracts in French and Spanish Louisiana: A Study in 'Notarial' Jurisprudence," 53 *Tulane L. Rev.* 1 at 9 (1978).

10. *Id.*

11. The edict is printed in 4 *Publications La. Hist. Soc.* 63 (1908).

12. The translation in the text is mine. The entire edict is translated and discussed in Dart, *supra* note 1 at 261 *et seq.* Further discussion of this edict can be found in Dart, "The Colonial Legal Systems of Arkansas, Louisiana, and Texas," 27 *Reports of the Louisiana Bar Association* 32 at 52 (1926).

13. Dart, *supra* note 12 at 267. The other districts were New Orleans, Biloxi, Mobile, Alibamous, Natchez, Yazoo, Natchitoches, and the Illinois.

14. Translated extracts from this order appear in 2 J. White, *A New Collection of Laws, Charters, and Local Ordinances of the Governments of Great Britain, France, and Spain, Relating to the Concession of Land in Their Respective Colonies* 439–40 (1837).

15. *Id.* at 440.

16. 4 M. Giraud, *Histoire de la Louisiane Française* 272 (1974). Ménard left the Arkansas in 1722 (*id.* at 275) and was in New Orleans in 1729. "Index to the Records of the Superior Council of Louisiana," 4 *LHQ* 349 (1921).

17. Dufresne appears in the Arkansas census of 1 January 1726; but on 21 October 1726, he is described as a "settler in Arkansas, but now domiciled with Mr. Tronquidy [in New Orleans]." "Index to the Records of the Superior Council in New Orleans," 3 *LHQ* 420 (1920). In 1727 there were no soldiers at the Arkansas, as Father du Poisson tells us that he took up residence in "the India Company's house, which is also that of the commandants when there are any here. . . ." *See* Falconer, "Arkansas and the Jesuits in 1727—A Translation," 4 *Publications Ark. Hist. Assoc.* 352 at 375 (1917).

18. For a charter from Tonty to Jacques Cardinal, one of his men at the Arkansas, *see The French Foundations* 396 (T. Pease & R. Werner eds., 1934).

19. Concession in fee by La Salle to Pierre Prudhomme, in *id.* at 32.

20. When Tonty petitioned for confirmation of his charter, he was evidently refused. The petition is printed in E. Murphey, *Henry de Tonti, Fur Trader of the Mississippi* 119 (1941). It is possible that La Salle did not have the power to make permanent grants and that may be the reason that Tonty needed confirmation. The letters patent of 12 May 1678, giving La Salle the right to explore "the western part of New France" in the king's behalf, also gave him the power to build forts wherever he deemed them necessary; and he was "to hold them on the same terms and conditions as Fort Frontenac." *See* T. Falconer, *On the Discovery of the Mississippi* 19 (1844). La Salle said expressly in 1683 that this allowed him to "divide with the French and the Indians both the lands and the commerce of said country until it may please his majesty to command otherwise. . . ." *See The French Foundations, supra* note 18 at 43. The language is ambiguous, but on one permissible reading it indicates a specifically reserved power in the king to revoke grants that La Salle made.

21. Quoted in Dart, *supra* note 1 at 249.

22. P. Pittman, *The Present State of the European Settlements on the Mississippi* 53 (1770) (reprinted with intro. by R. Rea, 1973).

23. The relevant documents are translated in Core, "Arkansas through the Looking Glass of 1743 Documents," 22 *GPHSB* 16 (1979).

24. This incident is reported and discussed in Faye, "The Arkansas Post of Louisiana: French Domination," 26 *LHQ* 677–78.

25. *See* Baade, *supra* note 9 at 7, 8.

26. *Id.* at 25.

27. 1 F. Pollock & F. Maitland, *A History of English Law* 218 (2d ed., reissued with intro. by S. Milsom, 1968).

28. *See* 12 W. Holdsworth, *A History of English Law* 70 (1938). *See generally* on the notary in England, Gutteridge, "The Origin and Development of the Profession of Notaries Public in England," in *Cambridge Legal Essays* 12 (1926).

29. 12 W. Holdsworth, *supra* note 28 at *id.*

30. 5 *id.* at 115 (3d ed., 1945).

31. 12 *id.* at 71–72 (1938); T. Plucknett, *A Concise History of the Common Law* 227–28 (5th ed., 1956).

32. As draftsman of wills, marriage contracts, and conveyances, *Mons. le Notaire* has survived in France as a much-respected person, especially in the country villages. He is a general non-forensic legal practitioner, his part in the legal scheme "being confined to voluntary as distinct from contentious jurisdiction." Brown, "The Office of Notary in France," *International Comparative Law Quarterly* 60 at 64 (1953). Indeed, the French notary is close to the equivalent of the English solicitor, except for the latter's participation in minor litigation. Thus one modern-day commentator opined that "a solicitor

would feel much at home in the *étude* of the French notary, though he would be surprised, and perhaps disappointed, by the cordiality of the morning post." *Id.* at 71.

Today in Louisiana as well the notary enjoys considerable powers. *See* Burke & Fox, "The Notaire in North America: A Short Study of the Adaptation of a Civil Law Institution," 50 *Tulane L. Rev.* 318 at 328–32 (1975); Brosman, "Louisiana—An Accidental Experiment in Fusion," 24 *Tulane L. Rev.* 95, 98–99 (1949). The Louisiana notary has the power "to make inventories, appraisements, and petitions; to receive wills, make protests, matrimonial contracts, conveyances, and generally, all contracts and instruments of writing; to hold family meetings and meetings of creditors; . . . to affix the seals upon the effects of deceased persons and to raise the same." *La. Stat. Ann.* § 35:2 (1964). When the Louisiana legislature defined the practice of law, and prohibited all but licensed attorneys from engaging in it, it therefore remembered to except acts performed by the notary which were "necessary or incidental to the exercise of the powers and functions of [that] office." *La. Stat. Ann.* § 37:212(B)(1974). A walk through modern-day New Orleans will reveal a number of signs proclaiming the existence of "Law and Notarial Offices," a combination that leaves an odd ring in the ears of an American common lawyer. The Louisiana notary is simply "a different and more important official person than is the notary public in other jurisdictions of the United States." Brosman, *supra* at 98.

33. *See* Baade, *supra* note 9 at 12.

34. *"Mémoire sur l'État de la Colonie de la Louisiane en 1746,"* ANC, C^{13A} 30:242–81 at 249. As the average family size in Arkansas in the middle of the eighteenth century was about four, this would put the number of *habitant* whites at the Post at about forty-eight.

35. For an abstract of this marriage contract, *see* "Records of the Superior Council of Louisiana," 13 *LHQ* 129 (1944).

36. *The Vaudreuil Papers* 136 (B. Barron ed., 1975).

37. "Index to the Records of the Superior Council of Louisiana," 24 *LHQ* 75 (1941).

38. *See* Din, "Arkansas Post in the American Revolution," 40 *AHQ* 3, 4 (1980).

39. What follows is based on a memorandum entitled *"Harrangues faites dans l'assemblée tenue à l'hôtel du gouvernment cejourdhui, 20 Juin 1756,"* ANC, C^{13A} 39:177–80.

40. Berryer to Kerlérec and Bobé Descloseaux, 14 July 1769, ANC, B 109:487–88.

41. "Index to the Records of the Superior Council of Louisiana," 22 *LHQ* 255 (1939).

42. La Harpe to Choiseul, 8 August 1763 (Transcript in Little Rock Public Library).

43. "Records," *supra* note 41 at *id.*

44. *Id.*

45. Baade, *supra* note 9 at 15–18.

46. "Records of the Superior Council of Louisiana," 25 *LHQ* 856–57 (1942).

47. De La Houssaye to Vaudreuil, 1 December 1752, LO 410, Huntington Library, San Marino, California.

48. *Id.*

49. *The Vaudreuil Papers, supra* note 36 at 152.

50. Records of the Superior Council of Louisiana, 11 February 1764, Louisiana History Center, Louisiana State Museum, New Orleans.

51. For a translation of this inventory, *see* Core *supra* note 23 at 22.

52. *Resancement General des habitants, voyageurs, femmes, enfans, esclaves, chevaus, beufs, vaches, cochons etc. de Poste des Akansa 1749*, LO 200, Huntington Library, San Marino, California.

53. On the Arkansas Vaugines, *see* Core, "The Vaugine Arkansas Connection," 20 *GPHSB* 6 (1978).

54. Faye, *supra* note 24 at 709.

55. 1 *Athanase de Mézières and the Louisiana-Texas Frontier, 1768-1780* 166 (H. Bolton ed., 1914).

56. *Id.* at 168–69.

57. *Resancement, supra* note 52.

58. H. Bolton, *supra* note 55 at 167.

59. "Index to the Records of the Superior Council of Louisiana," 17 *LHQ* 569 (1934).

60. *Id.*

61. *Id.* at 571.

62. Quoted in Dart, *supra* note 1 at 279.

63. *See* P. Pittman, *supra* note 22 at 53.

64. *Id.* at 36.

65. J. Delanglez, *The French Jesuits in Lower Louisiana* 445 (1935).

66. ANC, C^{13A}40:328–29.

67. ANC, C^{13A}40:306–12.

68. ANC, C^{13A}40:323–26.

69. Faye, *supra* note 24 at 716.

70. *Id.* at 715.

71. J. Delanglez, *supra* note 65 at 445.

72. For a list of these and the dates during which they commanded at the Arkansas, *see* Appendix I.

73. Faye, *supra* note 24 at 709.

74. Royal Letter of 21 April 1764, quoted in Baade, *supra* note 9 at 31, n.159.

75. For the details, *see id.* at 31–33.

76. *Id.* at 33.

77. *Id.* at 36.

78. Translations are available in 1 *La. Law Journal,* No. 2, 1 (1841); 1 *SMV* 108; 1 *American State Papers, Misc.* 350 (1834).

79. There is a translation in 1 *La. Law Journal,* No. 2, 27 (1841).

80. *See* Baade, *supra* note 9 at 40.

81. *Id.* at 35–36, 43, 89; Batiza, "The Unity of Private Law in Louisiana under Spanish Rule," 4 *Inter-American Law Review* 139 (1962).

82. Faye, "The Arkansas Post of Louisiana: Spanish Domination," 27 *LHQ* 629, 632 (1944).

83. De Clouet to Commandant, 14 February 1769, AGI, PC, *leg.* 107.

84. De Clouet to General, 14 August 1769, AGI, PC, *leg.* 107.

85. Demasellière to General, 15 July 1770, AGI, PC, *leg.* 107.

86. Demasellière to Governor (?), 4 March 1770, AGI, PC, *leg.* 107.

87. ? to Demasellière, 10 August 1770, AGI, PC, *leg.* 107.

88. De Virzaga to Governor, 4 October 1770, AGI, PC, *leg.* 107.

89. Governor (?) to Orieta, 7 November 1770, AGI, PC, *leg.* 107.

90. For the posts to which these *Instructions* were first sent, *see* Baade, *supra* note 9 at 37–38. Arkansas Post was not among them. Professor Baade very kindly supplied me with a copy of this document, which he found in AGI, PC, *leg.* 188A. There is another copy in the Missouri Historical Society at St. Louis, which I have also consulted. This document will be cited hereafter as *Instructions.*

91. *Instructions,* § 1.

92. *Id.,* § 2.

93. *Id.,* § 4.

94. *Id.,* § 2.

95. *Id.,* § 8.

96. *Id.*

97. *Id.,* § 6.

98. *Id.,* § 7.

99. Baade, *supra* note 9 at 39.

100. *Instructions,* § 10.

101. *Id.,* § 14.

102. *Id.,* § 15.

103. *Id.,* § 17.

104. *Id.*

105. *Id.,* § 19.

106. *Id.,* § 20.

107. *Id.,* § 18.

108. *Instruccion a que se arreglarian los Tenientes de Governador* . . . New Orleans, 26 January 1770 [cited hereinafter as *Instruccion*]. Unlike the *Instructions* to the civil commandants, this document was not printed. Professor Baade very kindly provided me a copy from AGI, PC, *leg.* 2357. I also made use of a copy of this document at the Archivo General de Indias in Seville.

109. *Instruccion,* § 1.

110. *Id.,* § 2.

111. *Id.,* § 3.

112. *Instructions,* § 1.

113. Bénard de La Harpe to the Duc de Choiseul, Minister of the Marine, 8 August 1763 (Transcript in Little Rock Public Library).

114. Lambert to Demasellière, 1 June 1770, AGI, PC, *leg.* 107; Francoeur to Demasellière, 16 June 1770, AGI, PC, *leg.* 107; Demasellière to O'Reilly, 28 June 1770, AGI, PC, *leg.* 107; Demasellière to O'Reilly, 15 July 1770, AGI, PC, *leg.* 107; Demasellière to ?, 15 July 1770, AGI, PC, *leg.* 107.

115. Governor (?) to Demasellière, 20 July 1770, AGI, PC, *leg.* 107.

116. What follows is taken from 1 *SMV* 377–82.

117. A partial copy of this ordinance has survived in AGI, PC, *leg.* 191.

118. De Villiers to Gálvez, 23 February 1780, AGI, PC, *leg.* 193A.

119. What follows is taken from *Declaraciones tomadas sobre el herido qe vaso de Arkanzas nombrado Francisco le Cler,* 19 August 1791, Judicial Records of Spanish Louisiana, Louisiana History Center, Louisiana State Museum, New Orleans.

120. What follows is taken from "Index to the Spanish Judicial Records," 8 *LHQ* 314–16 (1925). I have also examined the original papers in Montcharvaux vs. Francisco Ménar(d), 18 April 1771, Judicial Records of Spanish Louisiana, Louisiana History Center, Louisiana State Museum, New Orleans. This María Montcharvaux is the same person as Françoise Lepine who figured in the marriage contracts discussed *supra,* pp. 135–36.

121. Francisco Ménard vs. Anselme Billet, 29 August 1787, Judicial Records of Spanish Louisiana, Louisiana History Center, Louisiana State Museum, New Orleans.

122. Santiago Gaignard vs. Juan Batista Saussié, 25 January 1791, Judicial Records of Spanish Louisiana, Louisiana History Center, Louisiana State Museum, New Orleans.

123. There is a transcription and translation of the records of this case in "The Case of Pourée against Chouteau," 2 *Publications Mo. Hist. Soc.* 68 (1900).

124. Pourée's petition appears in *id.* at 69–71.

125. Chouteau's answer appears in *id.* at 72.

126. For examples of petitions in St. Louis civil litigation, *see* F. Billon, *Annals of St. Louis in Its Early Days under the French and Spanish Dominations* 131, 136, 151, 155, 162,

174, 179 (1886). In Douglas, "The Spanish Domination of Upper Louisiana," *Proceedings of the Wisconsin Historical Society* 74, 83 (1914), the author says of the lieutenant governor's court: "The proceedings were summary. The injured party addressed a petition to the governor setting forth the particulars of his complaint written in the French language."

127. De Clouet to General, 21 March 1768, AGI, PC, *leg.* 107.
128. *Id.* to *id.*, 26 July 1768, AGI, PC, *leg.* 107.
129. *Id.* to *id.*, 6 October 1768, AGI, PC, *leg.* 107.
130. *Id.* to *id.*, 21 March 1768, AGI, PC, *leg.* 107.
131. *Id.* to *id.*, 1 August 1769, AGI, PC, *leg.* 107.
132. *Id.* to *id.*, 15 August 1769, AGI, PC, *leg.* 107.
133. Demasellière to General, 15 January 1770, AGI, PC, *leg.* 107.
134. *Id.* to *id.*, 4 March 1770, AGI, PC, *leg.* 107.
135. *Id.* to *id.*, AGI, PC, *leg.* 107 (1770?).
136. Leyba to Governor, 24 June 1772, AGI, PC, *leg.* 107.
137. Demasellière to General, 7 October 1770, AGI, PC, *leg.* 107.
138. Leyba to ?, 27 July 1771, AGI, PC, *leg.* 107.
139. 4 June 1771, AGI, PC, *leg.* 107.
140. Leyba to Governor, 15 June 1772, AGI, PC, *leg.* 107.
141. *Id.* to *id.*, 24 June 1772, AGI, PC, *leg.* 107.
142. Governor to the General Chief of the Arkansas, 30 June 1772, AGI, PC, *leg.* 107.
143. What follows is based on de Villiers to Gálvez, 15 September 1779, AGI, PC, *leg.* 192.
144. Faye, *supra* note 82 at 693–94.
145. *Id.* at 694.
146. Orieta to Governor, 2 February 1771, AGI, PC, *leg.* 107.
147. H. Bolton, *supra* note 55 at 166–68.
148. *Id.* at 168–69.
149. *Id.* at 160–63.
150. Demasellière to General, no date, AGI, PC, *leg.* 107.
151. *Id.* to *id.*, 14 May, 2 June, and 4 June 1770, AGI, PC, *leg.* 107.
152. *Id.* to *id.*, 6 June 1770, AGI, PC, *leg.* 107.
153. *Id.* to *id.*, 16 June 1770, AGI, PC, *leg.* 107.
154. Brothers Francoeur to Demasellière, 17 June 1770, AGI, PC, *leg.* 107.
155. Demasellière to General, 16 June 1770, AGI, PC, *leg.* 107.
156. *Id.* to *id.*, 15 July 1770, AGI, PC, *leg.* 107.
157. *Id.* to *id.*, 16 June 1770, AGI, PC, *leg.* 107.
158. *See id.*

159. Demasellière to O'Reilly, 15 July 1770, AGI, PC, *leg.* 107.

160. *Id.* to General, 7 August 1770, AGI, PC, *leg.* 107.

161. *Id.* to *id.*, 11 August 1770, AGI, PC, *leg.* 107.

162. *See* Filhiol, "Description of the Ouachita in 1786," 20 *LHQ* 476 (1937). For a better translation, *see now* Dickinson, "An Early View of the Ouachita Region," 3 *The Old Time Chronicle* 12 (1990). Jean-Baptiste Filhiol arrived in the Ouachita country in April of 1782 and first settled at Écore à Fabri, the site of present-day Camden, Arkansas. E. Williams, *Filhiol and the Founding of the Spanish Poste d'Ouachita: The Ouachita Valley in Colonial Louisiana, 1783–1804* 18 (1982). In 1784 he descended to the site of present-day Monroe, Louisiana, and reestablished his command. Dickinson, "Don Juan Filhiol at Écore à Fabri," 46 *AHQ* 133, 140 (1987). He divided his district into two military units, one of which lay north of the confluence of the Ouachita and Saline rivers and thus entirely in Arkansas; the unit was supposed to muster every six months at Écore à Fabri. E. Williams, *The Military Tradition of Fort Miro and the Poste d'Ouachita in Colonial Louisiana, 1783–1804* 1 (1982). At the first muster of the Écore à Fabri unit, probably late in 1784, Filhiol auctioned off a tavern license to Pierre Cuvillier *dit* Champignolle. E. Williams, *Spanish Law, Justice, and the Church in the Colonial Ouachita Valley* 26 (1983). Perhaps the site was at or near Champagnolle in Union County, though it is possible that this was only his hunting camp and that his tavern was at Poste du Ouachita. Filhiol abandoned the Écore à Fabri muster after three years. E. Williams, *The Military Tradition of Fort Miro and the Poste d'Ouachita in Colonial Louisiana, 1783–1804* 2 (1982).

163. Filhiol, *supra* note 162 at 483–84.

164. *Id.* at 484.

165. *Id.*

166. *Recensement des habitants, femmes, enfants, et esclaves du Poste des Arkansas*, AGI, PC, *leg.* 107.

167. *Estada presente de todo los inhabitantes del Puesto de los Arkancas . . .*, AGI, PC, *leg.* 107.

168. What follows is based on de Villiers to Gálvez, 3 August 1777, AGI, PC, *leg.* 190.

169. *Id.*

170. De Villiers to Gálvez, 25 January 1777, AGI, PC, *leg.* 190.

171. *Id.* to *id.*, 2 March 1779, AGI, PC, *leg.* 192.

172. *Id.*

173. *Id.*

174. *Id.*

175. Their petition for asylum is in AGI, PC, *leg.* 191, as is a census of them taken 20 February 1778.

176. De Villiers to Gálvez, 2 March 1779, AGI, PC, *leg.* 192.

177. De Villiers to Gálvez, 28 April 1779, AGI, PC, *leg.* 192.

178. Gálvez to de Villiers, no date, 1779, AGI, PC, *leg.* 192.

179. These regulations are translated several places. I have used the version that appears in 2 J. White, *supra* note 14 at 231–33. The relevant portion is § 13.

180. *Id.*

181. Faye, *supra* note 82 at 639.

182. What follows is based on Din, *supra* note 38 at 4 *et seq.*

183. *Id.* at 13, n.28; Faye, *supra* note 82 at 671.

184. For the following, *see* Miró to Cagigla, 5 May 1782, AGI, PC, *leg.* 1305.

185. Din, *supra* note 38 at *id.*

186. Vallière to Miró, 16 May 1788, AGI, PC, *leg.* 140.

187. In 2 J. White, *supra* note 14 at 10, 11, an 1829 letter from White to Henry Clay appears in which White estimates that unsettled claims "in Louisiana, Alabama, Missouri, Arkansas, and Florida yet cover ten or twelve million acres."

188. The most complete compendium is the work by J. White, *supra* note 14.

189. J. White, *supra* note 14 at 220.

190. *Id.* at 230.

191. *Id.* at 231.

192. *Id.* at 231–33.

193. *Id.* at 234–40.

194. *See generally,* on the subject of Spanish land claims in Missouri, Violette, "Spanish Land Claims in Missouri," *Washington University Studies* 167 (1921). Also useful are 3 L. Houck, *A History of Missouri* 34 *et seq.* (1918) and J. Scharf, *History of St. Louis* (1883).

195. A. Stoddard, *Sketches of Louisiana* 245 (1811).

196. 1 Scharf, *supra* note 194 at 32.

197. 3 *American State Papers, Public Lands* 294 (1834).

198. The will, executed 27 July 1791, is included in the papers in a case brought in 1793 by Ménard's widow. *See* Spanish Judicial Records, Louisiana History Center, Louisiana State Museum, 14 February 1793.

199. *Instructions,* § 11.

200. *See Instructions, supra* note 79 at 49.

201. The will of Louis Lefevre, executed 13 October 1793, has survived in a number of copies. I have made use primarily of the one in *Probate Record Book AA,* pages 14–15, at the Probate Clerk's Office, De Witt, Arkansas. Deputy Circuit Clerk Tommy Sue Keffer brought this instrument to my attention. The witnesses to both the Ménard and Lefevre wills were Jean-Baptiste Duchassin, François Vaugine, and Manuel Reyes. The only other

will executed at Arkansas Post in the eighteenth century that I have discovered was that of Capt. Balthazar de Villiers. It is in AGI, PC, *leg.* 107. But this is a Spanish translation of a French original and the attestation seems not to have been copied; only a signature is indicated at the end. This will was executed on 14 April 1782, and a codicil to it followed in May.

202. The inventory is in AGI, PC, *leg.* 140 and covers four pages.

203. AGI, PC, *leg.* 191.

204. J. Holmes, *Gayoso: The Life of a Spanish Governor in the Mississippi Valley, 1789-1799* 67 (1968).

EPILOGUE

1. 2 C. Robin, *Voyages dans l'Intérieur de la Louisiane . . .* 265 (1807). *See also* the 1794 census in *Records of the Diocese of Louisiana and the Floridas,* 24 January 1795, where Arkansas Post is the third smallest of thirty-four reporting units. In A. Stoddard, *Sketches, Historical and Descriptive of Louisiana* 211 (1812), the author asserts that in 1804 the population of the New Madrid district, which included the settlements of New Madrid, Little Prairie (Caruthersville), and Arkansas Post, was only about 1350, free and slave. If this figure is correct, there could not possibly have been 400 persons at Arkansas Post.

2. 2 V. Collot, *A Journey in North America* 40 (1826).

3. Letter of Carlos de Gran Pré, 16 December 1796, Bancroft Library, Berkeley.

4. 4 *SMV* 103, 104.

5. G. King, *Old Families of New Orleans* 320 (1921).

6. *Arkansas Gazette, State Centennial Edition,* 15 June 1936, p. 13.

7. For the events of the transfer at Natchitoches, *see* 9 *Territorial Papers* 238; for those at St. Louis, *see* J. Primm, *Lion of the Valley: St. Louis, Missouri* 73 (1981).

8. *See* E. Williams, *The Military Tradition of Fort Miro and Post d'Ouachita in Colonial Louisiana, 1783-1804* 46 (1982).

APPENDIX I

1. This list draws on a very large number of sources for its content. Chief among them are Faye, "The Arkansas Post of Louisiana: French Domination," 26 *LHQ* 633 (1943); Faye, "The Arkansas Post of Louisiana: Spanish Domination," 27 *LHQ* 529 (1944); Thomas, "The Arkansas Post of Louisiana, 1683–1783" (M.A. thesis, University of

California, 1948); and Din, "Arkansas Post in the American Revolution," 40 *AHQ* 3 (1981).

2. Tonty doubtless had judicial authority since he was the feudal lord of Arkansas, but there is no evidence that he ever held court there. *See* text, *supra* at p. 128.

3. In May of 1722 a provincial council was established in St. Louis, with jurisdiction over the Arkansas settlement. But it is doubtful that this council ever adjudicated Arkansas cases. It seems more likely that those in charge of Law's colony did so. *See* text, *supra* at p. 127.

4. *See* note 3 above.

INDEX

Index

Index